Sworn Bond
in Tudor England

Sworn Bond in Tudor England

Oaths, Vows and Covenants in Civil Life and Literature

THEA CERVONE

McFarland & Company, Inc., Publishers
Jefferson, North Carolina, and London

LIBRARY OF CONGRESS CATALOGUING-IN-PUBLICATION DATA

Cervone, Thea, 1968–
　　Sworn bond in Tudor England : oaths, vows and covenants in civil life and literature / Thea Cervone.
　　　　p.　　cm.
　　Includes bibliographical references and index.

　　ISBN 978-0-7864-4983-5
　　softcover : 50# alkaline paper ∞

　　1. Oaths — England — History — 16th century.　2. Tudor, House of　3. Literature and society — England — History — 16th century.　4. English literature — 16th century — History and criticism.　5. Political culture — England — History — 16th century.　6. Great Britain — History — Tudors, 1485–1603.　7. Great Britain — Politics and government — 1485–1603.　I. Title.
　　GT3085.C47　2011
　　306.40942 — dc23　　　　　　　　　　　　　　2011023200

BRITISH LIBRARY CATALOGUING DATA ARE AVAILABLE

© 2011 Thea Cervone. All rights reserved

No part of this book may be reproduced or transmitted in any form or by any means, electronic or mechanical, including photocopying or recording, or by any information storage and retrieval system, without permission in writing from the publisher.

On the cover: The Magna Carta of 1215; Tudor Rose

Manufactured in the United States of America

McFarland & Company, Inc., Publishers
　Box 611, Jefferson, North Carolina 28640
　　www.mcfarlandpub.com

Table of Contents

Preface   1

Introduction   5

1. Defiance by Prerogative: The Coronation Oath of Henry VIII   19
2. The Matter of Resources: Sworn Bond and Biblical Example in *The Boke Named the Governour*   38
3. Additions and Admissions: The Manipulation of Sworn Bond in the Henrician Fealty Oath   56
4. Grudging, Muttering, and Horn Blasts: Aurality and Performativity in Reformation Polemic   77
5. Credibility Among Cynics: Coerced Sworn Bond in More, Bale, and Harington   102
6. Oath, Obligation, and Obedience: Fealty and Service in Three Plays About King John   134
7. Virtue by Degrees: Espousal in Spenser's *Faerie Queene*, Books III–IV   168

Appendix A. The French Version of the Anomalous Form of the Oath of Edward II   187

Appendix B. The Recantation of William Tolwyn, Recorded by Alexander Seton, and Reprinted by John Bale   188

Chapter Notes   191

Bibliography   207

Index   215

Preface

Sworn bond is pervasive throughout the history, literature, and culture of England; yet there is no more important period than the sixteenth century for the cultural development, political implementation, and literary expression of this concept. The sixteenth century is defined by the continuous implementation and discussion of oaths, vows, and covenants. It is odd, then, that so little cholarship exists on this issue. There are very few comprehensive literary studies of oaths; Douglas Canfield's *Word as Bond in English Literature from the Middle Ages to the Restoration* is one of the most recent.[1] Others deal with the subject as it pertains to one author or genre, such as Frances Shirley's *Swearing and Perjury in Shakespeare's Plays* or *Shakespeare's Promises* by William Kerrigan.[2] There are many historical studies of oaths, and many that focus on the early modern period. Conal Condren's *Argument and Authority in Early Modern England* and Edward Vallance's *Revolutionary England and the National Covenant* are studies of the seventeenth century that offer excellent background overviews on oaths in the Reformation period. For this study they have been very helpful.[3] I have also drawn on historiographical discussions of oath-swearing, pertaining to a larger subject. Robert Bartlett, in *Trial by Fire and Water*, examines the role of the oath or vow in the medieval ordeal system; and Eamon Duffy, in *The Stripping of the Altars*, discusses oath-swearing as part of the adaptations of custom and belief, which accompanied the changes of the Reformation era.[4]

Although all of these books are helpful to understanding the concept of swearing, none of these studies places the swearing of an oath or the taking of a vow at the center of the Tudor mindset. My argument is that oath-swearing belongs *precisely* at its center. Rather than being an issue

Preface

that accompanies changes in belief, custom, and literature, oath-swearing defines those issues for the Tudor era. In this book, I look at sworn bond in Tudor England as a cultural phenomenon that fuses political rhetoric, literary expression, and historical perspective. I look, as people in early modern England did, at the ways in which legislation, poetry, drama, and custom interconnected by way of performative bonds. I put together affected polemicists and affecting art, and I view them in the light of the waning of ceremonialism and the emergence of the modern state. I treat sworn bond as a fundamental aspect of sixteenth century culture, and not as a reactionary element or legal technicality. Sworn bond in Tudor England produces and reflects behaviors and attitudes, rather than functioning as an accompaniment or afterthought to them. It is held deep in the cultural memory of anyone who holds a pen or pounds the pulpit, and that is why it lies at the very heart of much, if not most, written material of the era. In writing this book it was difficult to resist cataloging different types of oaths, to provide an example of each kind; it was also difficult to resist representing equally the genres of literature, drama, or polemic, to establish a "fitting" sense of variety. Instead I focused on situations and circumstances that define the era, and looked for ways in which sworn bond allows us as readers to look deeper into a culture which has been analyzed many times over.

I do not wish to look at sworn bond in terms of moral subjectivity, as is so often the case with nineteenth and early twentieth century studies on oaths. Scholarship on the issue before the second half of the twentieth century argues Protestant versus Catholic points of view; it also sees the interconnections about which I speak as an allegorical pattern meant to justify (or invalidate) Victorian imperial rhetoric. Although I often found key insights and useful resources in older studies of oaths in Tudor England, I ultimately rejected the vast majority of them. I have also rejected discussions of authorship in the cases of works in which the subject has become a contentious issue: for example, I state my simple agreement with the theory that Thomas More is the author of the *Letter to Alice Alington*, with his daughter Margaret as a peripheral contributor. From there I wish to move directly to the subject of sworn bond that defines the situation More is in. I accept that *The Troublesome Raigne of King John* is an anonymous text, which precedes Shakespeare's later play *King John*. Whether

Preface

Shakespeare drew upon it, or composed it in part or in its entirety, is not my concern here. I wish to focus on the circumstances that define John's struggle to maintain the bond between himself and his people. I am less concerned with how or why Sir Robert Cotton acquired the emended coronation oath of Henry VIII than with the simple fact that this amazing document seems to have beaten the odds more than once, surviving where other documents have been discarded or burnt. I do, however, acknowledge that Cotton's assistants probably stole it, as they tried to satisfy their master's unquenchable thirst for collectible documents. As I researched this book I found that the more I addressed issues of authorship and motive, the less I focused on sworn bond itself. I wish to ask the questions of how and why, rather than of whom and when.

Neither is this book merely a rewritten dissertation. My dissertation, from the University of Illinois at Chicago in 1998, was indeed on oath-swearing; but for this book the entire concept has been rethought. In my dissertation I focused on a carefully chosen representation of "important" authors, each of whom depicts a certain type of oath in his work. Much of my concern (as with many graduate students) was for whether I'd forgotten someone or something. The dissertation therefore simply pointed out that oaths in literature existed, proclaiming, "There's one; and there's another one; here's a third type..." This project takes almost an opposite view. Focusing on circumstance as the framework for a cultural phenomenon has caused this book to reflect a completely different course of study. The sixteenth century is a turning point upon which the entire culture of late medieval and early modern England pivots as it reconsiders its past and its future. Its relationship with oaths allows the period to look all around itself. In this book I avoided making distinctions which the English themselves did not; although sometimes I tried too hard: a well-meaning colleague once approached me during lunch, and said, "I thought of you today. I came across a document with an oath in it." To which I replied, "I'm not collecting them."

I am deeply indebted to the staff of the Huntington Library, San Marino, California, for their assistance, support, and accommodation during the years I conceived, researched, and wrote this book. Thanks also to the many scholars I have met at the Huntington over the years, with whom I have discussed my topic. Many thanks also to the staff of the British Library

Preface

for their assistance and cooperation, for granting me access to their manuscript collection, and for granting me permission to use the reproductions of the manuscript folios that appear in the book. My gratitude to the staff of the University of Southern California Library and my colleagues at the English department at USC for their words of encouragement. Heartfelt thanks go to my friends and colleagues, who have sat patiently and listened to me talk about oath-swearing *ad infinitum*; and who have made helpful and welcome suggestions, namely Michael Lieb (University of Illinois at Chicago), Thomas N. Hall (University of Notre Dame), Mary Leech (University of Cincinnati), Larissa Tracy (Longwood University), Jeff Massey (Molloy College), and Larry Swain (Bemidji State University). Thanks also to the Society for Reformation Research, for allowing me to present several papers which became chapters of this book, especially Maureen Thum (University of Michigan at Flint), who organized several of the Society's sessions at the International Congress of Medieval Studies at Kalamazoo, MI. Special thanks to my family, and to my friends outside academia, who listened to me talk about oath-swearing during Christmas dinners, Super Bowl Sundays, Oscar nights, wedding receptions, shopping trips, and afternoons at Disneyland.

Introduction

Sworn bond is central to the history of ideas, especially as the concept relates to the profound changes of the Tudor period. The means by which the English people and their nation are bound to each other is central to issues of allegiance and service to the Crown, and to identity and community. It is at the heart of ideas of personal integrity and moral character; of faith and religion; of law; and of espousal and marriage. These bonds are acknowledged in drama, poetry, and polemical writing, and they act as both sources of and reactions to the legislation and social change of the period. They become instruments by which the voices of the monarch, the court, and the commons can engage each other. This dialogue is established with great difficulty, however; it is an engagement that draws its success from the extent to which its participants can overcome the ceremonialism that had determined the course of such communication for centuries. Tudor England faced a tall order in this regard. Sworn bond needed to be rethought, its connection to service, ceremony, and allegiance redetermined, so that the nation could successfully describe itself amid the changes it experienced. The changes in culture and legislation in the Tudor era could not have been successful if the English people had not reconsidered sworn bond in this way. It would not have been enough for the monarch to simply require new oaths, or for the court or commons to change their customs. Tudor England had to reconsider the entire concept of oath-swearing and its thousand-year legacy in Britain. It was necessary, for the first time in a very long time, to rethink what a sworn bond really meant. It was necessary to accept the risk of what such reconsideration would mean for the present and for the future. If successful, the reinterpretation of sworn bond would bring God's favor upon England. It would defend

Introduction

the English Church and legitimate the Tudor monarchs. It would determine, permanently, England's superiority over its continental neighbors. The alternative was God's curse. Theologians cited it, dissenters considered it, and the Tudor monarchs feared it, but the thought of God's displeasure did not leave the collective mind of Tudor England. At stake was the permanence offered by an oath as a sacred and irrevocable act. Once sworn, an oath performs by way of the divine security of God as paramount witness and guarantor.[1] To invalidate or break an oath is to destroy the bond between God and man described by scripture. It amounts to blasphemy — about this Tudor England was sure; and that is because they understood that swearing an oath amounts to far more than the invocation of God's name to secure an agreement. Sworn bond is a way for a nation to guarantee for itself the validity of the Abrahamic covenant and secure an exclusive politic relationship with God. Rife with ironies, it is a system by which human beings, in a hubristic fervor, mean to protect God from humanity itself. It is a system dangerously prone to subjectivities, hypocrisies and abuses; and the English, from the monarch to the clergy, from the aristocracy to the commons, knew this danger.[2]

Much of the challenge about rethinking the ancient practice of oath-swearing revolves around Henry VIII. The concept experienced its most comprehensive and longest-lasting changes during his reign. Still, many questions remain about the king's attitude toward sworn bond in relation to his changing views of kingship as he devised the royal supremacy. At the onset of his reign, Henry VIII had been a monarch who appeared comfortable with the ideals of medieval kingship which his predecessors had acknowledged. The king communicated with the English church in the established manner of reciprocal but cautious deference between the head of state and the authoritative spiritual body that made its home in his nation. He communicated with his court and his commons according to long-held feudal traditions that dictated, by legislation and custom, the relationship between the king and his people. The onset of the Great Matter changed all this. The years between 1533 and 1536 produced the royal divorce, the king's marriage to Anne Boleyn, the birth of Elizabeth, the Acts of Supremacy and Succession, the establishment of the Church of England, the executions of Thomas More and Anne Boleyn, and the king's marriage to Jane Seymour. By 1536 Henry VIII was different. Suspicious,

Introduction

changeable, and ruthless, the king had become the very picture of tyranny. Although the entire decade of the 1530s represents the full range of dates for this change, the years 1533–1536 mark the period in which the king's descent into tyranny becomes evident. The rest of the decade continued this trend. There was a torrent of legislation, a long list of those accused and executed, and oath after oath after oath. Henry VIII was aware that fealty oaths describe a king's relationship to his people. What he wanted to change was the traditional means of description that had bound medieval kings to their subjects. Rather than describing fealty to the monarch, Henry VIII wished for the Oaths of Supremacy and Succession to describe fealty to *him*. It was a radical idea, one which experienced limited success, and which many dramatists, polemicists, and poets would struggle with well into his daughter Elizabeth's reign. It was certainly egomania, but only in part; it was also the king's genuine belief that his actions determined the manifest destiny of England, and that they were pleasing to God.

The descent of Henry VIII into tyranny is the subject of much scholarship. G.R. Elton had determined that Henry VIII was not a tyrant at all, but a shrewd and keen ruler whose uncompromising attitude reflected his determination to establish the Church of England.[3] In the past decade or so, scholarly views of the king's attitudes and behavior during the early 1530s have been modified, and not without reason. Shrewdness and keenness are qualities that the king certainly had; but his behavior reveals paranoia, inconstancy of mind, and cruelty. He was desperate for an heir to the extent that he married successively, but never quite successfully; he bullied parliament; he executed enemies both real and imagined (as in the case of the unfortunate Henry Howard, Earl of Surrey); and, as chapter three of this book shows, he tried to get inside the minds of his people in ways which were impossible. Henry VIII was not insane; but aspects of his behavior as he devised the legislation that would change England forever reflected an irrational desire to see how far a king's power could go. His enemies used the term *caesaropapism* for a reason. G.W. Bernard, in *The King's Reformation*, confirms as much in a thorough examination of the complex relationship the king had with his people during this time.[4] A discussion of the king's legacy as it concerns this matter is also the subject of a recent volume entitled *Henry VIII and His Afterlives*, edited by John N. King, Christopher Haighley, and Mark Rankin. It also contains con-

Introduction

tributions by Dale Hoak, Peter Happe, and Alec Ryrie, among others no less influential or expert. The volume accomplishes much concerning the study of the king's legacy; importantly, it presumes his tyranny, but also his sanity. Greg Walker has also dealt with the issue extensively in *Writing Under Tyranny*, and finds the years 1533–36 to be key to understanding the king's descent into tyranny. Other studies, like Susannah Lipscomb's recent book, are less persuasive concerning these dates. Lipscomb argues that the king changed the most in 1536; but there is much evidence to argue that by 1536 the king had already changed profoundly.[5] Rather than 1536 being the year that changed the king, it is better to say that 1536 was the year the king changed England.

Tudor society developed the practice of oath-swearing as a part of its manifold history of conversion, assimilation, and conquest. The evolution of the concept, from Roman Britain, to the Anglo-Saxons and Danes, to the absorption of the Judeo-Christian tradition, is revealing of how English society learned to draw parameters for behavior within itself. As England experienced social, legal, and religious changes throughout its history, English culture determined its interpretive categories, along with the relations and boundaries between them.[6] When the Romans brought their campaign to Britain, they brought with them an accomplished sense of legality and formalism, which had been formed partly by their ideas about sworn bond between contractual parties and in courts of law. They, like the Greeks, defined a sworn bond as necessitating the calling upon of a paramount witness. The witness could vary: it might be the State, family honor, Caesar, or a god or the gods generally. This system was later appropriated by Christian Rome, which replaced these elements with God as paramount witness, and which assumed a ceremonial role as vows became sacramental in nature. Although the Romans generally shunned the philosophical analysis of morals which the Greeks favored,[7] legal and political councilors of the Roman Republic and early empire became interested in principles of moral philosophy which referred to legal issues and hypothetical, yet relevant circumstances. In fact, the concept of "good faith" comes from the Latin *ex fida bona*. Cicero illustrates this principle as he outlines explicitly the qualities of the ideal public servant in *De Officiis*, and provides an analysis of legal issues and terms in *De Legibus*. In Book III of *De Officiis* Cicero discusses the circumstances under which oaths

Introduction

should or should not be sworn, saying that a sworn bond is a covenant with justice, and that good faith in making bonds is a cardinal virtue. In Cicero's belief, an oath upon one's conscience (*ex animi tui sententia*) must be kept in order to preserve structure in Roman law and order in the Republic's courts. Although Cicero tries to maintain an attitude of utter practicality, he does admit in *De Legibus* that sworn bond is a moral issue, and that the wrath of the gods is ultimately relevant.[8]

When it came to swearing on behalf of the gods themselves, the Romans used a more personalized and emotionally invested form of sworn bond to make vows and covenants in supplication. In these covenants, the supplicant asked a particular god for a favor and swore to present the god with an altar or commemorative tablet in return.[9] This type of bond was used with a wider scope, and among a larger group of people, than the type of formal oath reserved for the Senate and for court proceedings among men in public offices. For example, during their military campaigns, Roman generals made covenants with their own gods, offering altars, inscribed tablets, and celebratory games, or *ludii*, in return for victory on the battlefield.[10] In addition to making covenants with their own gods, Roman generals would make similar votive supplications to the gods of their enemies. Such covenants offered even greater praise, more altars, and extended *ludii* to foreign gods if they would abandon their own people and award victory to the Romans in battle.[11] As the Romans became settled in Britain, this practice reestablished itself in the form of combined offerings to Roman and British gods by the Roman settlers and by the Britons themselves. Romans and Britons began to express a combined devotion to each other's gods as the two cultures — and their manners of swearing covenants — assimilated. Surviving tablets show that votive sacrifices had been made to gods with combined Roman and British names, as in the following two examples:

> To Mars Toutatis, Tiberius Claudius Primus, freedman of
> Attuis, willingly and deservedly fulfilled his vow.
> To the god Mars Braciaca, Quintus Sittius Caecilianus,
> prefect of the First Cohort of Aquitanians, fulfilled his vow.[12]

The Teutonic and Nordic invaders and settlers of the fifth and sixth centuries introduced the Romano-Britons to the concept of compurgation, in which the witnesses to a ritual oath or covenant swore along with the

Introduction

participant of the bond, whom they supported.[13] This method of assurance through sworn witnesses was closely linked to Teutonic law and could be specifically applied to witnesses who stood in support of someone accused of a crime. "Oath-helpers," as they were called, swore to the credibility of the accused so as to clear the charge. The Teutonic invaders had a distinctive system of legal institutions and procedures, which, when paired with the tradition of Roman law, and then incorporated into Christian philosophy, resulted in a pivotal system of mandated — and also ideally meritorious — behavior. Anglo-Saxon oaths thereby developed into a categorical system of *fore-oaths, rim-oaths, cyre-oaths, cyning-oaths, unceases-oaths, hyld-oaths, pundes-wyrth oaths*, etc.[14] One *cyning-oath* records a sum of thirty hides to be put up against an oath to assure its fulfillment.[15] Each type of oath referred to a particular circumstance in which a person should find him or herself; whether one was required to swear fealty, was accused of a crime, had a property or inheritance dispute, or became embroiled in a deadly feud, there was a particular type of oath to describe the specific event and create the proper obligation, depending on the citizen's worth. The determination of worth for free, hierarchical society was based on *wergeld*, or literally, "man-gold." The concept is directly linked to how much property or money a man could put up against his oath as assurance. In this construction, the higher a person's class, the greater his or her worth; and the word of a king was considered to be incontrovertible.[16] When combined with Christian ceremonialism, this practice developed an undeniable sense of materiality, which reformers would later attack with ferocity.

After the seventh century, however, a person accused of a crime who could not secure "oath-helpers" faced one other option: to give his or her bare oath and undergo an ordeal to provide assurance of his or her word. The custom of the ordeal is of Frankish origin, but spread to Britain as Franks and Gallo-Romans influenced Britain in the centuries after the fall of Rome.[17] Its graphic, almost gruesome elements represent a radical attempt to assure a sworn bond by the Danish and Anglo-Saxon societies who absorbed and eventually relied upon the practice. After swearing his or her oath, the accused was, for example, made to plunge a bare arm into a cauldron of boiling water to retrieve a small object, such as a stone or ring. If the arm became infected after a few days, the oath could not be

Introduction

assured; if the wound escaped infection, the swearer's oath could be upheld.[18] The adoption of the practice of the ordeal as a necessary accompaniment to an unsupported oath was made more explicit, and more consequential, as the first millennium approached.

As the influence of Christian philosophy passed into Britain, many ideas of the Roman and Teutonic invaders acquired a pluralistic sense. Instead of nullifying the cultural and legal traditions of the past, the Christianized Danes and Anglo-Saxons reinterpreted and adapted those traditions. Since the Romans had occupied England for four centuries, ideas that were introduced to England via the Roman-influenced church fathers were not altogether foreign to the English. Indeed, the institutional structure of the early Christian church was based on Roman ritualism and formalism, especially concerning votive prayer and sacrifice.[19] Furthermore, the Romano-British pagan tradition of votive supplication successfully paralleled the Biblical tradition of covenant-making as depicted primarily in Gen.17, in which Abraham makes a covenant with God. Biblical covenant-making asserts the principle of performative language, particularly in its depiction of the name of God in Ex.4:14 and in the explication of the law throughout Exodus, as a description of the covenant's obligations. Abraham's covenant with God refers not to a single battle or crop, but to Israel's destiny as a nation. It also acts as binding in an indefinite sense. Christianized Britons became attracted to these aspects of the tradition and accepted its influence upon their view of what it meant to be Christian, and English. Types of sworn bond after the seventh century, and throughout the Anglo-Saxon period, reflect significantly the extent to which ancient Roman and Teutonic customs were influenced by Biblical tradition and incorporated into an English Christian philosophy.[20] The institutionalism of Anglo-Saxon law eventually paralleled that of the church, causing sworn bond to become a defining characteristic of both secular and religious life. During the eighth through the eleventh centuries sworn bond developed into a powerful cultural marker which would profoundly influence the Medieval period and eventually the early modern period. The laws of the Anglo-Saxon kings demonstrate the extent to which sworn bond became institutionalized as an element of stability and order, as is shown in these three examples:

Introduction

> FROM I ALFRED: First we direct, what is most necessary, that each man keep carefully his oath and pledge... [If, however, he pledges what it is right for him to perform] and leaves it unfulfilled, let him with humility give his weapons and his possessions into his friends' keeping and be 40 days in prison at a king's estate...[21]
>
> FROM V ETHELRED: [And] deceitful deeds and hateful abuses are to be strictly shunned, namely, false weights and wrong measures and lying witnesses and shameful frauds and horrible perjuries.[22]
>
> FROM II CNUT: [And] If the oath is then forthcoming, the man who is there accused is to choose which he will have, whether simple ordeal or an oath worth a pound within the three hundreds, in a case of [stolen goods of] over thirty pence ... and if, however, they dare not give that oath, he is to go to the three-fold ordeal.[23]

Eventually, the practice of compensating perjury with payment of goods or a fine was replaced with a more explicit ordeal system which focused on physicality and ritualism, and which reached its height during the ninth through the thirteenth centuries.[24] This development is due primarily to medieval adaptations of Roman moral philosophy. Cicero and others had rejected the idea of monetary compensation for perjury, but material assurance of a bond was nonetheless attractive to medieval society.[25] This concession, when Christianized, strengthened the power of institutional religion by elevating the significance of holy relics, scriptures, or vestments to secure an oath. These objects could be used in place of putting up one's own goods to assure one's word. Holy vestments or relics were presumed to be more acceptable to God than personal goods because they represented treasures not of this world. It was well known that vestments, relics, and copies of the Gospels had great monetary value and were considered treasures on earth; but the assumption was that the ordeal would emphasize the spiritual value of these objects, and that God would be pleased with such a priority. During this period the accused could also be made to carry a hot iron or tread upon red-hot ploughshares, for example, in an offering of his or her physical body to the assurance of the bond. If God accepted the oath and the means by which it was sworn, he would demonstrate his acceptance by way of a successful ordeal. As a result of this tradition, the Anglo-Norman period developed a culture that stood as a witness to the terrifying power of immediate, rather than imminent, Divine performativity.

Each chapter of this book examines a situation in which sworn bond

Introduction

undergoes a comprehensive reconsideration, whether it be literary, cultural, political, or theological. Chapter one examines the rare and puzzling document which is known by the title "Coronation Oath of Henry VIII," although that is hardly what it is.[26] The manuscript, affixed to an account of the king's 1509 coronation, is actually a 1534 revision of the oath which appears in *Liber Regalis*. Just before the passing of the Acts of Supremacy and Succession, Henry VIII sought to use a revised form of his coronation oath to validate that legislation. A copy of the traditional coronation oath is interlined with the king's handwriting as he attempts to reestablish the contractual relationship between himself and his people. His revision of the document is hardly admirable. Much of what the king adds to the oath conflicts with English law and points directly to a desire for absolute rule. Moreover, the revision of the document suggests that Henry VIII was considering a second coronation, which, although it was not unprecedented, would likely have been unpopular. It is a mystery as to why the king took the experiment no further. It is also a mystery as to why the document was not discarded, and how it ended up in the hands of Sir Robert Cotton over fifty years later.

Thomas Elyot's *The Boke Named the Governour* is examined for the way it uses Biblical example to illustrate how covenants among nations ought to be made. As he instructs his student in the ways of a gentleman and prospective governor, Elyot uses the ninth chapter of the book of Joshua to illustrate how a Tudor gentleman can find contemporary political relevance in a Biblical source. Faced with keeping his covenant to the Canaanites or keeping his covenant with God, Joshua is placed in a quandary, which Elyot likens to that which might be experienced by a diplomat, a position Elyot himself had held. Joshua's covenant with the disguised Canaanites shows how a governor might make difficult decisions in the absence of his king, while still remaining pleasing to God. Elyot does so with a caution for which he is famous; and rather than demonstrating timidity or equivocation, Elyot shows a profound understanding of the relationship between the good servant and his word. He frames that relationship within the difficult task of offering counsel to Henry VIII, whose wrath he both feared and anticipated. His example of Joshua shows that Elyot is aware of the realities of political life; and part of that includes knowing when not to speak too boldly.

Introduction

Chapter three provides a close examination of two fealty oaths to Henry VIII which appear in BL MS Stowe 15. The oaths are informed by the Acts of Supremacy and Succession and were both given in an official capacity at the Henrician court. The first oath, composed before May 1536, was revised later that year on the folio facing it, with the first version remaining intact (fols. 8b and 9a). The revision of the oath is of great interest for the way it attempts to guarantee fealty by policing thought. In its first version, the oath requires a pledge of fealty; it then further requires the swearer to confess or relate any treason which is known to him or her. The oath thereby attempts to define both the body and the mind of the subject as the property of the monarch. Moreover, it seeks to appropriate the tradition of auricular confession by replacing the relationship between the sacerdotal figure and the penitent with that of the king and the swearer. The second version of the oath effectively undoes this effort in an acknowledgment of the problematic nature of the first version. In omitting the language of conscience, and replacing it with more general statements of fealty, the second version of the oath guarantees a more secure bond for both the swearer and the king. The significance of the revision process is augmented by the physical adaptation of the book itself to the purpose of swearing oaths. Without a doubt, MS Stowe 15 is one of the most fascinating artifacts of the Henrician era, for its preservation of the revision process of fealty oaths, and for its role as an example of the reappropriation of Catholic artifacts for use in the reformed state.

Tracts both in favor of and against the Royal Supremacy in chapter four show that sworn fealty is often hardly a quiet or stoic affair. Henry VIII delved into the milieu of literature when he imagined a dialogue between a lawyer and a divine on the subject of the Great Matter and the royal prerogative. Before long the two opponents find themselves in agreement that the King's divorce is warranted, his authority unimpeachable. Together, they wish for quiet in the realm, to an end to the dissenting voices that disturb the peace. Thomas Swinnerton was dissatisfied with the effect of the Royal Supremacy on English recusants. Their continued muttering produced, in his view, a deafening opposition which was impossible to ignore. John Feckenham had been loyal to Mary I, and supposed his fealty to Elizabeth I to be presumed by his cooperation with the institution of her Episcopate. It was not. He protested his loyalty in a short

Introduction

book in which he stated that as he was already sworn to the Royal Supremacy, a reiteration was unnecessary. Moreover, he claimed that the queen's government was forcing him to swear, and he refused as a matter of principle. His book outraged Robert Horne, with whom Feckenham had disputed both formally and in private. Horne "blasted" Feckenham in his own book, which justified swearing to the Supreme Governorship of Elizabeth I. Offended by the "Horne blast," Thomas Stapleton tried to drown out Horne's book with one of his own. Stapleton's work supported Feckenham's fealty, arguing that there was no need for him to swear anew. Hearing the din, John Bridges blew his own "horn," in a thousand-page book condemning the false fealty of papists. With each book the authors, Catholic and Protestant, shout louder and louder, with greater and greater resolution, about the efficacy of sworn fealty amid great subjectivity.

Despite the profound consequences associated with sworn bond in both this world and the next, there were those who approached the subject with cynicism. Thomas More, John Bale, and Sir John Harington may seem to be an unlikely group, but they all share a cynical outlook concerning the application of sworn bond as a coercive measure to produce expedient political results. Chapter five looks at how each man used his knowledge of the law, his polemical skills, and his wit to indict sworn bond as a tool of oppression. Thomas More uses the pretence of a letter from his daughter Margaret to her stepsister Alice Alington to ridicule the members of the king's council who seek to bully him into taking the Oath of Supremacy. Knowing that Cromwell will intercept the letter, More feigns a dialogue between himself and his daughter in which Margaret seeks to persuade her father to take the oath. Taking his cue from two fables related to Alice Alington by Thomas Audley, More throws the fables back into Audley's face with both wit and derision. He implies that Audley does not understand the consequences of the oath which he demands that More swear. Moreover, he uses seemingly lighthearted quips and jokes to accuse Cromwell, Audley, and Cranmer of using a forced oath to advance their careers. John Bale resents deeply the forced recantation of William Tolwyn at the hands of Bishop Bonner. He blames Bonner for using sworn bond as a tool of heretical repression, but he also blames Tolwyn for recanting under pressure. For Bale, the threat of being burnt alive is not sufficient to deter a man from an honest profession of his beliefs. Rather than recant,

Introduction

Tolwyn should embrace martyrdom; rather than tolerate such travesties of justice, the Crown should disenfranchise Bonner and all bishops. With his legendary vitriol, Bale uses contemptuous humor to mock those who accept forced recantation as a form of justice, excusing no one. True to form, Sir John Harington takes a lighter approach to cynicism. In his *Apologie*, published as an emendation to *A New Discourse on a Stale Subject*, Harington attacks show trials as hypocrisies constructed to promote the careers of the judges and jurors. Reacting to the offense taken by many at the Elizabethan court regarding the subject of the *New Discourse*, Harington imagines that he is being dragged into court to recant his philosophy that the world is a quagmire of excrement in need of a well-designed toilet. He reviews the jurors for their swearing-in, noting with great irony that each one of them enjoys a good reputation for maintaining his estate, but little else; moreover, each juror is closely associated with recusancy, and some are beset with lawsuits. If these are the men who will secure his recantation in the name of justice, jokes Harington, then his conscience will remain unperturbed.

Chapter six examines three plays about King John, each of which presents issues of sworn bond that reflect the Tudor era's continuously developing attitudes toward its historical past. John Bale's play *Kynge Johan* celebrates King John as a martyr and proto–Protestant figure, whose vow to protect England exposes him to the abuses of the Roman Church. The anonymous *Troublesome Raigne of King John* and Shakespeare's *King John* investigate John's legacy by way of an introspective look at the ceremonialism of oaths that describe loyalty and good service. Although all three plays are informed by the Reformation, each one takes a different view of ritualism as it relates to how well the concept defines fealty and service in the individual subject. Each play depicts King John as a complex and problematic figure, whose view of his royal prerogative challenges his subjects' sense of duty. All three playwrights examine King John's difficult relationship with his aristocracy, clergy, and commons, and all three plays use sworn bond as a means by which those relationships can be remedied.

Edmund Spenser's attitude toward sworn bond is discussed in Chapter seven. *The Faerie Queene* is a massive work filled with different types of sworn bond and swearers; but Book III presents three female characters whose experiences with sworn bond stand out from those of *The Faerie*

Introduction

Queene's male protagonists. Britomart, Amoret, and Florimell experience sworn bond as it relates to the concept of espousal. Each woman, through her experiences with betrothal and/or marriage, is given the opportunity to learn from her successes and her mistakes; and each woman displays varying degrees of success. Britomart is the most successful character. As she discovers her destiny and journeys to seek Arthegall, she develops a comprehensive understanding of her bond to him. She perfects that understanding by establishing chivalric leagues with other knights and by rescuing the imprisoned Amoret. For her sake, Amoret possesses a full understanding of her bond to Scudamore, but because she is held captive by Busyrane she is unable to fulfill her marriage bond. Despite Busyrane's tortures Amoret does not break her vow; but she is still unable to escape, and the emasculated Scudamore is unable to rescue her. Only Britomart, as an espoused woman in her own right, has the capacity to defeat Busyrane's magic and restore the couple to wedded unity. Florimell, however, does not possess a sufficient understanding of her bond to Marinell. She vows rashly and flees Gloriana's court impulsively as she desperately seeks her beloved, who she thinks to be dead. Her recklessness becomes a metaphor for the failings of the courtly love tradition, her view of her love vow a stark contrast to Amoret's steadfast suffering or Britomart's chivalric empowerment. As with the preceding chapters, chapter seven illustrates the reconsideration of sworn bond by an author of the Tudor era. Spenser, like the other authors of this book, reexamines the oaths and vows that bind subjects to their kings, lovers and spouses to each other, and humanity to God. It was a subject in which they were deeply invested and wholly informed; one which permeated England, its politics, religion, and culture, to the core.

   Writers of the Tudor era believed that they lived in a world where sworn bond performed the power of God immediately and completely. They debated and depicted oath-swearing with great fervor because they believed that the practice revealed truths about the destiny of their nation. The authors in this project demonstrate a sense of self-awareness and self-criticism, as they develop an understanding of their history in relation to the changes of the times. Even Henry VIII himself is represented, because he is trying to achieve this understanding as well. Distinct from prayer, sworn bond communicates with God by way of promissory statement

Introduction

rather than supplication. Divine response validates truths performed rather than sanctioning pleas for favors not yet granted. The chapters in this book illustrate the development of an idea, which allowed Tudor England to reinterpret its past, examine its present, and determine its future all at once. It gave Tudor England the opportunity to aver, profess, and assert its truths in the face of God; and from Him Protestants and Catholics, aristocracy, clergy, and commons, anticipated the utmost in validation, that what they believed, and what they performed, was right.

Chapter 1

Defiance by Prerogative
The Coronation Oath of Henry VIII

The idea that Henry VIII, in devising the royal supremacy, was attempting absolutism was a concern shared by some of the king's highest commissioners and officers. This concern is related in part to one of Henry VIII's most controversial efforts: the revision of his own coronation oath. If the king could successfully (and legally) revise the coronation oath, he could redefine the entire process by which a king was made. The coronation ceremony revolved around the oath and its lawful justification by the Holy Spirit. If Henry VIII could remake the ritual bond, he could profoundly, and single handedly, affect the relationship between the king, God, and the English people that the oath described. Moreover, he could do so apart from legislation, so that if Parliament failed to ratify the bills according to his provisions, the coronation oath could act as a sort of failsafe measure to secure the control he wanted over his role as head of Church and State. There was much wrangling between the king, his counselors, and Parliament in the autumn of 1534, and the revised coronation oath suggests much about how far he wished to take the exertion of his control. It reflects a desire to take pen in hand and make changes unencumbered by the advice of council or the cooperation of Parliament.

The king was dissatisfied with the coronation oath as it appeared in *Liber Regalis*, the book used at English coronations by the Archbishop of Canterbury, and which is kept at Westminster Abbey. This oath, considered by tradition to be authoritative and official, had been administered since the time of Edward I; Henry VIII had sworn this oath in 1509, when he was crowned at the age of eighteen. In 1534 the king instituted proposed additions to the oath. He ordered a new draft of the oath to be brought to him, which he amended in his own handwriting. This single sheet is now known as MS Cotton Tiberius E viii, fol. 100a. The revised oath was never used, and, after floating among piles of official and unofficial documents in the offices of the Palace of Whitehall, it was acquired by Sir Robert Cotton sometime between 1588 and 1612, and bound along with miscellanea, much of which concerns English and French coronations.[1] In the late nineteenth and early twentieth centuries published discussions of the oath assumed that it was amended by the young king in 1509, proving, as they said, that he looked toward the royal supremacy (or to tyranny), from the outset.[2] That argument was never really expounded beyond a cursory examination of the role of the coronation oath in the overall history of the English coronation. The date of 1509 was eventually discarded in favor of 1534, a date now offered by L&P and the British Library, and by my own intensive analysis of the king's handwriting. This argument posits that the emendation of the oath coincides with the period between the break with Rome in 1533 and the Act of Supremacy in 1534. There has been very little discussion of the king's revised coronation oath and its relationship to various acts of legislation and ritual during this period; yet the oath stands as a key document, one which sheds light on the king's actions, and which provides much food for thought concerning his circumstances at the time. It is reproduced here, following the oath as it appears in *Liber Regalis*:

> Coronation oath in *Liber Regalis*:
> This is the othe that the king shall swere at his Coronation; that he shall kepe and mayntayne the right and the liberties of Holie Churche and of old tyme graunted by the righteous Christen Kings of England; and that he shall kepe all the londs, honours, and dignytees righteous and fre of the Crowne of England in all maner hole, without any maner of mynysshement; and the rights of the Crowne, hurte, decayed, or lost, to his power shall call again into the auncyent astate; and that he shall kepe the peax of the Holie

Opposite: BL MS Cotton Tiberius E viii f. 100a. The text of the oath is written in a secretarial hand, and was probably drafted for the purpose of having the king make additions to it. No other draft was ever produced and the oath was never taken. The king's handwriting is found between the lines of text, and in the margins (© The British Library Board).

1. Defiance by Prerogative

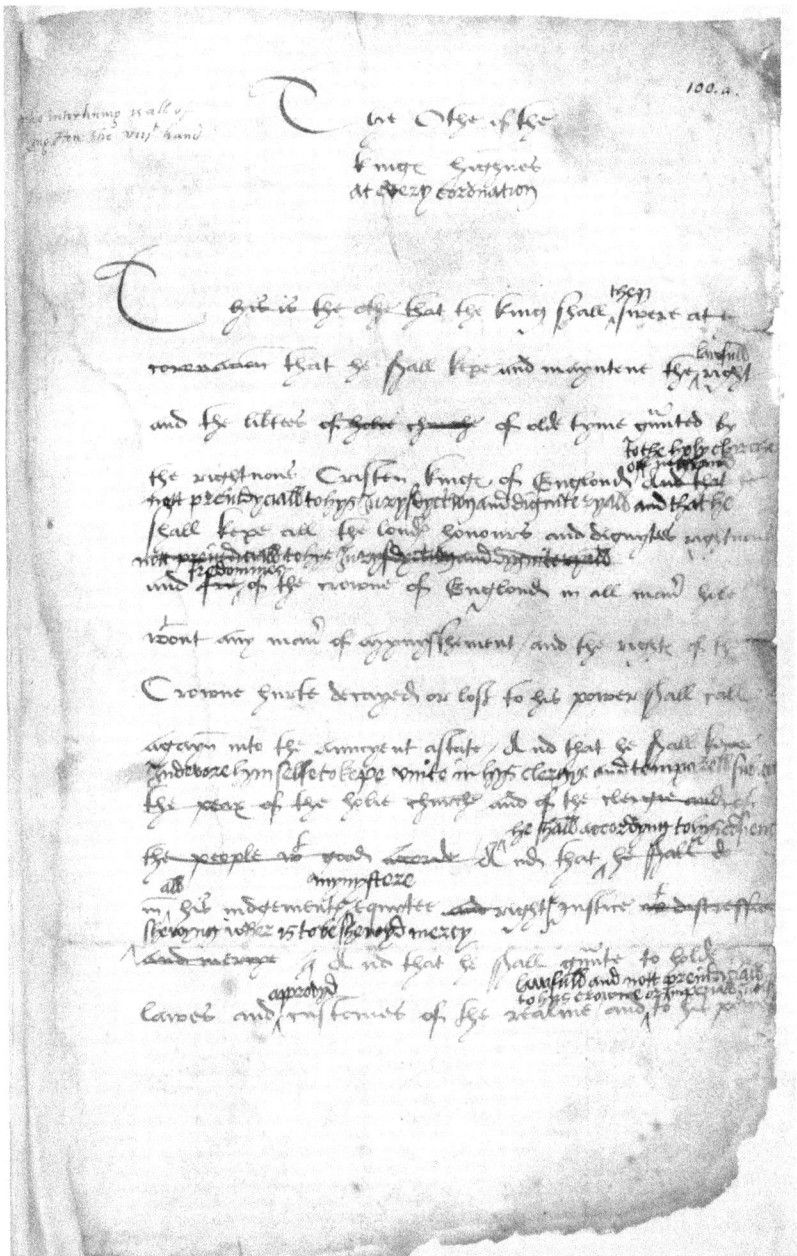

Churche, and of the Clergie, and of the People, with good accorde; and that he shall do in his judgements equytee and right justice, with discretion and mercye; and that he shall graunte to holde the Lawes and Customes of the Realme; and to his power kepe them and affirme them which the folk and people have made and chosen; and the evill lawes and Customes hollie to put out; and stedfaste and stable peax to the people of his Realme kepe and cause to be kept to his power.

MS Cotton Tiberius E viii f. 100a; Emendations by Henry VIII in italics (From anomalous form):
   The Othe of the King's Highness *at every Coronation*. The King shall *then* swere that he shall kepe and mayntayne the lawfull right and the libertees of old tyme grauntted by the rytuous Cristen Kings of England *to the Holy Chirche off England nott prejudyciall to hys Jurysdyction and Dignitie ryall, and that he* shall kepe all the londs, honours, and dignytees righteous, and fredommes of the Crowne of Englond in all maner hole, without any maner of mynysshement and the rights of the Crowne hurte, decayed, or lost, to his power shall call again into the auncyent astate; and that he shall *indevore hymselfe* to KEEP UNITE *in his* CLERGYE *and temporall subjects,* and that *he shall, according to his consciens in all* his judgements *mynyster* equytie, right, and justice, *shewing wher is to be shewyd mercy*; and that he shal graunte to holde the lawes *and approvyd* customes of the Realme, and *lawfull and not prejudiciall to hys Crowne or Imperial duty*, to his power kepe them and affirme them which the *noblys* and people have made and chosen *with his consent*; and the evill Lawes and Customes hollie to put out; and stedfaste and stable peax to the people of his realme kepe and cause to be kept to his power, *in that which honour and equite do require*.

From start to finish, the redrafted oath is problematic, insisting upon aspects of the king's prerogative and duties that conflict with legal tradition,[3] namely: "*At every coronation.*" This phrase offers a great deal of difficulty concerning the oath's legality. No king could require subsequent monarchs to follow a law or provision which he made, especially concerning the coronation. The coronation oath essentially binds the king to follow the law. Moreover, the oath requires the king to acknowledge that English law is derived in part from ancient tradition, by way of the people. In some cases these traditions go all the way back to Anglo-Saxon tribal laws and observances. The king must recognize that Parliamentary law and royal edict act in conjunction with these traditions. Coronations could be subject to stipulations which differed from monarch to monarch and which could indeed be personalized, as they later were for Edward VI[4]; but these

1. Defiance by Prerogative

differences did not change the sense of *Liber Regalis* and were agreed upon by the Archbishop, Lord Chancellor and Lord High Constable in advance of the coronation.[5] When the monarch takes the coronation oath, he or she constrains his or her own prerogative to the laws of his or her predecessors.[6] By requiring every subsequent monarch to take the new oath, Henry VIII was essentially working backwards.

"*Not prejudiciall to hys Jurysdyction and dignitie ryall*": This phrase appears just after the king's addition to the traditional oath which describes the "Holie Churche," causing the oath to read "*The Holie Churche of England.*" The phrase refers to the king's obligation to maintain the rights and liberties of the church and is rooted in the stipulations of Magna Carta. Despite Henry's insertion of the phrase "Church of England" into the coronation oath, this emendation is less than constructive. Henry VIII's version allows for his individual judgment to determine the English Church's rights and liberties based on whether nor not they conflict with his view of his own kingship. This is precisely the situation which caused King John to be forced to sign Magna Carta in 1215.

"[He shall] *indevore hymselfe to KEEP UNITE in his CLERGYE and temporall subjects*": Perhaps the least controversial of Henry's additions, this phrase seeks to establish the king as the party responsible for peace between the clergy and the laity. It does, however, have a double entendre: the phrase can suggest that to "keep unity in his clergy," means that the king has the right to ensure that his clergy is united under his Supremacy, and not divided in their loyalty between himself and the Pope. The same can be said for the laity. In this sense, the phrase diminishes the king's role as a peacemaker for the three estates of society as they relate to each other; it refocuses the relationship between the three estates so that they, as a unified group, relate exclusively to him. If the phrase were to be interpreted in this way it would conflict with traditional ideals of medieval kingship.

"*He shall, according to his conscience* [in] *all* [his judgements] *minister* [equity, right, and justice], *showing where is to be showed mercy*": "Conscience," is, of course the defining word of the Reformation, and in 1534, with Thomas More imprisoned in the Tower, the word was laden with meaning. Here, the king uses it to describe his own internal moral sense concerning how he will define and administer justice and mercy. Unfortunately, this phrase functions antithetically to the sense of the traditional coronation oath in *Liber Regalis*. The coronation oath is meant to be a check on the king's powers. It is not meant to defer to his individual conscience; rather, he must defer to the oath's requirement that he recognize that he is under the law. He must not determine justice and mercy; he must confirm and justify it.

"[and that he shall graunte to hold the lawes] *and approvyd* [customes of the realm]": Again, the king alone cannot determine which "customs of the realm" are approved. The oath, in the form having been used since Edward I (see exception below), took for granted that the customs of the realm had been determined by ancient traditions, both sacred and secular, and that those traditions were upheld by the people. Furthermore, Henry's emendation does not specify what an "approved custom" is, or how he will arrive at such a definition. His revision very likely looks toward future bans on pilgrimages, local superstitions, and saints' festivals, but it has dangerous connotations: it threatens to bring various aspects of English culture into conflict, and risks alienating people by region, especially in the North, where adjustments to the king's reformation was slower, the reception cooler.

"*Not prejudicial to his Crown or Imperial duty*": this phrase echoes the language of the Act in Restraint of Appeals, which was passed the year before, but which had gone through several drafts in earlier years. It adds the additional responsibility of imperial duty to the king's role. By recognizing England as an empire in his oath, the king thereby swears to preserve England's status as an empire, to keep the country independent from Rome. Despite the optimism it proposes, this phrase also conflicts with the traditional purpose of the coronation oath: it allows the king to decide which laws he will follow and which he will not. This language is echoed in the last line of the amended oath: "[and steadfast and stable peace to the people of his realm keep and cause to be kept to his power], *in that which honor and equity do require.*"

Percy Schramm, in his esteemed history of royal power as it relates to the English coronation service, points out that the theory of royal supremacy did not agree with the text of the traditional coronation oath and that, above all, it conflicted with the "Lytlingdon Ordo," or "little device" of Henry VII. This device of 1485 requires that the king should confirm the rights of the church *per* Magna Carta. Henry VIII included

1. Defiance by Prerogative

the "little device" in the second form of his oath, but he also included emendations which explained his revised view of his relationship to it. Interestingly, the text that Henry VIII amended himself was not the form of the oath of Edward I, as it appears in *Liber Regalis*. The form is actually based on the oath of Edward II; it is found in a printed collection of statutes of the fifteenth century, and it is slightly different. The form itself is not authoritative, and it is written in French, but the differences do not pose consequential legal issues.[7] In his study of the minor discrepancies that differentiate this oath from that of Edward I, Schramm wonders why the king would use an anomalous form in French:

> ...the compiler has merely expanded the oath of 1308 according to the rules laid down by the London author of the *Leges Anglorum* of the early thirteenth century... He narrowed down the first question of the real oath to a confirmation of the rights of the church. Then, borrowing from the legal textbook, he inserted the obligation not to alienate the Crown domains. Not til then do we get the promise of peace and justice. Finally, concessions to the people were combined: we get the security of old laws and customs from the first and fourth questions, the removal of the bad came from the text-book, while the second question provided the promise of peace, specially "al people de soun roiaulme." Most significant of all, the compiler turned the critical clause concerning the laws which the people *aura esleu* into "que les gentes de people averont faitz & elies," but in another version this dangerous promise has been made harmless by turning "averont" into "avont."[8]

Perhaps the collection of statutes was convenient — it was held by Clarencieux Hanley in the Heralds Office.[9] Perhaps the discrepancies were so minor that they were overlooked. Perhaps the king revised the oath in secret, using an anomalous form instead of *Liber Regalis* to keep the Archbishop from knowing what he was up to. Such hypotheticals inevitably arrive at dead ends, but Schramm does at any rate make a guess: that the inclusion of the oath of Edward II in a book of statutes was an error, and that it was translated into French, "along with the bunch"— had Henry used the proper form, Schramm states, he would have found it "more adequate."[10] This is possible but not probable; the anomalous oath merely rearranges several phrases without changing their meaning, or in some cases, wording. Both Schramm and Ratcliffe are right about one thing: since the purpose of the coronation oath is to place a check upon the king's power and prevent absolutism, Henry's amended form was a travesty.

Sworn Bond in Tudor England

In 1533 the king separated from the Roman Church and promoted the Act in Restraint of Appeals. He married Anne Boleyn, and awaited what he believed would be the birth of a son. As these events unfolded he crafted himself as the icon of Royal Supremacy, and by the end of the following year he had drafted a new version of his coronation oath. The redrafted oath is an exercise in the reinvention of kingship, and in the structure of iconography for a new age, and yet it is surprisingly cryptic and suggestive: Why was Henry VIII dissatisfied with the traditional form of the coronation oath? What were his intentions in redrafting the oath? It seems clear that at one time he intended to swear to its terms, but the circumstances in which that second swearing would take place are unclear. Did he mean to reswear the oath in the presence of Parliament? Did he mean to swear it secretly, as he had taken his marriage vow with Anne Boleyn? Or did he mean to perform a second coronation? Why was the oath eventually abandoned? Why was it not discarded? How did Robert Cotton obtain the oath, and how did it come to be bound with the materials that appear along with it?

It is difficult, if not impossible, to answer these questions, but the structure of the oath itself, and its milieu, provide much insight as to its role in a period brimming with activity. MS Cotton Tiberius E. viii fol. 100a displays examples of the king's casual handwriting, which is markedly different from his formal script. A poor calligrapher, the king hated writing, and told Wolsey so in a letter in 1520–21.[11] He needn't have made such an admission. It is clear from the autograph writing that the king had trouble with calligraphic forms. He describes writing as "tedius and paynefull," and from the letter one can see just how tedious it was: he is practically unable to replicate the forms of many letters. In the letter to Wolsey the king tries to be on his best calligraphic behavior as he asks the cardinal to "make good wacche" on the dukes of Suffolk, Buckingham, Northumberland, and other suspected traitors. He presses hard with the pen, making slow and deliberate, but unskilled strokes as he attempts to make the letters connect in the proper way. But in other, more private documents, his writing is more relaxed, the calligraphic forms that gave him so much trouble abandoned in favor of an abbreviated (and easier to read) hand. This is the hand found in two letters to Anne Boleyn, written just a few years later, and in many letters and notes written in the 1530s.[12] The writing is

1. Defiance by Prerogative

far more legible, the letters connected in an abbreviated fashion, and sometimes not connected at all. This is also the writing which appears on the oath, and which he eventually used in all communications by the 1530s.

The king wanted simply to write more quickly without being distracted by the act of writing. He made dozens of emendations on both official and unofficial documents.[13] In these documents the nib skips along the paper more smoothly; words are abbreviated, letters are made without flourish. He no longer wishes to emulate the elegant flow of legal hand; he wishes to get things done. In both his words and his actions, the king communicates that he wants for his future relationship with his subjects to be defined by rethought, restructured, and redrafted documents — especially oaths. This desire is especially apparent in the case of the Act in Restraint of Appeals.[14] In 1532 the king had remarked that clerical vows necessarily contradicted the oath that The Submission of the Clergy required. He sent copies of both oaths to Audley at the end of the 1532 Parliamentary session and demanded that a draft be prepared that more solidly described the clergy's role, explaining, "...that we be not thus deluded of our spiritual subjects."[15] In this case, the king's future attitude toward his clergy would be based on the critical examination, and eventual reconciliation, of these two oaths. The success of the bill literally depended on whether or not it would prevent dangerous equivocation. If the king was to have confidence in the bill, he must first have confidence in the oath it required. As it happened, the bill failed, and a new oath was not drafted. John Guy suspects that Cromwell recognized what he calls "Henry's proclivity toward Caesaropapism," and redrafted the bill himself with a more legislative eye.[16] Guy's suggestion here is interesting, as it argues that sworn bond had not been the crux of the issue; on the contrary, the king's concerns, and his actions, demonstrate that sworn bond was indeed at the heart of the matter. Although Guy's suspicion may be a bit dramatic, he has a point. Cromwell continued to work through the following year on a draft of the bill that became the Act in Restraint of Appeals. Rather than trying to rein the king in, however, Cromwell was trying to channel monarchic power into a constructive entity, and he did so by allowing many of the king's autograph additions into the bill. In one passage, Henry VIII inserted the words "of and from the said imperial crown and non other wise."[17] In their tone and intent, these words are very similar to those of the amended coronation oath, especially the passage which states, "lawfull and not prejudiciall to hys Crowne of Imperyal duty."[18]

The Act in Restraint of Appeals famously declares that England had always been an empire, and that as a result, it was "accepted in the world [that England was] governed by one supreme head and king, having the dignity and royal estate of the imperial crown of the same."[19] John Leland had been employed expressly for the purpose of constructing a suitable history for England which would argue this premise. John Bale, the "bilious" preacher and polemicist, was working on his own independent project on the same subject. Assisted by Geoffrey of Monmouth's propaganda masterpiece *The History of the Kings of Britain*, Leland and Bale ultimately "traced" Henry's lineage to Brutus by way of King Arthur, giving Henry VIII the ultimate in imperial legendary credibility. Redefining a nation's history to that extent can lead to redefining the role of its most important figure in such a way that redefinition gives way to reinvention. At the time the coronation oath was redrafted, reinvention had become a major part of the king's view of his reign. The king wanted an altogether new sense of his jurisdiction, of justice and mercy, and even of his own conscience, and he wanted those concepts to be tailored specifically to his unique view of his prerogative. To succeed, he would have to reinvent, not merely redraft, the English coronation oath, and effectively defy a thousand years of tradition and history.

By April 1533 the appeals bill had passed both houses, and in June Henry married the pregnant Anne Boleyn. Her coronation pageant, which followed shortly after, is considered to be one of the grandest and most ostentatious pageants ever staged by Henry VIII, as the king sought to reinvent not only kingship but succession as well. The coronation pageant of Anne Boleyn heralded her as the iconic mother of the New Succession, whose symbolism transcended the individuality of the child she would soon give birth to — although it was clear that Henry VIII expected a male heir.[20] Despite the fact that he was disappointed by the birth of Elizabeth in September 1533, the king wished nevertheless that the issue of succession be a part of his new coronation oath. He expected for Anne Boleyn to bear more children, and he expected to found a stable and long-lasting dynasty. The reinvented succession would be unique indeed, as it would be reiter-

1. Defiance by Prerogative

ated continually with the taking of each subsequent coronation oath ("The Oath of the King's Highness *at every Coronation*"), for an interminable number of generations. In this sense, Henry VIII appears to have looked far beyond the birth of his daughter and towards a reinvented succession that would justify and legitimize itself every time a new monarch was crowned. He appears to have considered that in doing so, each new monarch would at the same time assert his or her own legitimacy, and also that of Henry VIII as the architect of revised (or perhaps re-visioned) kingship. This idea is in stark contrast with the spirit of the traditional coronation oath, which justifies and legitimizes kingship generally, and focuses on the monarch's relationship to the people and to God. Furthermore, the traditional oath justifies the monarch being crowned as the accepted and elected legitimate *heir*; Henry's revised oath goes one step further and justifies him along with the future monarch being crowned. It emphasizes and re-emphasizes him as legitimate *progenitor*, even in his absence. This had been precisely the role of the king at Anne Boleyn's coronation pageant. Although the king did not attend, he was there nonetheless, legitimizing the pageant through his royal presence metaphorically, by way of heraldic symbol and ceremony, and physically, by way of the child Anne carried.

The king did not participate along with Anne in the coronation ceremony, but he could have if he wanted to: there was a well-established precedent of second coronations in English history. The most well-known of these was the second coronation of Richard I, Lionheart. In 1194 Richard devised a second coronation upon his return from capture in order to boost the confidence of the populace and emphasize his authority. He made the clever choice of Winchester, the ancient capital of Wessex, for his second coronation. At Winchester Richard was able to identify himself as the rightful heir of the Anglo-Saxon kings and a devotee to Anglo-Saxon saints, namely St. Edmund. The ritual reinvented him as an English King rather than a King of England and established England as the seat of his kingship rather than France, where he preferred to live. It reminded the people that Richard had, after all, been born in England and that despite the fact that he was descended from Norman conquerors, he actually represented the fusion of Norman and English cultures. It is most interesting that in performing a second coronation, Richard intended to justify his kingship by looking decidedly backward, in the direction of English cultural and spiritual heritage.[21] By way of his second coronation oath, Henry VIII intended to look exclusively forward, distinguishing himself from past monarchs and saints rather than identifying with them.[22]

There were two precedents from his Anglo-Saxon heritage upon which the king could draw: the first is that of King Stephen (1135–1154). Stephen was either formally re-crowned or simply wore his crown ceremonially, to reassert himself after having been released from captivity by his cousin Mathilda (called Queen Edith by the Anglo-Saxons), in 1141.[23] The second and more compelling precedent is that of King Edgar "The Peaceful," who was crowned in 973, fourteen years after he actually became king. Edgar was elected by the Northumbrians and Mercians in 957, when he was fifteen years old, and while his brother King Edwy was still alive. Edgar became king of all England in 959 at the death of Edwy.[24] During the interim he seems to have enjoyed a moderate level of success for an Anglo-Saxon king, organizing the English fleet, strengthening provincial administration, and doubling the number of mints. He enjoyed an especially productive relationship with Dunstan, Archbishop of Canterbury, with whom he reformed many of England's monastic houses. It was Dunstan who crowned Edgar in 973, and who introduced the tradition of anointing English kings in a magnificent coronation ceremony at Bath. In this case, Edgar was crowned at the culmination of his reign, as a means of recognition of his accomplishments and successes. Had he wished to, Henry VIII could have done the same thing, citing the Royal Supremacy as the pinnacle of his reign. He could also have taken the opportunity to anoint himself as the Church of England's first true priest. The Roman Church had long been disturbed by the fact that the anointing of the English monarch with chrism during his coronation, along with the garments he wore, paralleled the consecration of a bishop rather closely. These garments included buskins, sandals, a cope, a tunic, and a ring — all articles which bishops wore at their consecrations.[25] Jennifer Loach, in her important article, "Ceremonial in the Reign of Henry VIII," remarks that English kings were anointed in a manner defined by Pope Innocent III in 1204 as "belonging to the episcopate alone."[26] That tradition was newly relevant, and very persuasive, concerning the reformist claim that the royal supremacy symbolized the unification of ecclesiastical and temporal power.

1. Defiance by Prerogative

We can only guess at whether Henry VIII revised his oath because he wanted a second coronation after establishing the supremacy, but it is a viable possibility. Had it taken place, it may have cemented the establishment of a new, legal reign for himself and Anne Boleyn. It may have also caused riots. Anne's coronation was reluctantly attended by crowds who refused to remove their hats and who had to be paid to cheer. The more cynical persons in the crowd noticed that the elaborate banners bearing Henry and Anne's intertwined initials spelled out the words HA HA. Moreover, not all second coronations reflected success: amazingly, Henry VI had no fewer than *three* coronations: once just before his eighth birthday in 1429, at Westminster Abbey; once in Paris, as King of France at the Cathedral of Notre Dame; and once after his restoration to the throne in 1470 at St. Paul's Cathedral.[27] All three coronations carried omens of bad luck. At his first coronation Henry VI had been so small that the crown did not fit and had to be supported by two bishops. Five months later his coronation in Paris included only English clergy, causing the king to be snubbed by his own grandmother, Queen Isabel, who, although she was in Paris, did not attend the ceremony. The exclusion of the French bishops infuriated the French multitude, who mobbed the banquet hall in advance of the royals and ate most of the food. Henry VI was deposed by Edward IV in 1461, and upon his restoration was crowned again, but with little rejoicing: he was, by then, completely distracted by the great adversities and tribulations of the Wars of the Roses. He was murdered just a few months later. This precedent, far more recent in the minds of Henry VIII and his ministers than that of Richard the Lionheart, was certainly strong enough to dissuade them from plans for a second coronation. More unofficial, but no less dissuasive, were the long-standing (but unfounded) rumors about plans for a second coronation for King John after the signing of Magna Carta and one for Richard III after the murders of the Princes in the Tower. It mattered little that these were only rumors. For a king who had employed John Leland to "prove" that he was descended from King Arthur and Brutus, legend was just as powerful as history. For Henry VIII, being identified, even marginally, with Bad King John and Richard III could send the wrong message.[28]

It may have seemed prudent for Henry VIII to forgo a second coronation oath in favor of an argument for continued relevance and legality rather than a new sense of those things; the king's cause, in its legal, historical, and theological applications, was already making the case that long-suppressed truths were being revealed. Amid the apparent innovation of the many changes of the 1530s, the overall message reminds the English people that there isn't much happening that is new, after all. England had always been an Empire. There had always been a royal supremacy. Katherine of Aragon had never been the king's true wife. The Roman Church had long suppressed the genuine mission of Christianity, which the Reformed faith was now free to express. The true nature of the English Supremacy and Succession was being restored, not reinvented. It is therefore probable that the king did not take the oath, or insist on a final copy of the draft, because he did not need to. Oaths are difficult creatures because sometimes they exacerbate the problems they are supposed to solve. Then, as now, swearing an oath does not legalize a proposed idea or make a law. Earlier that year, the Acts of Supremacy and Succession had legalized the changes which were presented by the redrafted coronation oath; this legislation would have allowed the king to argue that he continued to keep the oath he had already sworn, at his coronation in 1509. This argument is actually stronger than one which would be presented by swearing a new oath. It cooperates with the tone, language, and overall message of reformist rhetoric concerning innovation; it strengthens the king's authority, and his cause, from the beginning of his reign. Had the king sworn a new oath, he may have created a mountain of controversy. It was in the king's better interest to legislate these issues rather than swear to them. It is therefore not surprising that the redrafted oath was quietly put away. The king's reformation might have argued against itself in the context of such a redundancy.

There are no apparent references to the draft of the oath in any official register, and no recorded discussion of it during Henry VIII's reign. It does not reappear after subsequent legislation or ecclesiastical policy, nor does it appear after the king's marriage to Jane Seymour or after the birth of Edward VI. Neither Jane Seymour nor any of the king's subsequent wives were crowned. Yet, somewhat surprisingly, the oath was not discarded — although this is probably due to oversight and a poor filing system. As far as its provenance can be traced (and even that is tentative), the oath lay in an unknown location, likely among a miscellaneous pile of

1. Defiance by Prerogative

loose sheets in a government office, for decades until it was acquired by Sir Robert Cotton sometime between 1588 and 1612.[29] It was common for documents to be stored in such a way, and as Kevin Sharpe points out in his biography of Cotton, it was not difficult to persuade the secretaries to lend them.[30] Unfortunately, Cotton did not always return things he was lent, and he did not always pay for additions to his library. It is amusing to think that the revised coronation oath may have been nicked. Although the oath is not an official document, it laid among state papers nonetheless. Cotton's connections in government made it relatively easy for him to acquire state and official papers — he was a member of Parliament, an adviser and unofficial secretary to the Lord Privy Seal and was a member of several government commissions. Men such as Ralph Starkey, an antiquarian, Robert Boyer, clerk of the House of Commons, and Francis Tate, of the Society of Antiquaries, along with various protégés, provided welcome assistance.[31] Cotton enjoyed collecting material on English aristocratic history, and was especially proud of his own heritage (he claimed kinship with James I). He expressed this personal and cultural pride via his collection, which included heraldic papers, chronicles, genealogies, and documents describing pageants, triumphs, jousts, and duels.[32] He was also interested in coronations.

According to Colin Tite, the book which became Tiberius E viii was probably bound at the behest of Cotton and/or his sons, although the book does not contain Cotton's binding instructions.[33] It was bound by 1612, when the volume was lent to Francis Tate, although it did not take on the title of Tiberius E viii until later. The now-famous arrangement of Cotton's books under busts of Roman Emperors and two Queens occurred between 1621 and Cotton's death in 1631.[34] The oath is bound together with various documents in English, Latin, and French, many of which describe coronations, namely: an account of the coronation of Richard II, along with an account of the procession and pageant; an account of the (first) coronation of Henry VI, along with the ordinance for the ceremony; observations on the (first) coronation of Richard I, and a document describing the coronation of Henry V and his queen. Also present is the record of Henry VIII's own coronation ceremony in 1509, along with an account of the pageant. There are two documents listing the officers to be present at English coronations, and their duties, and two documents describing the coronation ceremony for English kings. The majority of the other documents of the volume describe various ceremonies, rituals, and traditions. There is a list of the precedence of lords and ladies, and the forms of crowns particular to each; there are two descriptions of the prizes which are to be given at contests and jousts; and there is a document on the order of a herald, containing the oath of a herald. There is a genealogy of Edward III, and one of Elizabeth I, with those of various noblemen. There are seven documents listing and describing banners, heraldry, standards, and items to be worn by knights, heralds, officers of arms, and the Order of the Garter. There are three items describing royal funerals.

The revised coronation oath appears just before the description of Henry VIII's 1509 coronation. Interestingly, the oath does not follow the earlier account, to perhaps suggest a chronological progression, but is, as the item's description states, "prefixed."[35] Perhaps Cotton presumed the oath to be the one the king had taken in 1509, and perhaps he understood it as a later document; nonetheless, it is the overall context of the oath in relation to the other items in the volume which is of the most interest. Whether he believed the king to have considered the royal supremacy from the outset or not, it seems that Cotton intended for the oath to make a statement about Henry VIII and the royal supremacy precisely because of the other documents with which it is bound. In his discussion of the way Cotton developed his library, Kevin Sharpe makes the point that Cotton favored a utilitarian arrangement for his materials, binding them whenever he could with papers on the same and related subjects. Cotton expected those materials to be used in context by scholars, politicians, and courtiers using his library for research.[36] Although it is not completely cohesive, the volume is not, as Colin Tite has described, a book of "Miscellaneous Heraldic and Historical Papers."[37] There is more to it than that.

The volume reflects Cotton's attitudes toward the preservation of ancient rituals and traditions as they related to his own sense of patriotism. A committed Reformer, Cotton had wished to produce an ecclesiastical history of Great Britain which would emphasize that the English Church had always been independent from Rome. Cotton's interest in the revisionist antiquity of the Christian religion in England stemmed from the writings of John Leland, John Bale, and others, who promoted the view that England had been founded by Brutus, and evangelized by Joseph of Arimathea.

1. Defiance by Prerogative

About these efforts Sharpe states that Cotton believed that "knowledge of the past made men love and equipped them to serve their country."[38] That past was the one favored by Henry VIII, the one referenced so eloquently in the preamble to the Act in Restraint of Appeals and echoed in the revised coronation oath. Cotton intended for his collection to be an important resource for his contemporaries precisely because it was emblematic of the Protestant cause. His collecting can therefore be seen in a similar light to that of John Bale or Matthew Parker, who collected manuscripts for the purposes of constructing reformed histories of the English church.[39] Indeed, during his lifetime Cotton collected papers on the dissolution of the monasteries and Henry VIII's divorce, for the threefold purpose of historical preservation, legal reference, and promotion of the Reformist agenda.

In binding the leaves of Tiberius E viii together in the manner he did, Cotton seems to have done something quite clever — and extraordinarily equivocal. The context in one sense illustrates a dialogue among the coronations, their kings, and their traditions. In this sense the single leaf containing Henry VIII's revised coronation oath is not merely an attachment; it is part of an argument, made by the documents themselves, justifying the king's Reformation, and his right. One item, folios 248–250, describes "Articles of Agreement Between ... K. Henry VI. and Ric. D. of York, concerning [against] the title [of Richd. D. of York] to the crown [1460]." In this sense, the revised oath demonstrates Cotton's desire to argue in favor of a Tudor understanding of the past. Collected between 1588 and 1612, the documents of Tiberius E viii produce the same kind of language arguing for Tudor legitimacy that Shakespeare's histories do, or that Spenser's *Faerie Queene* does, in that same era. Cotton's documents speak to the cohesive nature of the kingdom's ancient rituals, which are clarified by the Royal Supremacy. It is therefore no accident that folio 243 is a letter on the marriage of priests, and that folios 264 ff contain an excerpt from one of Leland's books. Another item, near the end of the volume but speaking loudly concerning its odd (and perhaps ironic) placement, is a description of the shrine of Thomas Becket, which Henry VIII famously destroyed.[40] Rather than being attached to the end of the description of Henry VIII's 1509 coronation, the revised oath is *prefixed*. The royal supremacy is not an afterthought; it is an enrichment to an already great empire and its traditions.

In another sense, albeit less so, Cotton's placement of the revised oath alongside other coronations, observances and rituals can be seen as quietly subversive. In binding, cataloguing, and lending state and official papers, and papers which described ancient and privileged rituals, Cotton created a collection which provided a sometimes uncomfortably transparent view of kingship, one which could be open to the critical observations of commoners.[41] As the reign of Charles I approached its unfortunate apex, Cotton expressed the view that a king could expose his failings by comparing himself with earlier reigns.[42] Although Tiberius E viii was bound by then, it stood as a possible testimony to that idea, since the redrafted oath could be seen as an attempt at Caesaropapism by Henry VIII. This idea could speak volumes when compared with the reigns of Richard II and Henry VI, whose coronations also appear in the volume. Later in his life Cotton would be accused of possessing and circulating seditious papers against Charles I; the king's suspicion culminated in Cotton's library being closed, and Cotton is storied to have died of grief at the loss of his library. Context, therefore, stood dangerously close to intent if and when the king chose to read between the lines, especially if he knew, as most did, that Cotton was conscious of how he arranged his material as he bound previously unrelated sheets together in the same volume. In making his library speak for him, Cotton stood to emerge as an innovator, but also as a traitor.

The case of the revised coronation oath of Henry VIII is a strange one indeed, because it ultimately produces more questions than answers, more implications than evidence. In studying the oath the scholar is forced to reckon on behalf of Occam's razor more often than a scholar ought to. The fifteenth century book of statutes was probably convenient, and the anomalous oath of Edward II was probably translated along with other papers it didn't belong with; the oath was preserved *per accidens* by someone who was either too busy or too disorganized to throw it away. Perhaps it wasn't his job to discard it, in any case. Cotton likely stumbled onto the single sheet while he or his friends "borrowed" a pile of papers eagerly lent by secretaries who were running out of room for miscellany they hadn't paid attention to in years. It is not known how long Henry VIII considered the revision of his coronation oath. Perhaps he concentrated on the effort for a few months, or even a year. Perhaps he considered the option of a new oath, or even a new coronation, for only a day. Perhaps the oath was

1. Defiance by Prerogative

seen only by Audley and Cromwell; perhaps it was seen by other ministers or members of parliament. It is dramatic to think that the oath, rife with legal controversies, was proclaimed a travesty and taken away by Cromwell before the king could harm his own cause; it is more likely that the project was abandoned because it simply wasn't necessary. Despite such formidable variables, one fact emerges which overcomes the uncertainties of circumstances whose details have been long forgotten: where the king's reformation is concerned, there are no small issues or implications. The king knew that most of all, and he never let anyone forget it. The efforts of Henry VIII to reinvent himself, and kingship in England, relied upon oaths to keep his motives, his mission, and his prerogative dangerously relevant. In doing so, the king made sure that any oath that referred to his kingship was of the utmost consequence.

Chapter 2

The Matter of Resources
Sworn Bond and Biblical Example in The Boke Named the Governour

The courtiers and counselors in orbit around Henry VIII were expected to assert their loyalty continuously. They were expected to give much more than their obedience to the king's wishes or their assent to his legislation, however; they were expected to give the king their friendship and support him in fraternity. In doing so they aimed to justify their positions as men worthy of their hereditary privilege and status as Parliamentarians. It was necessary for a courtier to have a good notion of himself: he was to be confident, clever, mindful of his pedigree and station, and ready, but not eager, to advise the king if and when he was called upon to do so. To be successful, a courtier needed to walk a fine and sometime dangerous line; and Sir Thomas Elyot knew that fact as well as anyone. Elyot's career provides an example of how life in the king's service called for a combination of caution and assertiveness, the success of which was determined only by the king's reaction to advice given in his presence or decisions made in his absence. The courtier's only recourse was, in Elyot's view, a strong course of education and training. In *The Boke Named the Governour* Elyot outlines the type of education that will produce a successful career for the young man in governance: a solid foundation in the classics and Biblical scholarship, and a prudent framework of moral philosophy, along with occasional remarks concerning manners and behavior becoming a gentleman. Despite its typical structure, however, Elyot's book provides the gentleman with

2. The Matter of Resources

an important, and possibly life-saving reminder: when a gentleman is in the king's service, his word is not his bond solely; it is also the king's.

Much of Sir Thomas Elyot's work in *The Boke Named the Governour* revolves around his desire to develop new insights about the texts that formed the core of his prospective student's education. These insights were to help the student develop important intellectual skills which he could then apply to his political career. In his discussion of the Book of Joshua in Book III, Chapter VI, Elyot encourages new insight of the Biblical source by retelling and reinterpreting its narrative. He engages in this effort so that the source will cooperate with two concepts which Elyot feels will be important to his student's budding career: service to his lord, and sworn bond. In Chapter VI, Elyot retells Joshua Chapter 9, in which Joshua makes a sworn pact with a group of disguised Canaanites, and then keeps his word after the Canaanites are exposed. Joshua is portrayed as an ideal spiritual and political leader because of his ability to make, interpret, and keep a solemn oath under complex and momentous circumstances. In this short, but important example, Elyot places sworn bond at the center of good service. Joshua represents both his Lord and the Law, and yet his success is determined by a decision which he alone makes. Joshua's success infers much about Elyot's outlook on foreign relations, even if, as Greg Walker states, Elyot's stance on ambassadorial politics and foreign policy in *The Governour* is unpronounced.[1] Walker is correct that no specifics are discussed in these areas, but Elyot's example of Joshua shows that Elyot is willing to refer to these issues conceptually and abstractly. The student must make the connections in his own mind, via his own experiences, and Elyot was confident that a worthy and talented student would do so. To use a phrase often employed in Elyot's day, the governor must be a "friend to the king." It is a more complicated idea than the phrase suggests, but a discussion of how Elyot understood it sheds much light on what he intends for his student to be able to accomplish, and how Joshua becomes a good figure for illustration of the concept.

As a counselor, a governor in the service of his prince was expected to be a "friend" to his lord. As such, the role was tenuous: it took a wise and moderate counselor to interpret his duties correctly, and provide the prince with advice that would guide him toward virtue. If a counselor was expedient, or eager for fame at court, his "friendship" would quickly become flattery, and his counsel would fail to prevent the prince from becoming destructive, both to himself and the nation. The inevitable result would be tyranny. Elyot was familiar with the long-held maxims later made famous by Machiavelli's *Il Principe*, especially concerning flatterers. He was also familiar with what the Romans called *amici principis*, or "the friends of the prince," and he was prepared to make distinctions between the prince's true friends and ambitious courtiers who acted in self-interest. The role of the counselor, therefore, in Elyot's experience, was part of a contractual relationship between the king and his "friend." It was an unofficial bond, but it was one that was upheld by centuries of tradition concerning the ideals of kingship and counsel that stretched back to the days of the Roman Senate. A good king was expected to surround himself with wise counsel, to whom he listened and whose advice he considered carefully before acting. He was to expect that they would disagree with him from time to time, and when they did he was expected to weigh the evidence of their arguments with the nation's best interests in mind. In this sense, flatterers were seen as destructive elements in this relationship. Although they posed as "friends," their continuous agreement with the prince, and their willingness to indulge his whims, encouraged tyrannical qualities that would soon manifest themselves with tragic results.[2] In Elyot's book, the "friends" of the prince are more like Roman senators, who spoke for the common good of the Senate, and who spoke honestly and eloquently to their king.[3] The reciprocal nature of the relationship between the prince and his true "friends," therefore resembles a covenant. Bound to each other, and to the premise that they act in the greater interest, they cultivate their roles but forget themselves as men. Unable to do these things, the tyrant and the flatterer mutually destroy each other, and also the greater good. This idea is central to *The Governour's* promotion of the ideal counselor; but the way Elyot uses the example of Joshua is particularly telling. It reflects Elyot's desire to employ the idea in a specific situation in which a governor must make a decision in the absence of his lord. As a former ambassador who had to answer for the decisions he made (or failed to make) while at the court of Emperor Charles V, Elyot was familiar with the situation.

    Sworn bond is featured as one of the most socially relevant aspects of a nobleman's life in *The Boke Named the Governour*. He will encounter it in court, as testimony; he will make personal pledges between himself and

2. The Matter of Resources

others; and he will bear witness to political leagues between ambassadors and nations. A successful governor must be considered worthy to make a viable oath, and he must be faithful to his promise once he makes it. By tradition, a nobleman's worth was his right. He could have his bare word accepted in court without witnesses, and he could put up his word for a commoner to swear by.[4] Traditionally, the nobleman had been called upon to stand by his word as a man of action, a representative of the aristocratic-military complex that defended his lord, and his lands. In Elyot's time, however, political realities had changed, and warfare was no longer considered to be the chief occupation of the aristocracy. As Anne Wagner points out in her article "Idleness and the Ideal of the Gentleman," the Tudors had stabilized the monarchy to a great extent in the aftermath of the Wars of the Roses. With power concentrated in the office of the king, and with Henry VIII's interests in centralizing it, noblemen no longer felt the need to choose between the action-oriented career of the knight and the contemplation-oriented career of the clerk.[5] As he was in tune with his times, Elyot cooperated with the idea that the man of action should *study* action, and come to court as a prepared and modern figure.

Elyot's student was therefore encouraged to seek a career path that trained him as an administrator as well as a military figure. His view of his own word of bond was expected to adapt in conjunction with his view of his budding career, and it was expected that he would employ his word of bond as a "friend to the king." In his book, Elyot emphasizes the importance for a governor to be oath-worthy to the extent that he includes sworn bond in his discussion of the Cardinal Virtues in Book III. Elyot's discussion of the Cardinal Virtues is an idealized and romantic one, and it deliberately echoes courtly literature that promoted the nobleman as an idealized and romantic figure. *The Book of St. Albans*, by Dame Juliana Berners (1496), and *On Love* by Andreas Capellanus (1473) were two fairly recent well-known examples, but Elyot's generation was familiar with hundreds upon hundreds of similar books, both in England and on the Continent.[6] Elyot means for his discussion of sworn bond to draw upon such traditional sources even as it promotes modernity in the figure of the nobleman. It reminds the sixteenth-century nobleman that he is a figure in changing times. It reminds the reader of Elyot's book that the author is aware that the times are changing.

Elyot knew that his student had very likely been brought up to begrudge learning, and that many in the aristocratic and merchant classes believed that learning was a waste of time and money. As Anne Wagner points out, parents feared that sons who engaged in learning would neglect their families' estates, and put the inheritance of their siblings and descendants at risk.[7] Elyot tried to remedy this notion by encouraging young noblemen to accept learning as an essential element in their training, rather than as a substitute to their training.[8] Joshua is therefore a model example. He is at once one of the Bible's legendary prophets, and also a military man of action, via the Israelites' victory at Jericho. When he makes, and keeps, a sworn pact with his enemy, Joshua is compared to the Tudor man of action who is at once a keen political ambassador and a learned representative of the law. The example of Joshua's oath of goodwill with a group of disguised Canaanites allows Elyot to circumvent the stereotype of the effeminate man of letters who was unprepared or fearful of dangerous politics.

Elyot therefore uses sworn bond to provide a common ground for the combination of Biblical and classical sources in his discussion of virtue. In doing so he attempts to narrow the gap between two types of influence on his student's career: moral philosophy and literary/historical insight. My discussion here parts with Ruth Kelso's assertion that humanists quoted classical philosophy "quite as a matter of course, without regard for changes in circumstances."[9] In his example of Joshua, Elyot chooses his examples from Cicero and Aristotle carefully, so that they might help the student reach a new insight about Joshua's political abilities. Although Elyot does feel compelled to choose Aristotle and Cicero, his use of these sources is not superficial; he wants for these sources to complement the Biblical material so that his student will see how his materials can be used to justify each other mutually. Elyot therefore encourages his student to personalize his lessons, seek connections in his resources, and apply them to his own experiences in the service of his government.

Elyot falls short, however, of using moral philosophy to promote the cultivation of his student's individual persona. Although he believes that humanist learning contributes to the dignity of the individual, he does not use it as part of a theological or doctrinal discussion. Elyot was, of course, wary of the decadences of court life, and he bemoans the moral corruption of society throughout the entirety of his work. Even so, Elyot's use of Biblical examples throughout *The Governour*, and that of Joshua in

2. The Matter of Resources

particular, promote a general adherence to Christian virtue rather than a lesson in morality meant to cultivate his student's spiritual identity. Rather than producing a counterproductive text, this choice actually reflects a broader attitude that Elyot had toward Biblical text. As Paul Siegel notes in his discussion of English humanism and the Tudor aristocracy, humanists avoided allegorical discussions of Biblical texts, especially those which were considered "overly elaborate." They preferred instead to discuss the plain sense of Scripture, as it appealed to the natural intelligence of the student who understood it.[10] As it is, Elyot's example of Joshua is not particularly elaborate, *per se*, and although he allows it to encourage political savvy, Elyot does not over interpret it or cause the example to be explicitly theological. Moral philosophy in *The Governour* is meant to cultivate restraint in one's professional life; and so, even as he discusses oathworthiness as a Cardinal Virtue, Elyot does not consider the development of his student's relationship to his faith. Elyot's use of moral philosophy is meant to develop his student's prudent sensibility, but not necessarily his persona. This distinction reflects further on Elyot's legendary caution when it came to expressing his opinions in his work. Elyot's book contains instruction and example, but it is not polemical.

Elyot is careful sometimes to the point of ambiguity, or even blandness, and *The Boke Named the Governour* is famous for the extent to which it avoids a discussion of the King's Great Matter or of Luther's teaching or of Tyndale's books, all of which were subjects that dominated court life at the time of the book's publication. In the case of Tyndale and other reformers whom Henry opposed, Elyot is especially silent — likely because he had failed to capture Tyndale on the Continent on the way home from the Emperor's court in 1532. When it came time to express his opinion, however, Elyot did give it. Although he maintained traditionalist views, Elyot assured the king, via Cromwell, that he supported the Royal Supremacy. In a letter to Cromwell in 1536, just days before the execution of Thomas More, Elyot identified himself as a friend of the king rather than a friend of More. Interestingly, he used sworn bond as the means by which to define this friendship. In telling Cromwell that he intended to take the Oath of Supremacy, Elyot states that he had been More's friend "Usque ad aras," and that their friendship had ended when More refused the oath.[11] The proverb states, "Usque ad aram amicus sum," or "I am your friend, up to the altar." The adage in which it is found is Plutarchan; it was well known to humanists, and it had been repeated in recent years by Erasmus. Elyot's relationship to More and his circle was professional, and largely peripheral; but he made sure Cromwell understood that he was willing to defend traditionalism only up to the point where it became seditious. When it came to his oath, the king would have it.

Despite the clarifications offered by anecdotes and letters, Elyot's caution inevitably intrudes upon his pragmatism. His promotion of classical and Biblical ideals encourage his student to accept a sort of "Golden Age" of antiquity, complete with images of immutable justice, unwavering codes of behavior, and exemplary foreign politics. Greg Walker goes so far as to state that Elyot had an unrealistic attitude, and there is much in *The Boke Named the Governour* that argues in favor of that view.[12] Elyot might have been able to overcome this problem had he been able to discuss specific events and circumstances, but the naming of names and the discussion of current events was overwhelmingly dangerous. In this sense, part of becoming a successful governor is the student's ability to read the book and make the necessary connections himself, based on how observant he is at court, how well he listens to his elders, and how keen a mind he has. In this sense, the example of Joshua allows Elyot to use the subject of sworn bond as a springboard for discussions too risky to hazard in print: Elyot's example of Joshua's pact with the Canaanites seeks to provide political advice, give a moral example, encourage formal learning and promote ideals all at the same time. It is quite a tall order, and at times Elyot seems to struggle to keep all of his bowling pins in the air. As a political device with a Biblical source the story of Joshua's pact helps to hold Elyot's discussion together, as do many similar examples throughout the book; without *The Governour's* political agenda Elyot's idealism would overwhelm his narrative, and his work would cease to be relevant.

At the onset of Book III, Elyot presents his view of Joshua as an accompaniment to his ideas concerning the relation of the governor to the State he serves. In concordance with his legendary caution, Elyot avoids naming the King as the Supreme Head of such a State, but he does allow the king to emerge as a figure with an enhanced role in the new structure of governance ushered in by the Tudors. These ideas come mostly from Plato, who holds that the measure of a society's worth is the degree to which it

2. The Matter of Resources

observes its own standards of rectitude. These standards are evident in dealings between individuals, and also between nations, and they must be observed by those who possess an undeniable sense of virtue. Similarly, Aristotle's ideas in *Nichomachean Ethics* suggest that virtue results when choices made for their own sake stem directly from what he calls "a fixed and permanent disposition of character."[13] Here, Elyot sees a perfect outline for the young governor's attitude towards his nobility, and a perfect parallel with Joshua's behavior as God's representative for Israel. Elyot can emphasize his point that oath-worthiness is an ideal form of human trust, based upon an innate sense of virtue. From this "sense" an equally ideal form of nobility "naturally" progresses, and the student must therefore accept his duty to inherit it as part of his aristocratic privilege.

Before showing how Joshua embodies these ideal qualities, Elyot warns his student about the state of nobility, and of sworn bond, in his own country and time. Elyot bemoans the decadences of his own age, and encourages the young governor to adopt an idealized view of the ancient world as a remedy for contemporary moral decay. He says:

> But now to speke in what estimacion this vertue was of old tyme ... whiche nowe (alas to the lamentable reproche and perpetuall infamie of this present tyme) is so neglected throughout Christendome that neither regarde of religion or honour, solemne othes, or terrible cursis can cause hit to be observed ... Neyther seales of armes, signe manuels, subscription, nor other specialities, ye uneth a multitude of wytnesses be nowe sufficient to the observynge of promyses.[14]

Elyot is particularly concerned with the mere appearance of worth, especially at court. The semblance of worth is a sure sign of false friendship to the prince, and no amount of wit can make up for a lack of honesty. Maintaining esteem and reputation is essential, but only if such esteem is augmented by the governor's actual performance in society rather than by hearsay or appearances. Elyot says:

> As in praysing a manne for some good quailtie, where he lacketh iustyce, men will commonly saye, he is an honorable man, a bounteouse man, a wise man, a valiaunt man, savynge that he is an oppressour, an extorcioner, or is deceytfull or of his promise unsure.[15]

Moreover, craftiness and fraud are condemned by Elyot as "ungentill," making such people unworthy of their nobility.[16] He cites both Cicero and

Plato in his condemnation of fraud, or false swearing,[17] but he reserves his strongest statement for a common theological assertion: that since God is truth, fraud constitutes blasphemy. By way of this statement Elyot connects false statement with false action: perjury and falsehood "in covenaunt, bargayne, or promyse" are said to be "...as playne agayne Justice as if it were enforced by violence."[18] Justice, in this sense, is meant to refer allegorically to both God and the king; just as blasphemy had been used for centuries to describe the re-crucifying of Christ, perjury is used to describe the violent usurpation of the king's justice. Nevertheless, Elyot does not use this idea to try to unify the figures of God and the king; instead, he unifies the principles of moral rectitude and proper service. Perjury, whether used as part of a sacred oath or a political bond, is a form of violent attack upon justice in its paramount form, sacred or secular.

Elyot knew that measuring honor in Tudor society was difficult, especially after the political crises of the fifteenth century. Because the chivalric code was waning in relevance, Tudor politics relied heavily on circumstance and opportunity. Reverence, glory, and fame could be identified with the privileges of titles and offices, but there was little reference to worth, or specifically, what Elyot calls *fides*, in an abstract sense.[19] Despite Howard Norland's persuasive argument that Elyot, because he held intermediate government positions, avoided conceptual reasoning, Book III, and its discussion of sworn bond, shows that Elyot did employ it when the situation called for it.[20] The overall tone of Book III balances a condemnation of political expedience with an appeal to be patient with contemporary circumstances. Elyot therefore creates a sense of urgency for his student, encouraging him toward an eagerness to absorb positive example and carry forward an ancient past as part of a realization of his national identity.[21]

In Chapter VI of Book III, Elyot focuses on the Ninth Chapter of the Book of Joshua. Israel is visited by disguised Canaanites who desire a political league with Joshua, the nation's leader and keeper of the Covenant. The league is made in the form of a sworn bond. In the Biblical narrative, Joshua swears to the league in good faith, only to discover that his new allies are actually his sworn enemies.[22] He is therefore faced with a profound dilemma: as Israel's leader, he must either preserve the league and violate God's Covenant, or break the league and perjure himself in God's name. Ultimately, Joshua chooses to honor the pact. He thereby violates the Covenant

2. The Matter of Resources

generally, but preserves an oath sworn in God's name specifically. Elyot's example of Joshua's pact with the Canaanites makes the most of an example of the Bible's implicit political theory. It depicts a situation in which God's Covenant is used as the basis of a comprehensive justice system, but also in which Joshua is shown to make decisions based on his own judgment.

Elyot's reading of Josh. 9, although it is not literal, makes the most of its "plain sense." As he retells the story he allows the narrative to reflect on politics and faith in Henrician England. He paraphrases loosely and inserts commentary, but he basically allows the story to tell itself. Elyot emphasizes Joshua's sense of diplomacy and leadership in making a sworn league with the disguised Canaanites. Then, he portrays Joshua as ideally virtuous regarding his keeping of the promise once the visitors are found to be enemies. Elyot does provide, however, one important departure from the Biblical narrative: in Elyot's version of the story, Joshua's capacity for making and keeping the pact reflects upon him alone. Elyot de-emphasizes other characters who interact with Joshua in the chapter, especially those who have an effect on the pact. Elyot downplays the role of the Israelites in influencing the outcome of the incident, even though their participation appears in the Biblical text. Josh.9:18 states that the "princes of the multitude" make a collective decision to avoid God's wrath by preserving the pact, because it had been sworn in God's name.[23] Moreover, the same verse states that the other members of the "multitude" were not satisfied with the decision, and voiced their discontent.[24]

Elyot's depiction of the event as revolving solely around Joshua is consistent with the status quo of the Tudor monarchist view, which holds that magistrates are extensions of the monarch's will.[25] However, in downplaying the roles of the "princes of the multitude" and the other Israelites, Elyot is able to make reference to an important contemporary issue: the role of Parliament in the Great Matter and budding Royal Supremacy. Again, Elyot is cautious to the point where he can be accused of ambivalence, but despite his subtlety he is able to communicate his wary acceptance of the profound changes which were on the horizon. As the sole architect of the decision to preference the covenant over the individual bond, Joshua acts as the agent of the lawgiver. Here his role is ambassadorial, as Elyot's had been in the year before he published *The Governour*, but it is also decidedly aristocratic. As the successor to Moses, Joshua's innate worth is literally sanctioned by God.[26] That which is inherited as part of an ancient and sacred tradition must be cautiously updated but dutifully preserved. If the governor is successful, then he, like Joshua, will find favor with God and he will preserve his nation. One form of manifest destiny will, as a matter of course, therefore follow the other. At the center of this idea is the Tudor monarchy itself. Such an interpretation of the narrative allows Elyot to downplay any suggestion that the "multitude," or its princes, are Parliamentary figures. Had Elyot depicted the participation of the princes of the multitude, he would have offered too much praise for Parliament; moreover, the murmurings of the rest of the multitude would have suggested that more authority of the Commons was appropriate in deciding the legitimacy of the king's divorce, and the issues that surrounded the early drafts of the bills which became the Acts of Supremacy and Succession not long after. Elyot therefore chooses to tune the story toward the Israelites' collective and immediate support of Joshua's human, but divinely-sanctioned decision-making. In doing so he supports the king concerning a matter to which Henry VIII was sensitive.

Despite Elyot's suggestions that the chapter refers to the workings of the upper echelons of power, Elyot is sure to communicate the fact that Joshua acts with the entire nation of Israel in his interest. The political implications of Joshua's obligation to preserve God's Covenant serve to aid Israel in its battles with neighboring nations for possession of the land promised by God. Making a sworn league with a presumed ally is identified as a just action because it assures the preservation of requisite political safeguards that protect the "publicke weal." Joshua is therefore depicted by Elyot as a gentleman in service to his nation, and his focus on justice and *fides* is placed appropriately. The gentility of Biblical figures had been presumed by the authors of courtesy books for centuries, and in the sixteenth century they continued to do so; Dame Juliana Berners had divided the offspring of Noah into "gentylmen" and "churls"; and in Elyot's own time he witnessed the practice of creating genealogies that "traced" the lineages of Tudor monarchs to Biblical heroes.[27] Knowing his student to be familiar with these sources, Elyot wishes to convey a view of public governance, which, together with an innate sense of nobility, bears as much consequence on English society as Joshua's leadership has for Israel's identity as a nation. The more worthy the governor is, the more worthy is the

2. The Matter of Resources

sense of nationhood that develops from the "public weal." On this point I agree with Howard Norland when he says, "For Elyot the "publicke weal" must have priority over individual concerns, and it is the governor's duty through his counsel to insure that that precedence is maintained."[28] Although he makes an individual choice, and although that choice is based on his exclusive relationship with God as keeper of the Covenant, Joshua acts in the interests of the nation. True to his depiction of the governor as a dedicated and selfless servant, Elyot maintains the distinction between the governor's abilities and his persona. Joshua does not act out of concern for his soul, or out of fear that God will punish him individually; his concern is for Israel as a whole, and for its collective future. That being the case, Elyot does not allow Joshua to be seen as acting on behalf of the "common weal," in the Tudor sense. Joshua does not act without Supreme sanction, and he is not considered equal to the others. Indeed, the others, as they suggest Parliamentary and possibly sacerdotal figures, are kept in the periphery.[29] "Multitude" threatens to become an inconvenient word for Elyot if he fails to make this distinction, and so his interpretation of the narrative quietly controls it.

In order to make the point that a student of civil leadership can, indeed must, find close parallels between classical studies and Scripture, Elyot applies Ciceronian and Aristotelian principles to his interpretation of Joshua's skills as a political leader. Elyot especially draws examples from *De Officiis*, in which Cicero's view of an oath is clear: it is a sacred and solemn religious practice.[30] Cicero's statement further emphasizes Elyot's point that Joshua's responsibilities — and thus the Tudor nobleman's — are not solely political. In swearing the league he is bound to preserve the sanctity of both the Covenant and the individual oath as well. Fear and reverence for the Almighty are therefore primary requisites for deeming someone oath-worthy. Elyot says:

> Afterwarde it was discovered that they were Cananees, whiche if Josue had knowne before the leage made he had nat spared any of them, but whan he resolved in his mynde the solempne othe that he had made and the honour which consisted in his promyse, he presumed that faythe being observed unperrished shulde please all mighty god above all thinges.[31]

Elyot expects his student to recognize immediately the influence that Cicero has upon Elyot's interpretation of Josh. 9. Cicero says:

> Furthermore, we have laws regarding warfare, and fidelity to an oath must often be observed in dealings with an enemy: For an oath sworn with the clear understanding in one's own mind that it should be performed must be kept; but if there is no such understanding, it does not count as perjury if one does not perform the vow.[32]

Joshua's understanding of his oath is therefore reconciled with Elyot's understanding of Cicero. This connection demonstrates Elyot's focus on the legalism of war as well as on the sanctity of a sworn league. However, although Elyot's reading of Josh. 9 challenges his student to modernize the legendary Biblical paradox, Elyot is careful not to portray Joshua as a courtier. Joshua is not depicted as expedient or opportunistic concerning his relationship with God or concerning his privileges as a political leader. Instead, Joshua's sense of honor and justice is filtered through Cicero.

Elyot further encourages a classical interpretation of Joshua's sworn league by providing a connection to Aristotle. Elyot's presumption is that Joshua makes his choice to preserve the oath based on his belief that this particular action will please God best. Although preservation of the Covenant is Joshua's responsibility, Joshua's actions are made to reflect a sense of consequence for an individual circumstance. They also reflect a dedication to law as a general ethical concept. Here, Joshua considers the law in the absence of the Lawgiver, an ethical principle found in Aristotle's discussion of equity as a rectification for issues of legal justice in *Nicomachean Ethics*:

> ...law is always a general statement, yet there are cases which are not possible to cover in a general statement.... And this does not make it a wrong law; for the error is not in the law nor in the lawgiver, but in the nature of the case: the material of conduct is essentially irregular. When therefore the law lays down a general rule, it is then right ... to rectify the defect by deciding as the lawgiver would himself decide if he were present on the occasion and would have enacted if he had been cognizant of the case in question.[33]

In this view, Elyot emphasizes Joshua's wisdom concerning situational politics. The incident has afforded Joshua no other option: he must either break God's commandment to keep the Covenant, or break a specific oath made in God's name. He must therefore choose between a general rule and an individual circumstance by deciding which law to break. Again, Elyot makes a connection between Joshua and the Tudor nobleman, who saw, both in civil service and at court, a variety of situations which would

2. The Matter of Resources

affect him in totally different ways. Like many other men in government service, Elyot learned hard lessons about the politics of association and ambition. He had suffered professionally because of his connection to the fallen Wolsey. Despite having resigned his clerkship in the assizes to focus on the King's Council, Elyot failed to hold a government position of any importance for over a year until he had sufficiently disassociated himself from the Cardinal. Furthermore, he lost his position as ambassador to Charles V when he failed to win the Emperor's support for the King's divorce, and was replaced by Cranmer.[34] As Elyot experienced the complexities of Tudor government and ambassadorial politics he became increasingly aware of the importance of dealing with each situation as it arose. Joshua's choices allow him to remain reverent and pleasing to God, just as *The Governour's* sixteenth century reader is expected to maintain a just governmental or ambassadorial policy that is pleasing to the King in his absence.

Elyot is careful not to take this metaphor further; once he makes an initial comparison of God to King on the basis of provision of the law, he retreats from it in favor of a more general discussion of the governor's relationship to God. In the Biblical narrative, God does not respond to the decision of the princes of the multitude. God's inaction and absence in the immediate aftermath of the event presents a rather deafening silence; it leaves the Israelites, led by Joshua, to interpret for themselves whether God is pleased or displeased with their decision-making. On the one hand, God does not punish the Israelites for the transgression of the Covenant, and so Elyot assumes (as the narrative does), that Joshua has made the right choice. On the other hand, the ensuing victory at Jericho is seen as a reward for having done the right thing. Elyot is therefore able to use his reading of Josh. 9 to argue that the ideal qualities of a governor are ultimately pleasing to God because God behaves much like a Tudor monarch: if he is not displeased, he will say little, or nothing at first, and reward his servant at a later time.

Reality, however, is a recurring problem for Elyot. Despite his efforts to be pragmatic, he all but ignores the apparent absence of God's immediate influence upon the average sixteenth-century life. He also avoids an acknowledgment of Cicero's own candor about the role of the gods in Roman oaths. Cicero says that keeping an oath for the sake of moral right is preferable to keeping one simply to avoid Jove's wrath, but he also suggests that an oath might be proper and moral even if the gods are not party to the oath at all.[35] In Tudor England a statement like this was treated as a charming example of the unenlightened classical world; without an understanding of Christianity they could not have worked through such a conundrum. It was true, though, that a young gentleman serving as a justice of the peace, a member of the King's Council, or as an ambassador (all positions which Elyot held), could not realistically expect God's immediate reaction as a measure by which to determine justice. Nevertheless, Elyot remains optimistic, and selective with his sources. He avoids Ciceronian passages that do not contribute to his argument, but he is also careful not to allow the pragmatism of Cicero or Aristotle to disappear. Elyot believes that classicism cannot achieve equality with Scripture, yet he uses his sources carefully to encourage ways they might co-exist in the real world. In this case, the very relevance of God is a sticky point; Elyot must reconcile God's inaction in the Joshua narrative with Cicero's frankness. If Elyot fails to do so, his argument will fall apart because it will cease to be useful to the young governor's life and experiences. Although he does not always show it blatantly, Elyot is a master at managing sources, nudging them towards cooperation.

Members of any generation tend to look back fondly upon a bygone age, especially during periods of change. The fact that nostalgic views of the past are more mythical than real is beside the point; the purpose is almost always to distance oneself from the decadences of the current period.[36] It is an attempt for a society to orient itself in time by chasing its own lost dreams. Elyot's reaction to the continuing changes that characterized the slow death of the medieval period in England is one that focuses not on a lost world of chivalric ideals and feudal loyalties, but instead looks back even farther, past the generations preceding Elyot's own. Elyot wants for his student to look to the ancients, rather than to his own recent ancestry, to find the true gentleman for the current age. He wants his student to look for the source of his cultural, intellectual, and spiritual past, the well from which Elyot believes chivalric values had sprung.

In both classical and Biblical antiquity Elyot sees institutions that combine politics and religion, and which embrace the lives of their citizens.

2. The Matter of Resources

In classical antiquity Elyot sees a Golden Age of intellectual civility; in Biblical antiquity he sees a Golden Age of law and justice.[37] Elyot's application of a Golden Age to English life in Book III, Chapter VI is therefore carefully constructed. Instead of relying upon the most conventional images of classical or Biblical "Golden Ages," Elyot updates his conception of these ideal societies. Again, he uses sworn bond to establish a common ground. He forgoes the traditional example of Eden as the "Golden Age of Humanity" with its lack of material concerns or political problems. Instead, he chooses a postlapsarian vision of the nation of Israel in the time of the prophets as an ideal age of Divine law and immutable justice. It is an age which is characterized by a nation chosen, founded, and protected by God. He gives His laws and moral code exclusively to it, and he and his nation are bound by a Covenant. Both the *Nicomachean Ethics* and *De Officiis* also serve as models for a theory of a Golden Age of Greece and Rome. These nations are characterized by ideals of order, civility, service and patriotism.[38] They are nations which used oaths to ensure that their ideals were upheld, and sworn bond is praised by their greatest philosophical and political minds. Instead of pointing to a state of innocence, purity, or unspoiled humanity, Elyot harkens back to an age in which he sees the perfection of institutions of religion, law and politics in a most imitable form.

Interestingly, both societies — classical and Biblical — precede the Christian era. Part of what makes them imitable in Elyot's view is the potential they hold for success as the Christian era approaches. It is yet another subtlety of Elyot's book, but its implications would have been strong to readers like Cromwell, Cranmer, Audley, or the king himself. It suggests that a look back to the examples of classical and Biblical antiquity will produce a view of Christianity that avoids, both literally and figuratively, the history of the medieval church. Although Elyot was a traditionalist he had appreciated Erasmus' condemnation of clerical abuses, and of the superstitions of the relic trade and pilgrimage system. Although he and More moved in the same circle Elyot made sure Cromwell understood that, unlike More, he was not a papist. Ultimately, Elyot accepted the Royal Supremacy and continued to work in government. He was clear in a letter to the Duke of Norfolk in 1532, saying, "I am all the king's except my soule."[39] In promoting an idealized view of the classical and Biblical past he suggests that an appropriately modern governor be aware of, but not informed by, the medieval past. To do so would to be in line with what he recommends his student do: be a true friend to the king and support his positions. Elyot's support is given quietly, but clearly; it advises the king and encourages him toward wisdom and away from self-indulgence. It instructs but it also praises, and it communicates the loyalty of its author to the king at a very important time; as Elyot stated in a letter to Sir John Hackett in 1533, he was the king's sworn subject.[40] To make such a statement in that year was to invite the king to infer from *The Governor* anything which he felt supported his position. Elyot knew the king and Cromwell would do just that. In this way, *The Boke Named the Governour* allows Elyot to suggest that the abuses of the recent past be escaped from, but it allows him to avoid the subject of reform specifically.

Comprehensiveness, therefore, is the definitive point of Elyot's use of source materials in Chapter VI of Book III. It causes the student to view his own life in the context of a historical viewpoint, which he develops for his own sake. In doing so, Elyot's student learns his history and experiences it all at once. Within this assumption there exists a literary and historical coherence, in which the intent of the author and the experiences of the reader are united in the context of the work itself.[41] The experience of Joshua is therefore linked with the experience of the reader of the text. The ethics of the Greco-Roman philosophers remain meaningful and attainable in a similar way. One swears mindfully in court precisely because Cicero had; one considers the law in an abstract form precisely because Aristotle had. Herein lies the important distinction between Elyot's idealism and archaism: although the voices are ancient, the messages are not.

At times Elyot seems aware of the paradox he creates as a result of his agenda to unite ideals with practice. At other times he seems lost in an effort to reestablish an ancient structure based on wide-reaching principles of honor and trust that for the most part never existed. It is most ironic that Elyot's complaints about the diminished value for oaths and promises echo Cicero's own complaints about the diminished value for the same concepts in Rome. One passage from *De Officiis* to which Elyot fails to make reference is one in which Cicero looks back upon the ancestors of the Roman Republic and proclaims the high value they had for oaths, in those times.[42] Whether Elyot's omission of this passage is deliberate or

2. The Matter of Resources

not, it would seem that at least one of Elyot's sages is just as susceptible to illusionism as he is. Such is the paradox of any political or ethical principle that is re-imagined with an eye for agenda — it becomes suspended between historical fact and lore. The ideals therein threaten to become trapped in the narrative, unable to escape from their own roles as elements of an art form. Elyot's effort to keep his sources relevant and contemporary is partly rooted in his desire to keep the concept of oath-swearing from degenerating into a vague and ancient idea, with no place in the modern world. His caution, however, reflects a larger concern, one which was held by many but spoken of by few: if idealism were to become illusionism, then Tudor England's effort to redefine itself would be marked by delusion, and ancient and noble bonds of trust would fail to hold it together. The guidance provided by a friend to the king needed to caution the monarch and his government against itself; for Thomas Elyot, such guidance is found in what his book can show, but cannot say.

Chapter 3

Additions and Admissions
The Manipulation of Sworn Bond in the Henrician Fealty Oath

There were many voices speaking to and at the English people about the changes brought on by the king's divorce and the Royal Supremacy, not the least of which was Henry VIII's own voice. He was, as all monarchs were, duly advised; and although he appeared to appreciate his councilors the king answered their efforts with less and less regard as the 1530s advanced.[1] Henry VIII spoke most clearly through his legislation, and the oaths that secured the Acts of Supremacy and Succession required the English people to answer the king's voice by witnessing aloud their loyalty to him. The English people were asked to reconcile their consciences with new ideas about faith, and at the same time they were told that they had to obey the law and the King's policies, both political and ecclesiastical. As they did so they developed understandings, on various levels, about what the individual conscience was, and how it could contribute to the generation of one's own identity. They understood the importance of autonomy, but they also understood the dangers that loomed not if, but when, the individual conscience conflicted with royal policy. As the Acts of Supremacy and Succession were passed, it became clear that the fealty oath would present an opportunity for such conflict.

Much of the language regarding both politics and religion during the Henrician period relies heavily on specificity. At times it approaches a near obsession with detail. Fealty oaths are no exception. BL MS Stowe 15 offers a fealty oath in two versions: ffs 8b and 9a. Both versions of the oath were initially drafted about the same time and were revised more than

3. Additions and Admissions

once. 9a was written first, and appears to have been drafted after the Act of Succession in 1534. It was then revised at least twice over the next three to four years, with addenda to the text of the folio. 8b was also drafted in 1534, and shows major revisions concerning the content of 9a, with minor revisions (such as the additions of names) also appearing in the text. The first version (8b) presents specific language concerning the terms of the oath and the responsibilities of the swearer. The second version (9a) is shorter, and although it has the same sense of the first version its language is much more general, even vague. This oath illustrates some of the most problematic issues concerning the legislation of conscience which arose following the Acts of Supremacy and Succession. In its first version it seeks to determine the loyalty of the swearer on two levels: first, regarding his or her ability to profess fealty in person, according to the terms of the oath with his or her hand on the book; and second, regarding his or her ability to perceive disloyalty in others after rejoining society, and report it to the authorities. In its second version the oath dispenses with the stipulation that the swearer report treason by others and swear only to his or her own loyalty. In the case of this oath the specificity of language in the first version produces a failed attempt to quantify allegiance, while the more general language of the revision is more successful in reining in the liberties of conscience. The two drafts, placed side by side on facing pages in MS Stowe 15 show a clear effort to structure a relationship between the King and his subjects in terms of what they may, and may not, admit to each other.

The key to the success of this relationship lies in how both the King and his subjects understand the concept of guilt. This understanding has as its precedent the long history of negative self-image in Western Europe and the process by which it was generated, then adapted during the Henrician era.[2] For centuries, the clergy had acted as the agents of the sacrament of auricular confession, in which sin and repentance were reconciled through the concept of guilt. Despite their exclusive ability to give absolution, the clergy could not grant it without the self-efficacy of the penitent to examine his or her conscience and perform the confession.[3] A contractual relationship therefore existed between the laity and the clergy, which allowed the sacrament to accomplish the remission of sins, *ex opere operato*. Negative self-image, or guilt, is the catalyst that allows the sacrament to perform. Fear of oneself is central to this concept, especially because it bears directly upon the development of conscience.[4] In the centuries between the establishment of auricular confession as a seasonal observance in 1215, and the 1530s,[5] conscience had been viewed as a by-product of the self, rather than as an extension of the self. When conscience is held distinct from the self, it can be held as a standard — the actions of the individual can be made to oppose it or conform to it. If conscience is interpreted to be an extension of the self, then the individual is free, or more free, to rationalize his or her behavior.

Concerning this paradox of the self as it pertains to conscience, the development of auricular confession as a sacramental obligation offered the clergy an opportunity to apply continuous, and lasting spiritual pressure. The motive of the Church was twofold: firstly, it controlled the ability of the penitent masses to determine the extent of their responsibilities for their sins; and secondly, it had an enduring effect which lasted all year, so that the penitent were not only ready but eager to partake in the sacrament before the Easter observance.[6] In short, one's conscience is not really one's own in this model. It stands as a benchmark against which one's sins could be measured, because it represents the standards set by the Church. One cannot reconcile one's behavior with one's conscience without the sacrament of confession and the priest, God's agent. The application of spiritual pressure calls the sinner to reconcile with his or her conscience as a spiritual element distinct from the self, not as an extension of his or her individual self. T.N. Tentler addresses the subject of guilt before the Reformation, in his important study *Sin and Confession on the Eve of the Reformation*, saying, "A normal sense of guilt appears to act as a call not for the suppression but rather for the transformation and sublimation of impulses that are at odds with one's ideal self and relationship with God."[7] During the early modern era, the appropriation of the Catholic tradition of guilt became convenient to the power structure Henry VIII sought to build in the Roman Church's stead. Ironically, this appropriation clashed with new ideas about what Stephen Greenblatt has called the "artful process" of the development of the self, which occurred at the same time.[8] To assure himself of the fealty of his people, the King had to be sure that those who committed treason — or who even imagined it — would not be able to reconcile it in their consciences. Instead, their ideas about fealty would be

3. Additions and Admissions

forced to stand against the benchmark of the standards set by the Royal Supremacy. Rather than wrestling with new ideas about conscience, the king preferred, at first, to utilize old-fashioned guilt.

The relationship between the king and the people makes up a collective unconscious for which the fealty oath is an important symbol. As paramount witness for the sacred act of swearing, God binds the two parties together. The clergy had, for centuries, acted as the agents of the divine in this process. The Royal Supremacy effectively removes the role of the clergy from this act, yet the fealty oaths of the Herician era seek to reinterpret, indeed reform this relationship, as they preserve the part of the process which is automatic while replacing the clergy with the king as divine agent. Henry VIII's role, however, was far from benevolent. Both versions of the fealty oath of MS Stowe 15 were written in direct response to the Act of Succession and the Treason Act, and both are clear that subjects taking the oath are to swear their allegiance to the king, his queen, and their "heyres" without reservation. To do otherwise is treason. In order to be assured of the obedience of his subjects, the king needed to be in control of the swearer's personal relationship with his or her conscience, and this idea is reflected in the first version of the oath, folio 9a:

> "Ye shall swere and kepe fayth and truth and obedience all onelye to the kynges maiestrie [inserted in super margin: *supreme hed in erthe under god of the churche of England during his lyfe*] & to hys heyres of his bodie of hys most and entirely beloved lawfull [inserted in super margin: *late*] wife queen Anne [Anne is partially rubbed out, with "An" replaced by "Ja" to form the word "Jane"] begotten and [crossed out: *to be begotten*] and further to the heyres of any said sovraign lorde acordynge to the lymytacyon yn the statute made for the suertie of hys succession yn the [blank] of thys realme mencioned & conteyned (and not to any other within this realme nor foreign [rubbed out: *or potentate*])[9] acordyng to the statute and [blank] in that behalfe made and you shall do no felonyes nor treasons nor consent thereunto. And if you here or knowe of any you shall shewe the kyng and his counsell thereof. So god you help and all sayntes etc."

There is a great effort to avoid being misunderstood, by God, by the king, or by anyone else whenever the stakes are so high. In this sense specific language can promote clarity in fealty oaths; indeed, in the passages that outline fealty to Queens Anne, Jane, and their progeny, specific language is necessary. As long as Katherine of Aragon is alive, language that requires fealty to "the Queen" simply won't work. The same goes for Mary Tudor as heir. Language is therefore added, and admitted, so that the swearer must in turn admit that first Anne, then Jane is the rightful queen, especially as one literally replaces the other, and their heirs follow suit. The legitimacy of the oath is connected to the legitimacy of the heirs, and the specific language allows the oath's author (likely Cromwell) to admit the material into the oath as truths. At the same time it forces the swearer to admit *to* those truths and reconcile them with his or her conscience.

There is another factor at work here, though; and it stems from the stipulation in the oath that "...you shall do no felonyes nor treasons nor consent thereunto and if you here or knowe of any you shall shewe the kyng and his counsell thereof...." This stipulation refers to the process by which the king and his council redefined and reappropriated the aspects of auricular confession that had worked so efficiently for centuries. Despite arguments against (and the eventual ban of) auricular confession, the practice was ingrained in English spiritual culture. Reformers saw confession as an innovation of the thirteenth century, rooted solidly in the institution of the church; but they knew, as their traditionalist adversaries also knew, that theologians had long accepted the idea that confession was also rooted in rational and even natural reason. One was obliged to reconcile with one's sins and repent, thereby restoring grace and the favor of God. Even Luther himself agreed that such an idea had little to do with the Church's institution of seasonal confession.[10] Important aspects of this tradition therefore survived the Reformation precisely because they could be justified apart from their institutional applications to the Roman Church, especially the idea that penitents needed to reconcile themselves with their consciences, and that a pastor had to know his sheep so that he might detect heresy whenever it arose.[11] In this way, the king, the administrator of the oath, and the swearer could make a correlation between the stipulations of the oath and one's fealty and love for the monarch. If the swearer consents to treason, or knows of any treasons committed or plotted, he or she is required to "shew" it to the king and his council. In short, swearers must confess to what they know about treason because they feel guilty.

The fealty oath of MS Stowe 15 9a differs from that of 8b because it was not written with auricular confession in mind, although its composition is affected by it culturally. The overall sense of the practice of confession,

3. Additions and Admissions

had, over the centuries, become part of the culture of Western Europe, and of England in particular. In 1534–37, the time period in which the oath was revised, there was a variety of opinions as to what role auricular confession should have in England's future, and the king still favored it. Even by 1539 auricular confession had not been banned, but instead was supported in the Six Articles, with the final article being devoted to it. Although not all of the king's councilors agreed that confession was absolutely necessary, Cranmer and Latimer (along with several others) agreed that it was nonetheless expedient.[12] The power held by institution over conscience and penitence was shifting rather than disappearing.

The stipulation of the oath that the swearer confess to what he or she *knows* about treason goes right to the heart of the medieval practice of the examination of conscience by the penitent in the presence of the confessor. It had been part of the Church's institutional objective in 1215 to regulate the relationship between the pastor and his flock by causing the priest to engage in what Jean Delumeau calls an "interrogatory dialogue" with his penitents.[13] Basically, it was the confessor's job to hear the penitent's sins and pose questions meant to clarify the confession by judging the religious knowledge of the penitent. In doing so he would root out heresy, ensure the obedience and piety of the community, and, most importantly, know his parishioners. Although radicals dismissed the role of confessor as a relic of a superstitious and corrupt age, the fact remains that there was a surge in confessors' handbooks at the turn of the sixteenth century.[14] Confessors' manuals focused on the priest's role in the sacrament, and on the process of the ritual, but they also contained scripture and legal text for the purposes of precedent and authority.[15] In a sense, MS Stowe 15 serves as a *de facto* confessors' handbook. Although it was certainly not constructed for that purpose, the book did acquire that purpose once the oaths, especially 9a, were written in it.

The book in which the oath appears predates the Henrician era by many centuries, and was used in a myriad of ways until the Henrician fealty oaths were penned into it. MS Stowe 15 contains twelfth-century lessons from the Gospels in Latin, including narratives of the Nativity, Baptism and Passion, along with most of the Gospel of John.[16] It also contains miscellaneous notes and records relating to the business of the Exchequer, notes of committal of sheriff's attorneys, and notes of dues from various counties.[17] The records are dated in the reigns of Edward I, Henry VI, Edward IV, and Henry VII. There is a contemporary reference to the capture of Berwick on 30 March 1296, to the marriage of Richard II to Anne of Bohemia, and to the coronations of Henry VI and Richard III. In addition, the book contains hymns for the vigils of Sts. Katherine and Nicholas, and for the Vigil of the Ascension.[18] The fealty oaths to Henry VIII are placed on two blank facing pages, falling in between notes of debts due to the exchequer and of the release of sheriffs' attorneys and others in the reign of Edward IV (folio 8a), and a hymn for the Vigil of the Ascension, called "Eterne Rex Altissime" (folio 9b).

No one knows why this particular book was selected, and it may not have been selected for any reason beyond the fact that it had useful blank pages in it. Following scribal tradition, the first form of the oath was penned on a "fresh" page — the "a" side of the folio, in a spot that was conveniently blank. When the oath was revised, the scribe (perhaps guided by higher authorities in government) placed the second form of the oath on the immediately facing page — 8b. One reason for this placement has to do with the fact that Henry VIII was not of a single mind when it came to oaths and their modifications and revisions. Often the earlier version of an oath was preserved and not thrown away.[19] The fact remains that even though 9a was replaced by 8b, it was neither crossed out, nor pasted over with a blank piece of vellum, nor torn out of the book. It remained permanently, and perhaps uncomfortably, next to its own revision. This act allowed the two oaths to be viewed at once by whoever administered it, and caused the revisions made to both forms to be undeniably apparent.

The administrator of the fealty oaths of MS Stowe 15 had, as his primary authoritative texts, the Acts of Supremacy and Succession, which were presumed by the oaths in the book. But he likely saw the Biblical text and legal records that accompanied the oaths not as mere miscellany, but as representations of both sacred and secular authority which made the oaths in his book relevant and consequential in their overall context. In the book he could also see the revisions which had been made to the first form of the oath. Those revisions, the crossouts, marginal notes and rub-outs (in one case done awkwardly with a wet thumb), told him what he should expect from the swearer in front of him. In the case of folio 9a, they tell him to expect an examination of conscience, an admission of the

3. Additions and Admissions

knowledge of faults, and if necessary, a return to confess new or further knowledge of future faults. In the case of 8b they tell him to modify his expectations. It is, in a sense, his confessor's manual. MS Stowe 15 has roots in the confession manual not in its substance, but in the attitude of its necessity, as the Tudor era adapts and appropriates existing texts and sources for new meanings and uses.

Still, the administrator could rely on one ancient precedent for its own sake: he knew that the bulk of the responsibility for making a good oath lay with the swearer. By tradition, a confession could only be considered successful if it was both "good" and "complete," and the meeting of those criteria was the sole responsibility of the penitent. Despite the development of auricular confession as a seasonal observance with support from Scripture,[20] the medieval Church nonetheless recognized that the sacrament could only succeed if the penitent wished it to. Penitents were instructed to examine their consciences thoroughly, and confess well, leaving nothing out due to pride or shame. Moreover, the penitent had to acknowledge that there may have been some sins which were forgotten. If there were, the penitent agreed to confess them at the proper time and place (even if it was the following year, before Easter).[21] The examination of conscience had to discover not only one's sins, but the "aggravating circumstances" that made them more blameworthy and offensive to God's law.[22] In return the penitent received absolution and grace — but also a much-desired sense of self-improvement, and the knowledge that he or she had been an active participant in maintaining the strength of the moral fabric of society. In much the same way the swearer of the fealty oath of MS Stowe 15 is the one who determines the validity of the oath. At first the swearer makes a profession of loyalty, and then he or she is instructed to make a confession, to admit to what he or she knows. Nothing must be left out, and if anything has been forgotten, or if the swearer hears of any new treasonous

On the following two pages: The fealty oaths of BL MS Stowe 15, fols. 8b and 9a, as they appear in the book. Folio 9a (right) is the older of the two oaths, with 8b (left) representing the revision. In both versions the name "Anne" has been rubbed out, with the name "Jane" replacing it. In the supermargins of both versions the word "late" has been added above the word "Jane," to denote the death of Jane Seymour. These minor changes were probably made by the Remembrancer himself (© The British Library Board).

tempus non modicū et gravamen &c contra formam ordinacōis nos volentes dcām ordinacōem in omnibus
suis articulis inviolabilit observari tibi precipimus
et iniungim̄s q̄̄ ita est omnipotencia illius coram p̄fatis consil-
iariis n̄ris in cuius p̄dcā obedire non recusaueris ac
formam ordinacōis p̄dcā &c.

¶ Sacr̄m tenementū Rege a[nn]o iij Wh[.]
..... p successores ad onus et Jur-
amentū Consiliarii d[omi]ni Regis Anglie.

Ye shall kepe and bere feith and trueth and obeyence alto the kynge magestye and to his heires of his body [most]
most and entierly belonyd laufully wyfe Anne la-
fully begotten and to be begotten[s] furthyr to the heyres of
oure said soueraigne lorde acordyng to the lymytacyon and
statute made for the surety of his succession men-
cyouns of this reame mencyonyd & conteynyd and
also shall faith and trueth to any othyr soueraigne lord
his heyres and nor any othyr oughte yeut, this due
[...] ys true for the acquitall of R. that ye shall
.... soueraigne lorde so god you help
all saynts &c.

Secund p̄senta qui sunt nyht p̄ successione
Regis h. viij Jeno sonsortis sue Regina Angl
                                    [sidest?]

Ye shall swere and besto shall and truly and
 onlyne hit in ooth and yet at the chu'ch of Englo sheryng hys lie
obedyence oth only to the kynge liutiestie & to his heyres
of his bodie of hys most and entesly belovyd lautull
Wife quono Jeno begotten and to be begott· · and
fryther to the heyres of any other conteyned lorde
ccordyng to the kymytacyon yn the Statute made
for the suertie of hys succesion yn the chosone
of thys realme mencioned & conteyned And not
to any other wyyn thys realme nor foreyn
~Auctorite~ or ~pretended~ ccordyng to the statute
and lawes in that behalf made And you shall bo
no felonye nor treason nor consent thereunto
And if you here or knowe of any you shall shewe
the kyng and his councell therof So god you
help and all saynts &c

information, he or she must return to the King and his administrators and confess it. Such "aggravating circumstances" only serve to make the swearer more blameworthy, more offensive to the King's law because it puts him in league with the traitors he knows, or knows about. As a reward for his confession, the swearer is promised the love and protection of the monarch. He or she acquires the same sense of self-improvement, the same sense of being a constructive member of the community that auricular confession had offered.

Much of the legislation about treason in the 1530s revolves around the idea that when treason is committed, even by thought or intent, there must be institutional satisfaction for the government and the Royal Supremacy. The State, therefore, developed the exclusive right to determine the qualities of conscience which would allow such thoughts to be policed effectively. The issue of scrupulosity was as important to the Henrician state as it had been to the medieval church. Individual discernment concerning conscience was dangerous to the enforcement of the sort of stipulation found in the oath of MS Stowe 15 9a, and yet such discernment was emerging steadily as the development of persona so often called "self-fashioning."[23] It is no wonder then, that there is much emphasis on the dire consequences of developing an internal sense of compunction that conflicts with the King's idea of "conscience." The deaths of Thomas More and John Fisher had already demonstrated that those consequences were very real, and the legislation and fealty oaths that followed their deaths sent a message to future swearers, which also paralleled the Roman Church's model.[24] MS Stowe 15 9a presumes pathological anguish before judgment, an escalation of doubt, a rumination on fault, and a fixation on death.[25] In the Henrician model the king establishes himself as above deception or delusion.[26]

All of this amounts to tyranny, and one of the reasons why folio 9a was revised is because it tries to accomplish something which is impossible, but which Henry VIII nonetheless sought to do: get inside the minds of his subjects and dictate policy from there. The king tried, via the oath of folio 9a, to drive a wedge between his subjects and their attitudes toward themselves that would allow them to decide whether they were loyal or not. Although English men and women were developing those attitudes, it was far from easy, as Stephen Greenblatt points out in his discussion of self-fashioning. "One had to make choices, and there were few certain

3. Additions and Admissions

guides beyond your own conscience. Consequently, the worlds of righteousness and secular self-interest became confused as never before."[27] One literally had to discern between one's newly discovered (and much appreciated) self-interest, and submission to the absolute powers of Church and State. Where loyalty was concerned, this conflict could be extremely difficult. Even if one wished to support the king, he or she had to do so carefully. Not doing enough could bring charges of treason — and so could doing too much; this conundrum is what lies behind the frustrated equivocation of Thomas Cranmer and Richard Rich, and behind the frustrating caution of Thomas Elyot. Greg Walker makes a series of excellent points on this matter in *Writing Under Tyranny: English Literature and the Henrician Reformation*. Although Henry VIII had not been a tyrant when he acceded the throne in 1509, by 1534 he was well on his way to becoming one, and by the time of his death he was known throughout Europe as a legendary tyrant.[28] The Great Matter and the split from Rome subjected the English people to a host of demands with which they had to acquiesce or die. One of the things the king despised most at this time was public obedience and private dissent — what Walker terms "loyal resistance."[29] He says, "There was an entire cadre of English scholars and intellectuals who were not in favour of the divorce or the pace or direction of religious reform, or both, who nonetheless remained in royal service, working for the king and government to the best of their abilities."[30] These are the men who would have taken the oath in MS Stowe 15, as the book was kept in the office of the Remembrancer and used primarily for those in royal service and at court. They knew that they served a monarch who could perceive disloyalty even he if he observed loyal service. They also knew that he reserved the right to determine what disloyalty was, who had committed it, and who knew about it.

The stipulation that the swearer of the oath admit to what he or she knows about treason, or that he or she return to confess further knowledge of the same, is meant to extend the king's own attitude toward his subjects to the people themselves. They in turn are expected to suspect each other. The Treason clauses of the Acts of Supremacy and Succession had caught only those who wrote or acted against the king's marriage to Anne Boleyn, but had failed to root out all of them.[31] The Treason Act added the provisions that plotting physical harm to the king was to be included. In a *coup de grace*, the Treason Act proclaimed that it was treason to refer to the king as a tyrant. Those who aided and abetted were to be held as guilty as the traitors themselves, and sanctuary was abolished for this crime.[32] These acts of legislation cast a wider and wider net, seeking out traitors wherever they might be. Since the king and his ministers could not be everywhere, fealty oaths such as folio 9a saw to it that those loyal enough to swear would become the king's eyes and ears. They would do so, presumably, by perceiving their colleagues, friends, and neighbors in relation to the Other — a threatening, outside influence which sought to undermine the authority of the monarchy. The culture of fear which attacked that which was hostile or strange included the traitor among those figures it considered to be arcane, and alien, such as heretics, witches and infidels.[33] Those who swore fealty to the king were expected to know whom to hate, and they were expected to remove these figures from society by exposing them — or perhaps merely their intentions — to the king.[34] As MS Stowe 15 9a and 8b show, however, what the king wanted was not always what he got. The plan to cause courtier to turn on courtier and neighbor on neighbor was more idealistic than effective, and this is one of the reasons for a second draft of 9a.

The oath of folio 9a fails in several ways. Where specific language works in the passage that refers to the queens and their progeny, it does not work in the stipulation which requires that the swearer admit to knowing or hearing of treasonous acts and/or persons. The language fails in the passage precisely *because* the oath attempts to emulate the ancient process of confession as an action resulting from negative self-image. Through this specific language, the oath seeks to penetrate what the swearer will consent to, and even know, in the future. Conscience is meant to be the catalyst that forces the swearer to turn him or herself in and confess, or admit, to having known treasonous or forbidden things. In this case, the oath seeks to unify thought, word, and deed the way auricular confession does. The only problem is, it doesn't work. The self gets in the way. The takers of the oath who are having their thoughts policed are at the same time developing their identities. Having a personal relationship with one's identity, which is not defined by proscriptions from either church or state, is a phenomenon of early modern individualism. As Greenblatt points out, "Emphasis fell on the individual conscience, but when and how conscience

3. Additions and Admissions

was to be applied became a vexing question. Should conscience test and possibly reject custom and law? Or were custom and law appropriate guides to the conscience?"[35] The fact of the matter is, some people decided one way, and some the other. And very often they decided for themselves.

Amidst the changes in politics and religion in the Henrician era, there were also intellectual and artistic developments concerning conscience and the human identity. The 1520s and 30s were filled with young people who enjoyed the art of polemic — of arguing cases, of "one-upmanship" in argument, and in rhetoric as it pertained to all subjects. Henry VIII and his fealty oaths shared the company of an entire generation which valued its ability to determine and argue its point. The continued use of exempla, and classical and biblical examples allowed people to employ imaginative and critical aspects of their understandings of contemporary events — including the king's new policies. This situation is further explained by Greg Walker:

> In a political environment in which it was treason simply to imagine the death or deposition of the king, such recourse to biblical or classical analogy, and the hypothetical "put-case," gave well-read English men and women a vocabulary in which they might discuss the failings of their sovereign and contemplate the redress of grievances, thereby engaging critically with national political issues from which they were otherwise excluded.[36]

The specificity of the language of 9a therefore operates antithetically to its objective: it allows the swearer alone to determine what he or she knows, based on how that person interprets the behavior and knowledge of others. Moreover, the language requires the swearer to report treason that he or she has *heard of*, regardless of any speech or acts that he or she has made in response to it. The swearer, in his or her conscience, simply may not feel that the thoughts, intentions, or actions of others are treasonous. The swearer might also be deliberately deceptive, and claim (quite correctly) that no one can know what he or she thinks unless speech or acts proceed from those thoughts. It becomes difficult to determine whether the oath is valid, despite the effort of the authorities to wedge themselves between the conscience and the self. This means one can break the oath while keeping it. The first version of the fealty oath of MS Stowe 15 is therefore a travesty: it fails in its mission to police thought through negative self-image and threatens to become a vehicle for passive resistance. Furthermore, it allows

Sworn Bond in Tudor England

for exactly the situation the king despised most: a court, perhaps a nation, consisting of subjects who thought one way but behaved in another. Norman Jones, in his study of public virtue, notes that as long as people "felt sure" in their consciences, they could behave according to what they felt was right. He says, "As traditional certainties shattered, they had to invent the rules as they went along, conducting the business of their lives as their understanding of their place in society evolved ... it gave the individual more choice, depending upon conscience and self interest as regulators."[37] This was true for courtiers and tradesmen alike, and it was especially true for those who found themselves faced with the fealty oath of MS Stowe 15 9a. If the authorities cannot determine whether the oath is valid, not only upon its taking but for an undetermined period afterward, and if they are unable to extract the innermost thoughts of the swearer, the oath must be revised.

Folio 8b, like 9a, was initially composed during the lifetime of Anne Boleyn. Although its overall sense is the same, and although it shares minor revisions with 9a, it also shows major revisions, which adapt and change its intent:

> "Ye shall swere and kepe faith & truth obedience auctoryte to the kynges maestye & to his heyrres of his body of his most & entirely beloved lawfull Quene Anne, [rubbed out] Jane [written over, with "late" inserted in the super margin] begotten & [crossed out] to be begotten & further to the heyres of any said sovraign lorde accordynge to the lymytacyon yn the statute made for the suertys of hys succession in the [blank] of thys realme mencyoned & conteyned and also shall (kepe)[38] fayth & truth to any other sovraign lorde his heyres and pity all suche put (that do suche [blank])[39] aside due to hys [blank] for the [blank] of [blank] that ys gold of any said sovraign lorde so god you helpe and all saints etc."

Here, the language is far less specific, making no reference to what the swearer knows, either now or in the future. It makes no reference to anyone the swearer knows of who has committed treason, or any information the swearer has heard. Such a revision is neither incidental nor inconsequential; rather, it is a deliberate attempt to make the oath more effective and authoritative. The second form of the oath serves as a recognition that the first form was too problematic to be administered, and this is demonstrated by the very fact that the stipulation about the swearer's knowledge is missing. Ironically, the authorities had had less control over the effectiveness of the

3. Additions and Admissions

oath when it was more explicit. With that information edited out, the authorities were able to exert more control over the sworn bond by simply saying less. This is not to say that their minds had not been changed regarding the policing of thought; the king, and Cromwell, believed that it could. The revision has more to do with what is legally prudent and defensible than what the swearer knows or consents to after the oath is sworn and the authorities are absent. It allows the King alone to decide who has upheld the law and who has not.

The second oath effectively polices the actions associated with the swearer without taking his or her thoughts into consideration. It presumes that action will follow thought, because it is guided by the swearer's conscience, not in spite of that fact. The more general, more vague language of folio 8b ultimately gives the state more power than the first oath of 9a does. The second form of the oath gives the state the exclusive ability to discriminate the circumstances of the swearer's conscience. The state and not the swearer maintains the privilege of presuming what the swearer must have known. Guilt can therefore be imposed, externally, upon the self by the institutional authority of the Royal Supremacy rather than derived internally by the swearer on behalf of the self. The state is able to accuse the swearer of committing treason without having to compete with the swearer's conscience. The first form of the oath aims at a formula for determining guilt by association. The second form of the oath actually accomplishes this. The simpler form of the oath allows the authorities to control the development of the self by laying claims to which forms of self-determination are acceptable and which are not. It allows the state to determine what was known, or heard, and by whom. It makes guilt by association easier to implement. By saying less, the king gets more, simply because the swearer is denied the opportunity to withhold information — or even discern its value to the fealty-swearing process. Rather than asking the swearer to police the thoughts of his or her associates and neighbors, the second form of the oath presumes that the king's government will do so, and proceed against the swearer accordingly.

Both oaths exist, in part, as a facet of the government's attempt to quantify allegiance. Fealty oaths, like those required by the Acts of Supremacy and Succession, were intended to provide a means by which the king and his counselors could literally "count heads" and determine who was loyal and who was not. The first version of the oath of MS Stowe 15 seeks to identify the loyal and the traitorous in real numbers. Quantifying allegiance was a major concern for Henry VIII and his government, but the process of doing so was deeply flawed. The failure of the oath of folio 9a shows how easily such flaws could appear in a system of "head counting." Alec Ryrie, in his study on allegiance in the English Reformation, shows just how difficult it could be to determine loyalty at court and in communities, and how problematic even the most well-intended system could be. He says, "The majority of [the] reformers are known only because they fell foul of the heresy laws under Henry VIII or Mary Tudor. We are therefore dealing only with the very hardest core of outspoken reformers — the committed, plus a handful of the unlucky."[40] Henry VIII and Cromwell were no more able to "count" the loyal and disloyal than scholars are today, either in terms of the heads that swore fealty or the heads that rolled. Both traditionalists and reformers claimed large numbers in their respective camps, and often the king received conflicting reports from across the country about the opinions in one area or another. The oath of folio 9a seeks to guarantee fealty by providing the king with an assurance about the uniformity of opinion among the takers of the oath. The problem was, no such uniformity existed, either at court or in the towns. There was conformity though; but the sort of conformity the king got was not necessarily the kind he wanted. Rather than acting against each other out of fear, people often supported each other by way of saying and doing very little.

What Henry VIII wanted (via his agent Cromwell) was a machinery of authority and repression which would identify the loyal and root out treason. He meant for fealty oaths to accomplish these goals by imposing a conformity of fear among the swearers and those who knew them and lived among them. Instead, a different sort of conformity resulted: a conformity of survival. Despite the terminology, conformity of survival in the 1530s and 40s did not rely on desperation and fear of imminent persecution. Instead, it relied on a mode of rationale made possible by the developments of conscience in those decades. One of Stephen Greenblatt's major points about the paradox of individual conscience in the sixteenth century is that the energy devoted to attacking the alien in the name of authority (of the state, the church, or the king himself) often

3. Additions and Admissions

threatens the authority it sets out to defend.[41] He says, "For the men and women living through the Reformation the question was more often 'What do I do now?' than 'What do I believe now?' In that sense, he says, people very often simply got on with "the business of living."[42] Self-preservation, then, took precedence over actions which the king would have identified as either overtly loyal *or* disloyal. Norman Jones agrees, pointing out that as people's conceptions of public virtue became confused because of the rapid changes of the times, they used their notions about conscience to give themselves more choices that allowed them to conduct business, relate to family members, and sustain their communities.[43] This is not to say that fealty oaths were redundant exercises in futility; it is to say that they failed to quantify allegiance, either through guilt or repressive conformity.

Folio 9a especially shows how the wording of a Henrician fealty oath can illustrate the problems which inevitably arise when one tries to do things by the numbers. Scholars have records of those radicals who were committed to their causes, such as Elizabeth Barton (The Maid of Kent), John Frith, and Anne Askew, not to mention Thomas More, John Fisher, and scores of others. But scholars also have the knowledge that most people were not interested in martyrdom. Knowing this, Henry VIII hoped to use fear and suspicion to persuade people to conform to the ideas presented by the Acts of Supremacy and Succession. Folio 9a attempts to make an ideologue out of the swearer. It seeks to use the conscience of the swearer as a tool to conform the consciences of others who may or may not take the oath themselves. This is an attempt to construct a comprehensive public opinion, to determine its terms and set its parameters. In this sense the goals for this oath are set so high that they ultimately allow the conscience of the swearer to subvert them. "Public opinion," if it exists at all, is different for different groups of people in different places at different times. It also varies within the same community when age, gender, and class are concerned. Folio 8b is a much more effective oath because it omits the problematic specifics of 9a. 8b accomplishes more by focusing on the one swearer standing in front of the book rather than the whole community standing behind that person.

In the 1530s and 40s the book known as MS Stowe 15 was in the possession of the King's Remembrancer (a man named Christopher Moore) and was kept in the offices of Westminster Palace.[44] Despite the book's varied contents and its long history, when the fealty oaths to Henry VIII were added the book was appropriated exclusively for oath-swearing. On the reverse side of the book there is a large bronze gilt crucifix, which had been produced separately and was attached with small bolts to the back cover of the book. The crucifix itself is of unknown origin, and was removed from a larger ceremonial or decorative object, or from a wall, or perhaps even from another book. At first, the crucifix appears misplaced from the point of view of the reader of the book, since when the reader holds the book and then closes it the crucifix appears on the back cover rather than the front. Upon my initial examination of MS Stowe 15, I turned the book over, and, assuming the crucifix to be upright on the front cover, opened the book, only to discover upside-down text. Upon further examination, the purpose of this odd placement of the crucifix became apparent. The crucifix is affixed onto the reverse side of the book for the convenience of the administrator of the fealty oath. After the oath is administered, the book is closed by the administrator from the back to the front, not from front to back as books are commonly closed. This motion would place the book in the administrator's left hand. The crucifix is now atop the book, and is in direct proximity to the swearer's right hand. The swearer can now place his or her right hand onto the crucifix and swear. The book itself is part of an automatic and self-contained process, constructed to facilitate many oath takers.[45]

This fact represents the ultimate facet of the book's function, especially as the fealty oaths contrast sharply with the context of the book's other material. The whole book is an exercise in Henrician adaptation and revision as one set of uses replaces, but does not completely negate, another. The older material is consigned to the realm of the peripheral, which is evident by the bolting of the crucifix onto the back. The whole purpose of the book is permanently changed, but the content is still relevant to the culture that possesses the book, albeit in a different way. The coexistence of the Henrician oaths with the medieval material on the rest of the pages is a fitting metaphor for the uncertainty of the 1530s and 40s, as England wrestles with its medieval past in an effort not to eradicate it, but to own it. The moving force behind change in the Henrician age was political pressure; and yet, it is often difficult to determine just what effect that pressure had on the populace as a whole. The oaths of MS Stowe 15 were

3. Additions and Admissions

The gilt crucifix on the back cover of BL MS Stowe 15, which was attached after it was bound. Note the holes bored into the hands and feet of the crucifix, which indicate that it was once attached to a larger decorative object, such as an altarpiece or wall decoration. It was affixed to MS Stowe 15, to facilitate oathtaking (© The British Library Board).

administered from Westminster Palace, for the benefit of those who lived in London and/or who were at court; but other oaths based on the same legislation (albeit with variants in wording) were taken to monasteries, cities, and aristocratic estates. To what extent could the king rely on anecdotal information from those swearers and administrators? Could fealty oaths clarify allegiance to the point that it could be quantified? Could they assure the king that there was a public opinion to be determined, or that one could be formed? The oath of 9a expects that the swearer's conscience will allow him or her to participate in the enforcement of the Acts of Supremacy and Succession and their treason clauses. 8b, however, shows that the author of the oath, who was probably Cromwell, understood that it was far more common, and far more traditional, to expect passive obedience. 8b demands that the swearer pledge his or her loyalty to the king, his queen, and their heirs, and that he or she will give no money to a foreign ruler. In 8b the swearer is permitted passive obedience, and is excluded from participation in the enforcement of legislation. These two oaths, appearing side by side, demonstrate some of the most enduring ironies of the Henrician period: that amidst efforts to break from the traditions of the Roman Church, there were many situations which implemented those traditions; that alongside the development of the individual conscience, there were efforts to repress it; and that despite the king's innovations concerning the Royal Supremacy and Succession, he ultimately relied on old-fashioned feudalism to make his point.

Chapter 4

Grudging, Muttering, and Horn Blasts

Aurality and Performativity in Reformation Polemic

It was a noisy Reformation. Between the king's proclamations, the people's murmurs, and volleys of accusations, defenses, avowals and disavowals, the changes of the Tudor era took place amidst a clamor of voices. From the 1530s on, polemical tracts flew back and forth among those who supported the Royal Supremacy and the king's ecclesiastical policies, and those who did not. Often addressed to the author's personal enemies, or even to one person in particular, the tracts formed an ongoing argument that escalated with each publication. As the Henrician era passed, these arguments in print continued, and often revolved around appropriately placed loyalty in the face of changes in the Tudor monarchy itself. Polemicists argued about whether Edward, Mary, and Elizabeth warranted the same type of loyalty that Henry VIII had demanded for himself. They argued about whether the Royal Supremacy was to be perceived differently to cooperate with each monarch's different faith. They argued about whether the Oath of Supremacy, sworn to one monarch, necessarily described fealty to the next. They criticized each other's ability to communicate his ideas; they accused one another of heresy and treason; they shouted each other down in print and demanded to be heard; and they always refused, out of fear of damnation, to listen. They described themselves as unwaveringly loyal, and they all claimed to possess a sublime understanding of the Royal Supremacy and the oath which was required.

Early on, Henry VIII had made his own effort to persuade his subjects to hear him on the matter of the divorce in *A Glasse of the Truthe*. Thomas Swinnerton wrote in response to the dissident voices of opponents of the Supremacy in *A Litel Treatise Ageynste the Mutterynge of Some Papists in Corners*. During the reign of Elizabeth I, the Catholic Thomas Stapleton wrote in support of John Feckenham, erstwhile confessor to Mary I, and the Protestant Robert Horne and his ally John Bridges wrote against these tracts, all of them trying to drown out each other with successively louder "horn blasts."

For educated men of the sixteenth century, oration had been a primary form of discourse in their university training, much of it stemming from Ramist influence. Although the study of oratory concerned the art of speaking, it also concerned the act of hearing. As D.R. Woolf points out in his study of speech and hearing in Renaissance England, polemical writers thought of their senses as complementary. He states, "In the well-ordered body, each performed its function in harmony with the rest."[1] An education in rhetoric necessarily trained the senses to better absorb the material, and then reproduce it via one's own sensibilities. Polemicists therefore thought of the world in aural as well as visual terms, and they communicated this understanding by depicting sound and noise in their work. Despite the number of university-educated men who participated in Tudor era polemic, the vast majority of the society in which they lived was illiterate. Polemicists, like their illiterate countrymen and women, most often *heard* news items, rumors, and official information rather than saw them on the printed page. When they did experience text, they brought their lifelong experience of aurality to it, both when they read and when they wrote. As Woolf theorizes, "The frequency of metaphors of sound rather than sight in Renaissance texts suggests that the writers who employed it thought of their works not as silent artifacts to be studied exclusively with the eye, but as instruments for the conveyance of their authorial voice to a public which in turn was conceived as an audience."[2] Seeing and hearing, therefore, are not exclusive sensory experiences for Tudor polemicists; rather, the two senses work together to produce a single means by which an argument performs. Aurality in polemic is as important as voice, especially when the polemical tract concerns the subject of sworn fealty — a speech act. Therefore, even within the silent form of the printed word, the argument can

4. Grudging, Muttering, and Horn Blasts

rise to an absolute, and very real, din. The task of the polemicist is to persuade the audience to hear him as he shouts to sound an alarm, or blast his horn, as is the case with the Elizabethan polemical tracts discussed here. He must employ a significant amount of imaginative force, what Aristotle called *energia,* to bring as much dynamism to the piece as possible. He must convince his audience that they hear what he hears; or, he must complain about the noise his enemies are making; or, he must, with great skill, invite his readers to listen closely, so that they might hear the enemies of the monarch whispering, muttering, and plotting in secret.

The subject of orality versus textuality is central to the work of Walter J. Ong, on the subject of rhetoric in the sixteenth and seventeenth centuries. In Ong's view, the act of reading in the medieval period had been oral and aural, as texts were read aloud to an audience, while the early modern period had refocused sensory experience on text to the visual, as mass printings and more access to education allowed people to read to themselves. While Ong's view describes an important aspect of changes in the Western world when it comes to cognition and style, it treats these senses as exclusive. Rather than arguing in favor of a transition from oral/aural to visual, I will discuss the Tudor period as a time when modes of expression transcended such exclusivity. During this period, ideas about the performativity of speech and its relation to sensory cooperation represented readers' understanding of the full implications of individualism. The act of writing and reading polemical tracts which make heavy use of sound metaphors allows the reader to literally witness the clash of ideas described within the text. He or she hears it and sees it. As a speech act which is presented as text, and then which must be vocalized and witnessed, an oath which affirms the Royal Supremacy illustrates the extent to which multisensory perception represents a way for writers and readers to enhance what they already understand, instead of representing a transition from one type of perception to another.

One of the aims of the Henrician Acts of Supremacy and Succession was to invoke the voices of the loyal in taking the oath which justified the statutes, and then immediately to assure that those same voices would remain quiet. The oath which referred to the Act of Succession required its takers to swear "without fraud or guile," and to "keep to their cunning wit" the contents of the oath to the utmost of their abilities.[3] This language of course refers to the intent of the swearer, and it preempts any qualification of the act of swearing after the fact. Therefore, the language of the oath seeks to secure intent within the act of swearing. One cannot take the oath with the intent to disqualify it in private, or worse, to claim to fail to have understood, or to have forgotten, what was in it. As Greg Walker points out in *Writing Under Tyranny*, the king was deeply disturbed about the gap which lay between what people said as they swore, and what they said about what they swore, after the fact. Walker says:

> Through the oaths attached to the Acts of Supremacy and Succession [the king] specifically states that outward subscription to [the swearer's] claims was not enough: English men and women must swear the oaths without inward grudge or scruple, and they should not grumble or qualify their statements afterwards."[4]

In short, the king wanted more than a singular vocalized performance of the oath in its taking; he wanted a continued performance of the oath in the form of an absence of speech in the aftermath of its taking. More intolerance of complaint came with the Treason Act which accompanied the Act of Succession. It became treason to:

> ...maliciously wish will or desire by words or writing, or by crafty imagine invent practise or attempt any bodily harm to be done or committed to the king's most royal person, the queen's or their heirs apparent ... or slanderously and maliciously publish and pronounce by express writing or words that the king our sovereign lord should be heretic schismatic tyrant infidel or usurper of the crown.[5]

The message was clear: the king equated verbal complaint with acts of physical violence. What one thought, one was likely to say, and what one said, one was likely to do. The fealty oaths (in various forms) which followed these Acts in the next decade sought to unify how the oath read as text, how the taker heard and therefore understood it, how the taker swore it, and how the taker continued to validate orally what he or she swore afterward.[6]

The issue of public quiet in the face of royal proclamation was on the king's mind before the Acts of Supremacy and Succession were brought to Parliament. In 1532 he produced a treatise entitled, *A Glasse of the Truthe*, on the subject of the Great Matter, and published it via Thomas Bertelet. Written in the form of a dialogue between a Lawyer and a Divine, the

4. Grudging, Muttering, and Horn Blasts

piece seeks to showcase Henry VIII's skills in rhetoric, both after the elegant fashion of the Erasmian humanists and the invective of Protestant reformers. With an eye toward rhetorical and literary innovation, Henry pushed the boundaries of both styles of written argument to produce a text which he believed would be uniquely persuasive; and in his own mind, it was.

The book identifies itself as interpretive, claiming to make "pure truth" out of the overblown language of the two experts in the dialogue. Its prologue assures, "...where we be nat sufficient to supplye the same [i.e., eloquence and drift of argument], to content your selfe with this our rudenesse, declarynge the pure truth alone: which you shall be right sure to fynde in this poore treatise."[7] The truth, he states, is plain and simple; in it are found none of the characteristics of iniquity: no "...obstinate and forward bablynge, no malicious backbytynge, no sclaunderous and factious enforcynge ... [it is] without all vayne ostentation, without inventynge or borrowynge of ydell titles and inscriptions, with colourynge, dissemblynge, pretense and all outward payntynge."[8] Amidst the descriptions of noisy, distracting talk, all of which is depicted as inconsequential chatter, and therefore a prelude to treason, is a condemnation of language which is falsely painted, a *trompe l'oeil*.

Despite the fact that the dialogue presents itself as an argument between the Lawyer and the Divine, before long the two achieve a unity of opinion, albeit from two points of view, as to why Henry VIII is correct in divorcing Katherine of Aragon. The moment they realize that they actually agree is an illuminating one for them. The Divine states, "...it is great pitie, that lerned men specially, regarde nat more the worlde to come than the worlde present: and that they unyte nat them selfe in opinion."[9] Their agreement renders the matter indisputable, and the remainder of the treatise outlines the justification of the Great Matter on the points of their agreement, with examples from both the statutes and scripture. The Lawyer especially wants to have his opinion justified by concordance with the Divine's opinion, and asks that the Divine iterate his view. The Lawyer wants to hear what he already agrees with, so that he might more perfectly understand it — nothing is as persuasive as the sound of one's own voice.

The book reflects the king's attitude toward the Acts and accompanying oaths that would appear in the next two years: simple compliance is not enough. One must truly believe that to which one assents. Afterthoughts, grumblings, and regret signify that the truth has not been seen clearly. One must look deeply into the glass, through its obscurity, to see the truth. The tract's very argument is that where the Great Matter is concerned, argument is nonexistent. As the Divine ponders the "unnatural demeanor" of dissent, and wonders how it can be that a subject would even think to "mysdeme" his prince,[10] the reader understands what Henry VIII is getting at: the king is trying to imagine disloyalty, and he is unable to do so. He cannot put himself into the shoes of a dissenter, and he therefore cannot depict an opposing argument in his treatise. He cannot even go so far as to reiterate the arguments of others (as rhetoricians did) before refuting them according to their various points. The book closes with a deep suspicion on the part of both the Lawyer and the Divine, for the man whose word cannot be trusted, even upon his oath:

> LAWYER: I answere that the lawe in his due course exercised, oughte to be directed by truthe onlye.
> DIVINE: And what call ye truth? That which apereth in dede only: or that by report? And if by reporte, whether that which some men say & depose is true, or onely that all men say and holy agree unto is true?[11]

This exchange is quickly followed by their agreed condemnation for those who accept the oath of Katherine of Aragon, that she had not consummated her marriage with Prince Arthur.[12] The Lawyer quips, "And truly no man is to be bileved in his owne matter."[13] As if to drive home the point, a note in the margin at this point reads, "None to be beleved in his owne cause."[14] The provisions against complaint and begrudgement that followed in the ensuing legislation reflected the king's comfort with his own conscience, and no one else's.

At first Henry published the piece anonymously, then instructed his agents to gradually spread the word that the work was the king's own. He in effect "whispered" his defense of his own actions in a prelude to the much louder proclamations which would follow. This effort, which Christopher Warner calls "a ventriloquial technique,"[15] parallels the king's descent into tyranny; the rhetoric used in the dissemination of his voice precedes the mandated language of the statutes and oaths that by 1532 he certainly had in mind. Indeed, the king's voice is a massive presence, and anyone who bought, or was given a copy of *A Glasse of the Truthe* likely

4. Grudging, Muttering, and Horn Blasts

knew from the start who its silent author was, and read it with as much attention as they would a royal proclamation. This is precisely what Henry VIII wanted. The reader's experience in hearing the "argument" would have been superseded by the presence of the king's voice despite the form of the dialogue. The reader was therefore expected to assume that the dialogue represented the king's own opinion rather than the opinions of two allegorical groups (ie, civil lawyers and divines). Ultimately, the book presented the opinions the king wanted his subjects to hold. The "argument" was nothing of the sort. It was a proclamation, and its effectiveness relied upon the ability of the reader to hear properly what he or she was actually being told — or be accused of treason.[16] If one listened carefully, one understood that to swear the Oath of Supremacy and support the king's legislation was to speak as he would, albeit not in his voice. That privilege was his alone. His subjects, if they were loyal, were expected to perform their fealty ventriloquially.

There were, of course, dissident voices. Among those opponents and/or critics of the Supremacy were those who chose a clandestine form of communication, in order to avoid persecution. These voices disturbed Thomas Swinnerton, an evangelical preacher who had been educated at Wittenberg and who was an avid supporter of the king and a licensed preacher to boot. He wrote two treatises promoting the Royal Supremacy, including *A Litel Treatise Ageynste the Mutterynge of Some Papists in Corners,* in 1534.[17] Much of the language in the king's own treatise had focused on the quieting of the king's conscience and of the realm, on the peacefulness which agreement and assent would bring and then maintain. Swinnerton hopes to satisfy the doubts of those who still support the pope, "...to the intent that after they knowe the truthe they shulde be ashamed to clatter in corners ageinst it."[18] His treatise reveals a preacher whose support for the king relied predominantly on his audibility. Licensed by the Archbishop of Canterbury to preach throughout the country, Swinnerton proclaimed the Royal Supremacy boldly, and to an audience of eager listeners. Confident that he is successfully getting through to the king's loyal subjects, Swinnerton publishes his treatise not to attract the audience his voice fails to reach, but to get through to those who have heard, but have deliberately chosen not to listen.

Belligerent, disobedient, and disloyal, the enemies of the Royal

Supremacy plot and whisper; they are not like thieves, however, but like outmoded scholars in a library filled with out-of-date books. They will not hear Swinnerton (or the king) because they rely too heavily on the precedent set by the ancient written word. Swinnerton argues that the forefathers of old, the authors of these books, were "blynd and in a wrong beleve,"[19] concerning the Pope's power to rule the Christian church, because they have come to rely too heavily on the custom of putting their faith in ancient texts, without the benefit of critical voices. He states, "Wherefore, if any of our forefathers, of ignorance, or for their own glorie or lucre, have broughte any custome into Christes churche, contrarie to truthe and his holy doctrine we oughte of dutie (refusinge suche erroneous custome) to folowe the truthe."[20] Dissenters place too much importance on the authority of ancient, and in Swinnerton's view, redundant and irrelevant texts, for the sake of tradition. Those texts, the work of the Church fathers and medieval theologians, must submit to new ideas, new voices. "Custome must give place to the truthe," he continues, "For who doubteth that custome oughte to give place to the truthe ones published?"[21] Here, he calls for text to submit to the audible word. The truth has been discovered, and is being proclaimed throughout the country. Moreover, it has been published. In arguing this premise Swinnerton consigns the old texts to a fictive realm, filled with delusion and doublespeak. The plain speech of the evangelical preacher represents a new truth which cannot be denied once it is heard — an idea taken from the Gospels, which exhort those with ears to hear the message delivered by Christ.[22] These new truths have been spoken in the pulpit, but the dissenters have not been present to listen. Publishing these new ideas allows them to ring true precisely because Thomas Bertelet publishes *cum privilegio*; and this fact allows Swinnerton to align his polemical agenda, the Royal Supremacy, and the Word of the Gospel. Had the whisperers been better scholars, they would have seen this connection, as the reformers apparently did. He states: "For if they [the reformers] them selfe hadde not, by their diligent studie, sought out his [the Pope's] false fraude, the popyshe form shuld never have ben refourmedde..."[23]

For Swinnerton, the muttering of papists tucked away in corners is actually a deafening form of protest, for the simple fact of its persistence. Neither the plain speech of the evangelical preacher, the license from Cranmer that speaks for itself, or the publishing of the truths of the Royal

4. Grudging, Muttering, and Horn Blasts

Supremacy *cum privilegio* can drown out the muttering and the whispering. Moreover, the producers of such mutterings hear only those quiet voices with which they surround themselves. In his frustration, Swinnerton accuses the persistent whisperers of affecting the reception of others, of producing idle talk and complaint among those who, because of their ignorance (and perhaps illiteracy), are the most vulnerable. Swinnerton protests that even after hearing his bold defense of the Supremacy in the pulpit, the common folk, distracted by papist mutterings, will turn to folk sayings. He says:

> "Whereas it hath ben spoke of many and divers, that it was a mery world before men spake of any suche matters, that is to witte, to have any reformation among them of the clergie, and before that men beganne to sette light the pope, and to call hym the bishop of Rome: that is as wyse a sayenge and opinion, as this is of them that sey, sens the crienge down of Galy halfpens, the lernyng of Duns never prosperedde, and also sens Tenterden steple was builded, Sandwich Haven hath ever more decayed."[24]

In their confusion, and because of dissident mutterings, people turn to long-held, but foolish *post hoc propter hoc* folk beliefs. Such absurdities sound familiar, and make people feel comfortable, but they ultimately replace truths with delusions, the word of the king and the Word of God with idle babbling. It had not, in fact, been "mery" before men spoke of these matters, before reformers like Swinnerton made such noise. The learning of Duns Scotus did not wane because Henry IV banned the Gally halfpenny; and Goodwin Sands did not erode because of the building of Tenterden Steeple.[25] Swinnerton claims that it is the muttering papists who make the real noise; he and other reformers seek only to bring the country "from trowble and grievous vexation to quietnesse and reste."[26] They make noise so that there may be quiet.

Swinnerton's defense is typical of the attitude held by supporters of the Supremacy, who, following Thomas Cromwell (and sometimes promoted by him),[27] argued that the oaths that stemmed from the Acts of Supremacy and Succession merely reiterated the prerogatives the king already had. The oaths required of the loyal subject reaffirmed fealty rather than established it. In this case, begrudging indicated that the subject in question was unwilling to swear to something that was already true and, moreover, was supported by Divine Law. The persistent noise of dissent, even mutterings, pointed to loyalty that never existed. The Acts of

Supremacy and Succession, and their oaths, were therefore meant to make a distinction between those were always loyal and those who never were. Understanding the problem this posed for English Catholics, and in concert with her efforts to repeal much of her father's legislation, Mary I retracted the Act of Supremacy and annulled its oath. Elizabeth I reinstated the legislation upon her accession, however, and made several adaptations to the Act of Supremacy which would reignite arguments between Protestants and Catholics about how loyalty was to be defined in England. Many of these arguments revolved around those who had enjoyed privilege during Mary's reign but who, upon the accession of Elizabeth, refused to swear to the new Act.

John Feckenham, Abbot of Westminster (d. 1584), was one such person. A former Benedictine monk, he had assented to the Royal Supremacy under Henry VIII after the dissolution of Evesham Abbey, where he resided, in 1540. Although his career continued during the 1540s, he opposed the Henrician ban on sacraments and the Cromwellian condemnation of ideas from abroad.[28] He presented these views in a sermon at Paul's Cross in 1547, which was recorded by an informer.[29] He was imprisoned in the Tower by Edward VI, and remained there throughout Edward's reign, although he was released briefly to take part in several debates and public disputations with figures such as Thomas Cranmer, Hugh Latimer, and Nicholas Ridley. Feckenham interrogated both Jane Grey and Princess Elizabeth (but was unable to convert either one), and urged Mary I to exercise restraint when it came to the fate of her half-sister. Upon Mary's accession, he became her chaplain and confessor, and eventually became Dean of St. Paul's and Abbot of Westminster. He was known for having a strong and persuasive argumentative sense. Feckenham was still Abbot of Westminster when Elizabeth I acceded the throne, but by the Settlement of 1559, which reinstituted the Royal Supremacy, he refused his assent and denied the Oath of Uniformity which the Settlement required. He was sent to the Tower again, where he penned a treatise defending his refusal of the Oath, and soon after was transferred to the household of Robert Horne, Bishop of Winchester.[30]

Bishop Horne (d.1579) had been imprisoned in the Tower by Mary and also exiled; upon his return he was pardoned by Elizabeth and thereafter pursued the goal of reforming the ministry. In 1559 Horne was

4. Grudging, Muttering, and Horn Blasts

appointed as one of nine men chosen to engage conservatives in debate in the Westminster dispute, in which Feckenham was a key participant. Horne had been impressed by Feckenham's apparent openness of mind and argumentative talent. He sought debate but got resistance instead. In response to Feckenham's stubbornness, Horne "answered" Feckenham, in print, producing *An Answeare Made by Robt. Bishoppe of Wynchester, to a Booke, Entitled, "The Declaration of Suche Scruples, and Staies of Conscience, Touching the Othe of the Supremacy," as M. Iohn Feckenham, by Wrytynge Did Deliver Unto the Bishop of Winchester, with his Resolutions Made Thereunto.*[31] His aim in reproducing his debates with Feckenham in written form was to reiterate his views in the face of Feckenham's stubbornness. It also served the purpose of clearing himself of any pending accusations that he may have been too easy on Feckenham, or that he did not wholeheartedly support the Supremacy.[32]

Feckenham had been in residence at Horne's household, and despite the apparent conversations and debates between the two there was apparently much unsaid. For Horne, that material existed in the form of Feckenham's book, which had been disseminated abroad. As he begins his attack on the book, he makes an accusation of secrecy and dissemblance similar to that which Swinnerton had made decades earlier. He says, "It is nowe an whole yeere paste, since I herde of a book secretly scattered abroad by M. Feckenham emonge his freendes.... I stoode in doubt what to doo, whether to discover the man by writinge, or to shake him off with silence."[33] Ultimately he decides that silence is not a fit form of protest against secrecy among whispering papists, and he responds with a point-for point refutation of Feckenham's book. Feckenham had agreed to swear the oath to Elizabeth, albeit on limited grounds. Although he had no intention of recanting his Catholicism, or his demonstrated loyalty to Mary, he nonetheless conceded that the oath is "...a saulfegarde to be had of the Queenes royall personne and of her highness most quiet and prosperous reign."[34] Horne refused to believe him.

For Horne, the taking of a fealty oath to the monarch is more than a performed act, and much of his cynicism for Feckenham's protestation of his loyalty revolves around Horne's disdain for the ritualism that Feckenahm's Catholicism brings to the tradition of oath-swearing. Horne believed the Catholic oath to be archaic in its focus on ritual and performance, since the outward actions allow the swearer to perform the act of swearing while inwardly qualifying his or her statement with grudging and regret. He states,

> "How so ever by wordes you woulde seems to tender her maiesties saulfty, quietness, and prosperous reigne, your deedes declare youre meaninge to be cleane contrary.... How much prosperitie you wishe to her Majesties reigne appeareth, when that with diepe sighes and grones you looke daily for a chaunge thereof, and tharche Heretique of Rome, your God in earthe, to reigne in her place."[35]

Feckenham's loyalty, says Horne, is nothing more than flattery. The accusation of flattery was an insult which cut deeply into its intended target. It suggested that a person was a mere speaker rather than a subject, someone who performed in order to be seen by others, but who failed to act with appropriate sincerity. This person could be no friend to the monarch.[36] For this reason Horne rejects Feckenham's offer to guarantee his intent with a corporal oath: it will only represent seeming speech; Feckenham's sighs and groans reveal his true meaning.

For Horne, as for many Protestants during Elizabeth's reign, the sworn fealty of a Catholic was to be considered void until the person's Catholic faith had been recanted. Feckenham can never be believed, argues Horne, corporal oath or no, because he is forsworn to the Pope, and will therefore always be loyal to his first oath. As long as Feckenham believes that he will earn the Pope's curse upon such recantation, no new oath can be accepted on his part.[37] Here, Horne's attitude reflects the mistrust that many Elizabethan Protestants felt toward Catholics who had come through Edward's and Mary's reigns. Those who were defiantly Catholic in the 1560s were viewed differently from those who resisted the Royal Supremacy in the 1530s and 40s. By Elizabeth's reign dissenters were seen by Protestants as entrenched, especially defiant as they waited for a reestablishment of Catholicism in England by way of a Spanish invasion, a French marriage for Elizabeth, or a final surrender by the Queen to the Pope's curses, excommunications, and bullying. As Horne points out, Feckenham himself had admitted that he had been "sworn chaplain and most bounden," to Mary.[38] He attacks him on this point:

> Like an unfaithful subject contrary to your othe made to kinge Henry, and continued all the reigne of king Edward, you helpt to spoile Queene Mary, of

4. Grudging, Muttering, and Horn Blasts

famous memory of a principall parte of her royal power, right, and dignitie, which she at the beginninge of her reign had enjoyed and put in use. The same obedience & subjection, with the like loyaltie and faithfulness, yee will sweare to observe & perfourme to Queene Elizabeth. But she thanketh you for naught, she will none of it, she hath espied you, and thinketh yee profer her to muche wronge.[39]

Because Feckenham had sworn fealty to Henry VIII, and because Feckenham had observed that fealty throughout the reign of Edward VI, Horne argues, he was bound by that oath to be loyal and recognize the supremacy of the following monarch, whatever her faith. Although Feckenham had claimed to do so, Horne argues that the abbot in fact failed, because his oath had never been valid in the first place. His true bond had been to Rome, and to the Pope, not to Mary, who he therefore "spoiled" of her prerogative. Horne had some cause to make this accusation. Upon her entrance to Westminster before the religious service that preceded the opening of her first Parliament, Elizabeth I had been greeted by Feckenham and his monks, carrying tapers and waving censers. She had snapped at him, saying, "Away with these torches, for we see very well."[40] Several weeks later, when the uniformity bill was passed, Feckenham had been deliberately absent from the chamber.[41] What the queen saw, and what Horne saw in Feckenham, was a defiant papist bent on demonstrating his true intent via his actions. He condemns Feckenham for his misplaced fealty, and also for his attempt to justify it under the guise of loyalty to Mary as monarch. In doing so Horne demonstrates his observance of his own sworn bond to the Henrician Act of Succession. Despite Mary's Catholicism and Spanish marriage, Horne claims to respect the Succession, and claims that rather than being loyal to the English monarch, who happened to espouse Catholicism, Feckenham had misinterpreted his bond and placed his fealty with Rome with Mary as its agent. In Horne's view, the two are not the same.

In his book, Feckenham inquires as to the manner in which he will be required to swear. It is a cynical request: "And touchynge the rest of the othe, whereunto I am required presently to sweare ... how and by what meanes, I may sweare thereunto, without committinge of a very plaine and manifest perjury.... And of your parte to provoke me or require the same, it is no lesse damnable offence."[42] Horne responds to this claim by accusing Feckenham of "waverynge inconstancie,"[43] stating that Feckenham had assented to Henry VIII's oath — why did he now refuse and claim perjury? Horne is "blasting" Feckenham, so to speak, with the loud noise of his answer, in the hopes that the "Horne blast" he produces will serve as an alarm, a shock to the senses, the same way such a sound would awaken a sleeping (or perhaps daydreaming) and inconstant man. By these proofs he expects Feckenham to yield: "...wherefore you will now I trust, yeelde herein, & recken your selfe well satisfied, take upon you the knowledge thereof, and to be ready to testify the same upon a booke othe, for so have you promised."[44] He expects that Feckenham will awaken to the performative reality of the oath, abandon his fantasy, and thus yielding, express his assent. Feckenham must answer the "call" of Horne's "blast"; he must vocalize his fealty, perform the oath, and break the silence of his disobedience.

Much of the debate between Horne and Feckenham, and much of the debate about them, which would continue over the course of the next decade, revolves around the subject of casuistry. Long used as a rhetorical device in the universities, casuistry encouraged the dwelling upon of nuances of speech for the purposes of persuading the speaker's audience of the innocence or culpability of his subject.[45] The Henrician Reformation had appropriated discussions of conscience and the vocalization of fealty in order to identify the ideological Other. This redefinition of conscience defined the Tudor discourse of power, and made the king's prerogative inviolable on both secular and sacred grounds, as a means to eliminate the Other.[46] By 1559 the Elizabethan government sought to both define and control the device of casuistry so as to reconcile the Other to the monarch's own conscience, and to the collective conscience of the loyal Protestant majority of London. This had been one of the goals of the Westminster debate, and it was what Horne had hoped for in his discussions with Feckenham at his home.

Because of its ambiguity and its ability to reason around a problem, casuistry was a real threat to the Elizabethan Supremacy. It threatened to undermine the authority of the legislation of the Settlement, for which Elizabeth had fought hard and compromised much. As Lowell Gallagher points out, casuistry was:

> "...ostensibly the vehicle through which the voice of conscience performed its stabilizing, normative function, [but] it was also the harbinger of the disinte-

4. Grudging, Muttering, and Horn Blasts

gration of communally recognized signs of what belonged inside and what outside the structure of cultural norms."[47]

The Catholic was not to be permitted to reason around — or out of— his obligation to be loyal to the monarch, and this is precisely what Horne accused Feckenham of doing. Since Feckenham had been in Mary's service, and since he claimed to have been loyal to the Henrician Act of Succession under those circumstances, it was a particularly sensitive issue. Polemicists of Elizabeth's reign needed to be careful about how well they employed this concept in their work, since Catholics could employ it too, with dangerously persuasive results. Horne, like other Protestants in Elizabethan London, knew that casuistry had a long history that paralleled the rise in auricular confession in the thirteenth century.[48] Casuistry became a traditional form of reasoning through problematic situations, and for reformers of the sixteenth century, it came to represent the method by which the Roman Church sought to reason itself out of accusations of hypocrisy for centuries.[49] Horne would not tolerate it from Feckenham, and neither would Horne's supporters tolerate it from those who chose to defend Feckenham. Although these arguments and accusations were bound to take place, and did take place, Elizabeth did not wish to encourage them among her ministers and bishops. She had voiced her opinion on the matter at the opening of her first Parliament, with a speech given by Nicholas Bacon, her Lord Keeper of the Great Seal and trusted minister. Her Parliament was specifically instructed to avoid the traditional (and now typical) polemical techniques which had defined arguments surrounding the Supremacy for decades. They were to avoid "all sophistical, captious, and frivolous arguments and quiddities." Moreover, they were not to insult each other like pamphleteers, with terms like "heretic," and "papist."[50] If the queen's ministers and bishops observed these guidelines in their respective chambers, it was another story when they wrote to, for, and about each other. Horne and Feckenham had been two bishops engaged in heated debate; and this debate provoked responses that did not recognize the queen's demand for civility.

The noise generated by Horne's answer to Feckenham echoed across the realm, and across the sea as well. In 1559, the very year in which Horne and Feckenham began their debates, Thomas Stapleton (d.1598), a staunch Catholic, fled the country without license to seek refuge in the Low Countries. Having obtained his degree from Oxford during Mary's reign, he, like other exiles during the 1560s and 70s, believed that they were merely waiting out the Elizabethan settlement. The Tudors had once rescinded their own Supremacy and faith, and it was believed by many Catholics that they would do so again. Unbeknownst to Stapleton, the Elizabethan settlement would be permanent, forcing him to spend the rest of his life in Louvain and Douai.[51] Stapleton returned to England just once during his exile, at a request from his father in 1563 to attend to an unknown matter of business. He was swiftly arrested and presented with the Oath of Supremacy. He agreed to swear, but only to the part of the oath that gave Elizabeth supremacy in temporal affairs. In response, Bishop Barlowe deprived him of his position as prebendary of Chichester, and Stapleton and his family were permitted to leave the country.

In 1567 Stapleton published his own book, a defense of Feckenham against Horne's accusations. It was called, appropriately, *A Counterblast to M. Horne's Vayne Blaste Against M. Feckenham.*[52] Stapleton supported Feckenham not only because they shared Catholic sympathies, but also because their refusal of the oath of Supremacy had been based on similar grounds. Many Catholic exiles and recusants during Elizabeth's reign seemed willing to swear to the temporal aspect of her Supremacy but not to its spiritual aspect. If Horne's criticism of Feckenham is to be considered a horn sounding an alarm to jolt the dissident from his spiritual sleep, then Stapleton's "counterblast" is nothing short of a blaring noise meant to drown out, rather than awaken or signal to, the voice it opposes. He "counterblasts" Horne loudly and profusely, signaling not only his desire to shout down his opponent but to shout *over* the Elizabethan Supremacy in England, which by 1567 was threatening to have intractable staying power. Stapleton's book defending Feckenham's refusal of the oath is about five times the length of Horne's book but covers the same material. Stapleton, like Horne, produces a lengthy history which seeks to prove that kings had deferred to popes in ecclesiastical causes.[53] But in outdoing Horne, by making the material so much more profuse and exhaustive, Stapleton makes a significantly louder and more antagonistic protest than Horne had in his cause. This amplification stems from Stapleton's own experience of having been presented with the oath. He had accepted in part, but it had not been enough. He had been disenfranchised and exiled, left shouting outside the door, and now he felt the need to escalate.

4. Grudging, Muttering, and Horn Blasts

That escalation quickly causes Stapleton's book to admit a secondary focus: a personal attack on Horne. Horne had indeed made personal remarks against Feckenham, but the short length of the book kept the focus on the oath and on Feckenham's lack of persuadability. Stapleton's much longer book gives him plenty of opportunity to attack Horne personally, from calling him a whoremonger (based on his acceptance of clerical marriage) to calling him a bad scholar. He says, "...you interlace twice these words (as one that had the cure and authorities over all) and againe, in the same leaf (as one that had authoritie over them) which you find not in your Authors ... so you springle in these words (by his [Theodoretus'] supreme authoritie) to your narration out of the said Theodoretus."[54] He accuses Horne of being unlearned and unpracticed, a poor performing artist with a bad instrument. He suggests that Horne's "blast" merely pleases the majority audience, where the critical power resides, and acts as a distraction from the deficiencies of the Supremacy, which demands the vocalization of loyalty while it quietly defies scripture. As Stapleton claims, "For a Supreme governour is he, that hath the chiefe governmente of the thing governed, not in those actions that may any way properly belong to the subiect or thing governed ... but in those actions that belonge to the end, whereunto the governour tendeth."[55] He continues, outlining the Biblical precept that servants should be subject to their masters, as sons are to their fathers, as students to their schoolmaster, as sailors to the mariner, and as kings are to God; or, in Stapleton's interpretation of scripture, the spiritual powers.[56] Stapleton accuses Elizabeth of demanding sworn fealty that permits the monarch more authority than that which historical precedent and scripture warrant. In doing so, he says, she has elevated royal pretensions to a higher degree than even Henry VIII had.[57] In an interesting reversal of Horne's premise (based on the Henrician statutes) that the Supremacy asks for nothing more than that which is *already* due to the prince, Stapleton argues that the Supremacy must not ask for anything more than that which was *ever* due to the prince. Both Stapleton and Horne, each in his own way, argue that royal supremacy is based on truths that already exist; and that the oath which thereby binds subjects to their monarch cannot require anything which is not already true. Even the monarch must obey the spirit of monarchy — he or she cannot devise an oath which requires unjust or unprecedented things. He or she is bound, by the coronation oath, to this observance.[58]

Sworn Bond in Tudor England

Despite the personal attacks and historical precedents, Stapleton does not lose sight of his primary focus: the oath. Proceeding from his argument that Horne is a poor scholar both of rhetoric and scripture, Stapleton criticizes Horne's understanding of the oath and its sense. He contrasts it with Feckenham's understanding, saying:

> And now see, howe even at the first entraunce, he playeth fowle play and wrangleth. For M. Feckenham doth not maketh difference betwixt *to testifie in conscience*, and *to declare in conscience*,[59] as Maister Horne sayeth, he dothe: but betwixt to take an othe that the Queene's Majesty is supreme Heade in all causes, and to declare the same in conscience, which are two things ... for a man maye and many doe (the more pity) take an oathe for feare, love or rewarde, quyte contrary to their consciences. Men may be persuaded to take the othe, which is an externall facte, by external respects of force, feare, or frayltye: but perswaded to declare the other in his conscience, no man can be without an internall persuasion of hart and minde.[60]

Here, Stapleton accuses Horne of parsing mere words, of deliberately extracting from Feckenham's understanding of the oath a sense which is not there. He concedes that the mere act of swearing an oath out of fear, weakness, or force, does indeed cause a gap between action and intent, an interruption of the harmony between the vocalization of sworn bond and its performance. But, he claims, Feckenham's understanding of the oath does not make this distinction. Horne's "wrangling," is depicted as a wrestling of the word from its sense. Stapleton uses similar violent and dissonant imagery to describe Horne's mangling of texts, his "cries," "blusters" and "bragges." This imagery accompanies Stapleton's identification of Horne as a heretic "...as proceeding from the Devill the spirit of dissention, not from God, who is the God of unity, peace, and concorde."[61] For Stapleton, Horne's distinction is pure noise that distracts from the true sense of the oath, which Feckenham, in his defiant silence, better understands, and therefore refuses.

John Bridges (d. 1618) was still in pursuit of the DD when he published a response to Stapleton's *Counterblast* in 1573, entitled *The Supremacie of Christian Princes*.[62] Bridges had earned a name for himself by preaching at Paul's Cross and having at least one sermon printed, and by printing a translation of Rudolph Walther's *175 Homilies on the Acts of the Apostles*. He eventually became Bishop of Oxford. Known as a controversialist, he engaged in print disputes with Catholics and Calvinists alike;

4. Grudging, Muttering, and Horn Blasts

his work provoked a mention of his name in the famed "Martin Marprelate" *Epistle* of 1588, subtitled, *Oh Read Over Dr. John Bridges, for it is a Worthy Work*. *The Supremacie of Christian Princes* is a massive tome of more than a thousand pages, and serves to illustrate the further escalation and profusion of an argument which is traced by Bridges himself to a short treatise by Feckenham, in defense of his refusal of the oath of Supremacy. Bridges seeks to outblow Stapleton's *Counterblast*, and in doing so he employs so many attendant issues, references, and examples, that Feckenham's refusal of the oath nearly gets lost in the book's cacophony of words.

Like Stapleton, and Horne before him, Bridges reprints a great deal of his opponents' books, citing large amounts of material from Stapleton and Feckenham. Although such reiteration was a common rhetorical device (which served in part as a convenience to the reader who did not own the books being responded to), it served a further polemical purpose. The format "speaks" by way of the inclusion of the opponent's voice. The presence of the opponent's voice prevents the argument (here, by Bridges, but also by Stapleton and Horne) from becoming a soliloquy or tirade. The reader experiences a debate which seeks to reproduce the form, if not the spirit of the public debates that the peers of these authors (and sometimes the public) often witnessed. The point is to keep the discussion open, audible, and accessible in contrast with the "hucker mucker" of papist mutterings. Bridges here reiterates a claim which, by 1573 was longstanding, that papists whispered their dissent throughout the land. He condemns their clandestine dissidence, especially those whispers which appear in writing:

> ...your invective pampheletes dispearsed abroade in hucker mucker, her Maiesties subiectes here quiet at home, to make them mislike his highnesse regiment: but also to slaunder hir abroade to other nations, besides your continuall whisperers, whom ye sende aboute, instilling into the peoples heades, a hope or feare of a chaunge to come.[63]

In addition to disturbing the quiet of the realm, the continued muttering of papists fills the people (particularly recusants, who Bridges believed to be persuadable) with the false hope that the Tudor government would revert to the government established by Mary I. Bridges exhorts Stapleton to listen to his own words:

> Ye do wisely, M. Stap. to mitigate the matter by your owne hearing: ye coulde heare all things that sounded against the Protestants, wherein you

were as quicke of telling as of hearing. But for any thing, that should sounde against the Papists, although it rang in the eares of all men, he have on your harvest eares. But and if ye could have heard on that side the eare, that sheweth out the Papistes practices, he sould have heard of many their conspiracies, and other their wicked attempts, bysides their mutterings that they dare not utter, which if they durst, no doubte ye shoulde heare thereof.[64]

Bridges makes the assertion that the whisperings of the papists, and their silence in refusing the oath, denotes guilt. If their true intentions were spoken aloud, and loudly, no one would deny their error. Moreover, he argues, an answer to Stapleton had been too long in coming, and that Protestants, in their failure to answer Stapleton promptly, had echoed the error of their enemies, even if to a lesser extent. For Bridges, a defense of the Supremacy requires an immediate answer.

In Bridges' argument, part of Stapleton's deficiency in defending the indefensible is a lack of rhetorical skill. He states that Stapleton is unable to make a solid point and accuses him of talking all around the Oath of Supremacy instead of swearing it. Ironically, Bridges demonstrates this assertion by talking all around the Oath of Supremacy about the various deficiencies in Stapleton's skills. But he does have a point: the validity of an oath, especially one which refers directly to the monarch, is affected by how people talk about it, and also by how they talk around it. The substance of the oath is not merely contained within its specific words; it is contained outside the audible act of swearing, outside the text of the oath as it is presented to the swearer. Attitudes toward the monarch, and toward faith, learning, and custom will ultimately contribute to a person's decision to swear or deny the oath upon its presentation. Bridges therefore parses terms, deconstructs examples, and provides references with as much profuse fervor as Horne as Stapleton have. By discussing the larger issue he hopes to encourage his reader to understand the consequence of words.

Feckenham, by way of this assertion, had been wrong is assuming that he was required to swear, although that was what he had claimed. Bridges maintains that no such requirement was made of him, and that in making that claim Feckenham is simply trying to martyr himself. Part of this martyrdom, he says, is Feckenham's citation of those who stood as witnesses to his claim that the oath was being forced on him, and who offered their testimony to his defense and their support of his position as

4. Grudging, Muttering, and Horn Blasts

abbot of Westminster. He says: "Here M. Stapleton maketh much adoe to convince the Bishop [Horne] of an untruth, and to make it seemeth more probable he citeth divers *honorable* and *worshipfull* to witnesse, and al nothing to the purpose in hand ... but by silence confessing that, that he was charged withal."[65] Attendant upon one's acceptance or rejection of the oath is the pedigree one brings to his office, and the credibility of his witnesses to speak on his behalf. These things accompany one's intent and actions to demonstrate one's worthiness to be believed by one's enemies as well as by one's peers. In his study of piety among the Elizabethan elite, David Hickman observes that testamentary affirmations, which helped define the social order, were expressed through a whole range of rituals and observances, and a man's ecclesiastical career was no exception. Testamentary benefactors were essential in confirming one's eligibility for one's career, and many testators displayed what Hickman calls "a particularly rigorous attitude towards the definition of honesty."[66] Bridges' conclusion is uncompromising: Feckenham is not only falsely loyal, he is also a false bishop, because his career is characterized by false testament to its validity. Interestingly, this issue had affected Horne as well. When Horne had administered the oath to Bishop Bonner, Bonner had refused on the basis that Horne was not a true bishop. Because Elizabeth was a woman, and because he considered the Supremacy to be dubious, Bonner had argued that Elizabeth was not capable of consecrating a bishop. Legislation would eventually resolve the issue of the ambiguity of Elizabeth's bishops and would establish a precedent for their future consecration. Stapleton and Bridges, in their respective books, also accuse Horne [via Stapleton] and Feckenham [via Bridges] of not being true bishops.[67]

The desire for Bridges to answer Stapleton, as with that of Horne to answer Feckenham, points to the idea that the Royal Supremacy must continuously be reiterated. Otherwise, it will lose its power to withstand the pope's attempts to absolve the people of their fealty, and Protestantism in England will be destroyed. Feckenham's Henrician fealty failed to make him immune to the call that he retake the Supremacy oath. In Feckenham's refusal Bridges sees, as Horne does, an avoidance of the opportunity to accept that which is indisputably true. Bridges even goes so far as to define the oath not as a thing required, but as a thing offered: in taking the oath which is offered to them, those loyal to the Supremacy accept its truths, and perform their existing fealty rather than taking on a new sense of loyalty. Like a gift, the oath can be accepted without reserve by the swearer, who is happy to receive it. The swearer is now free to perform his or her true obedience. This liberating aspect of the Supremacy oath is contrasted with the tradition of Catholic oath taking by Bridges. Oaths in the papist tradition bind, says Bridges, whereas the oath offered by Elizabeth I to her people frees them from Rome and breaks the bond that keeps them from their true loyalty to their monarch.[68] Rather than connecting the oath to a familial bond or bond of espousal (as Elizabeth herself did), Bridges employs the language of liberation. He suggests that the oath which secures the relationship between the queen and her people is something which is seen as *required* only by those who are not loyal. Feckenham and Stapleton view the oath as a requirement because they are forsworn to Rome. Bridges argues that no papist can accept the oath, despite the fact that he swears. Loyalty to Rome carries with it perjury in all cases.

Bridges includes a long history of princes and their relationships to priests, just as his predecessors do, and he also includes a list of heretical Christian sects who have, in their error, disrupted the relationships between princes and their people and damaged the Christian Church. One of his most intriguing examples is that of Priscillianism, a fourth century Gnostic-Manichaean sect which built a cult around its founder Priscillius, and which was suppressed by the Church as heretical. To enhance his point that sworn fealty to Rome makes the papist unworthy to swear to the Supremacy, Bridges accuses Stapleton and Feckenham of behaving as the Priscillianists apparently did:

> [they] had among them, *iura periura secretum prodere noli*. Sweare and forsweare, bewray not the secrete: not only like the dissembling papists among us, that will sweare and forsweare themselves to the Prince with false hollow heartes in truth, and yet in falsehood trustie to their confederates, will not bewray their secrete conspiracies: but also like the rule of your pope, and all his perfect faythfull ones, *nulla fides tendenda haereticis*. No fayth must be kept to Heretickes as ye call us. But syth ye protest to be so unfaythfull, you might call them fooles to, that would believe, either any open or dissembling papist.[69]

The group had been oath-bound to its leader, Priscillius; and the sect's adherents, who practiced an esoteric form of asceticism, were permitted to forswear themselves it if was for a righteous purpose. The Church

4. Grudging, Muttering, and Horn Blasts

executed Priscillius and dissolved the sect, depicting the Priscillianists as people whose faith was based on lying and perjury. Here Bridges connects English Catholics with perjurers and liars whether they take the oath or not. Like the Priscillianists, he says, papists in England swear only to forswear; they lie to protect their own heretical sect, and are oath-bound to their egomaniacal leader, who is also a sorcerer. It is one of Bridges' most radical statements in a book filled with radical statements, but his comparison says much about how high the stakes were taken in the 1570s. One cannot be a Catholic and a loyal subject to Elizabeth I. Even if the oath is taken, the recantation will remain suspect. A heretic's word can never be accepted. If such an assertion is true (and Bridges believes that it is), then why pen over a thousand pages devoted to the effort to persuade such an adversary? Bridges wonders the same thing. Seven hundred and eighty-seven pages into his book he asks, "Why should a man use so many words with such a brabbler? Who though he have enough to say, yet will never leave saying, of that which is nought to purpose?"[70] The answer lies in the issue of audibility itself. Bridges' opponent is deaf to the argument, but his audience, he hopes, is not.

One of the biggest differences between the Henrician and Elizabethan Supremacies is that Elizabeth was Supreme Governor, rather than Supreme Head. This was a concession to her gender, but it also reflected the way she would define herself as monarch, and enforce her Supremacy in conjunction with Parliament, which her father had not done. That cooperation accounts for the difference in voice between Henry's expression of his Supremacy and that of Elizabeth. Like her father, Elizabeth demanded to know which voices supported her Supremacy and which ones muttered against it; but unlike Henry, Elizabeth chose to avoid direct participation in polemical writing. When she spoke, her voice was mingled with that of the collective body of her Parliament, of which she was Supreme Governor. The King's voice, in contrast, came from him alone, and was extended *from* his body *to* his Parliament. This fact allowed him greater freedom to express his conscience and participate in an argument which he felt was going on all around him. At times Elizabeth's wishes were vocalized in public by Bacon or Cecil, especially when Parliament convened; but she never hesitated to speak in her own voice, as perhaps in a letter, to her Bishops when she felt it was her duty to interfere. Even upon such interference, Elizabeth's voice to defend and (if need be) protest her royal prerogative was expressed via what she called "the mere will and motion" of the monarch. This aspect of her prerogative authorized official decisions and grants, but it also served as an aspect of her private conscience.[71] As she stated at the opening of her first Parliament (through Bacon), she was not "...so wedded to her own will and fantasy that for the satisfaction thereof she will do anything ... to bring any bondage or servitude to her people or give any just occasion to them of any inward grudge whereby any tumults or stirs might arise as hath done of late days."[72] Where Elizabeth hesitated to impose her fantasy upon the controversies of her reign Henry had seized the opportunity to do so. Where she wished to avoid giving "just occasion" for her opponents to grudge or become tumultuous, Henry provided punishment for the deed having been done. Henry had blamed inward grudge upon the disloyal subject; but Elizabeth, it seems, was ready to blame herself.[73] She had high hopes that the concessions and compromises she was prepared to make would prevent such grudging from making a travesty of her government. She spent the next four decades alternating between triumph and disappointment in her struggles with the recusants in her realm.

Elizabeth I used concession as a form of calculation in these matters. Via such consistency she hoped to manipulate the consciences of her subjects into a willing obedience. She knew that the full acquiescence of her subjects would come neither quickly nor completely, but she understood the same principles of assent her father had understood, only perhaps in an inverted sense: if subjects vocalized their loyalty, they were likely to apply their speech to their actions; and if they behaved loyally, they would eventually think loyally. What her subjects saw and heard during this process would always be of vast importance, as thought and sense cooperated totally to produce lasting effects upon the individual persona. Those polemicists who were loyal to their monarchs understood this principle and applied it to their writing in an attempt to influence not just the behavior of their audiences, but their very personalities as well. The true subject is loyal in one's whole person, not just in his or her discrete thought, speech, or behavior. The complementary nature of the senses was, for Protestant polemicists, a key element in persuading the persona, and therefore producing not merely loyal subjects, but a form of abstract fealty that

4. Grudging, Muttering, and Horn Blasts

emanated from the work itself. For this reason Catholic polemicists worked as hard as they did to produce the opposite effect. The result was often cacophony, even amid the calls from the monarch for quiet, and wishes from the public for the same. The noise of polemic persisted quite simply because although all parties involved seemed to desire quiet, they did not at all desire silence. Silence seemed too dangerous, too much of a deprivation to the senses; it threatened to provide ample spaces in which opposing discourse could appear, as though to fill the void. Even the din of blasting and counterblasting horns seemed to take up that space in a way that comforted the authors of such books, and their audiences as well. Even the monarchs who publicly wished for quiet privately understood the danger of uncomfortable silences in arguments. Noisy polemic was a bane to civility and intellectual discourse; it inverted the standards of good rhetoric and reduced pious and educated men to propagandists — but silence was worse.

CHAPTER 5

Credibility Among Cynics
Coerced Sworn Bond in More, Bale, and Harington

Not all those who were called swore eagerly to the various fealty oaths and changes in ecclesiastical policy that occurred during the Tudor era. Having a difference of opinion on such matters could result in being forced to swear, or being forced to recant. Making a critique of such matters could result in being brought into court to disavow one's statements; and not all those who were called to testify did so with enthusiasm. The king, his counselors, and his bishops often found themselves amid dissent from papists and protestants alike. Some, like Sir Thomas More, voiced their opposition from a traditionalist point of view; others, like John Bale, felt that the King had not gone far enough to establish a truly progressive regime; others, like John Harington, mocked the theatrics that threatened to overwhelm English fealty altogether. These men expressed their dissent with cynical literary responses to the situations in which they found themselves, their cohorts, and their families. More's *Letter to Alice Alington*, penned in conjunction with his daughter Margaret Roper in 1534, illustrates his utter disdain for Thomas Cromwell, Thomas Audley, Richard Rich, and Thomas Cranmer, among others, for their demand, on behalf of the king, that he swear to his acceptance of the Act of Succession.[1] John Bale, writing nearly a decade later, delivers a vicious tirade against Edmund Bonner and other English bishops for the forced recantation of the protestant William Tolwyn in *Yet a Course at the Romyshe Foxe* (1543). Although their ideas are absolutely polarized, these works by More and Bale had a

5. Credibility Among Cynics

profound effect on future generations in terms of attitude and style in dissent. Writing during the Elizabethan era, John Harington used similar rhetorical devices, and much the same outlook, to publish a cynical reaction of his own to what he saw as the proclivity of the law courts to compel sworn retractions of courtiers who did not behave according to the status quo. His *Apologie* appeared as a supplement to *A New Discourse on a Stale Subject, Called the Metamorphosis of Ajax* (1597). In the *Apologie*, Harington imagines that he is set before a jury, where he will be made to give testimony retracting his premise that society is an excrement-filled entity, which, by way of the flushing toilet, can cleanse itself. Although their writings were produced years apart, and although their writings are completely different, all three men display a keen sense of wit that reflects their disdain for the concept of compulsion and recantation in sworn bond. As they mock their enemies, sometimes subtly and sometimes overtly, More, Bale, and Harington each make a strong case for the idea that despite efforts by the church or government to establish, or perhaps contrive, normalcies and settlements, the individual conscience prevails. They challenge the credibility of their opponents, and empower their scorn, skepticism, and outrage with wit and humor. As coping mechanisms in the face of coersion, wit and humor allow the swearer to assert his worth in the face of those who would revoke it by force.

More, Bale, and Harington all take cues from Erasmus when it comes to expressing cynicism for one's adversaries. Each in his own way, they are influenced by Erasmus' letter writing, storytelling, word play, and allegorical role-playing.[2] But the similarities end there, and none of them refer to Erasmus extensively. The influence of Erasmus extends rather to the attitudes that stem from each writer, and the way each piece sends a flick of denigration to the sycophants in society, church, and government who believe that compelled oaths are genuine, and that a conscience can be bullied into accepting official truths. In the Erasmian mode, More, Bale, and Harington each write under pseudonyms or as characters in a dialogue or allegory, but none are especially concerned about the total concealment of identity. Their concern lies within the ability of the pseudonym to promote the cynical attitude of the piece. More poses as himself (and perhaps as his daughter Margaret) in a letter, which tells a story about a letter; and Harington adopts the character of Misacmos, who is an allegory of a naughty courtier much like himself. Both More and Harington assume that their adversaries will perceive their identities and attitudes in the piece, and that those enemies will be appropriately perturbed, to the authors' amusement. Bale makes the strongest attempt to hide his authorship, but only from the king's agents who would seek him out on the Continent and persecute him, as they had done with William Tyndale. Bale presumes that his allies will easily identify "Iohan Harryson" as Bale, and be appropriately satisfied, to the author's vindication. In all cases, these authors seek to mortify and confound their enemies in order to communicate to the reader that credibility, in the case of sworn bond and for the sake of conscience, lies with the author and not with the representatives of monarchic establishment, whether they be bishops, counselors, or judges. Pseudonyms therefore contribute to the overall statement each author makes about displaced voice in the public sphere, about the idea that recantation, retraction, or compulsion of sworn bonds amounts to putting another's voice into one's own mouth. Like an allegorical character or an alias, a forced sworn bond is a fantasy of the self, a false representation of the individual conscience. From this aspect of each piece the same question arises: why is such a thing so desired, and so accepted, by those in positions of power?

Thomas More's skill in cynicism is manifold, and widely demonstrated throughout his career. The *Letter to Alice Alington*, however, provides an example of More's devious wit, of his ability to combine humor, indignation, and momentous consequence in a short and (by all appearances) casually written piece. By the 1530s, irony, sarcasm, and humor had become popular weapons in the ideological battle between traditionalists and reformers, and More had employed no small amount of wit in his exchanges with Martin Luther, William Tyndale and Simon Fish, among many others. More also employed regularly the use of the dialogue, which was also an established medium for written arguments.[3] The format of the personal letter was a less common genre for a witty dialogue than a longer piece with far more structure, sources, and development. In this sense the *Letter* presents itself rather innocently, but actually functions as a piece which accomplishes the same thing as a longer treatise or book: to point out the foolish ambition of the king's counselors, to vindicate More's own position as correct, and to accomplish these things with a wink to those clever enough to understand what is really going on. Just as *Utopia* had been an indictment of the hypocrisies of Christian Europe, the *Letter to Alice Alington* is an indictment of the hypocrisies of ambition within the king's inner circle.

The letter employs the fable, or "merry tale," a device which More had used earlier in his career, in *A Dialogue Concerning Heresies*, among other works. In the *Letter*, however, More makes the most of the deadpan wit that was well known but little appreciated by those who neither knew nor understood him well. As Rainer Pineas fittingly points out, "More often joked with such a solemn face that it was impossible to tell whether or not he was in earnest."[4] In such a case, the recipient of the joke must be at least as clever as the humorist to understand and appreciate it. More presumed as much for his family, for whom the *Letter* is officially intended. More did not presume as much for Audley, Cromwell, and Cranmer, who he knew would intercept the *Letter* and attempt to derive meanings for their own benefit. Writing to those who are to laugh, and also to those who are to be laughed *at* is no simple task, especially considering the brevity and apparent simplicity of the piece in its letter form. As Louis Martz states, the *Letter* points to More's great rhetorical skill: suggesting improvisation, "[it] seems informal, extemporaneous, spontaneous. It allows for long digressions, excursions, and familiar asides, but in the end it reveals, lying under and within all its apparent wandering, a form and central line, a teleological structure based on a goal never forgotten."[5] That goal, of course, is to emphasize that he would not compromise his conscience for an oath he felt he could not swear.

More's political theory is tied to his theory of poetics in the sense that, like Plato and Aristotle, he believed that literature was a force for shaping human action, for leading the citizen to exercise reason freely.[6] In this view the limits of reason in politics are defined by the presence of tyranny, and by the willingness of the ambitious careerist to tolerate and promote it. From his youth More had been intrigued by what causes widespread irrational and unreasonable behavior among the citizens of an otherwise well-structured state. More understood that reason and rationality suffered when people failed to laugh at — and therefore recognize — human folly.[7] His wit, in his epigrams, dialogues, and letters is not merely meant to entertain himself or his family and friends; it is intended to influence civic behavior.[8] As he faced death, his cynicism for the view of sworn bond held by the king and his counselors took on a dark tone. He still meant to instruct, and to lead by example, but in the *Letter to Alice Alington* he demonstrates a profound resentment for the foolishness of those who would determine the course of his life for the advancement of their own careers. The *Letter* is an interesting prelude to the *Dialogue of Comfort Against Tribulation*, which followed it. Although the *Dialogue* employs similar writing styles, especially the use of the fable, it is less cynical and less antagonistic than the *Letter to Alice Alington*. Although the *Letter* is a bitter document, it does not go so far as to suggest that More had stopped taking the process of swearing seriously. What More disparages, in a most ironic fashion, is the ridiculousness of the ambitious political character who believes that More's conscience can be altered after a lifetime of the cultivation of Platonic reason. The act of swearing is not the central theme of the *Letter*, even though More employs it as the catalyst for the discussion between himself and Margaret. The real theme of the *Letter* is ridicule.

For John Bale such sophistication was neither warranted nor welcome. Forgoing wit, Bale preferred expressive word usage as a way to pepper his accusations that Edmund Bonner, like all English bishops, was a fraud, an agent of Rome, a subversive creature who sought to displace the authority of the king in favor of that of the Pope. Bale had demonstrated his interest in word play and alliteration from his earliest works, and relied heavily upon the most shocking terms he could muster in order to make his point. In *Acts of the English Votaryes* (1560), for example, he regales his reader with lurid reports of the clergy's transgressions from their monastic vows. One paragraph heading proclaims, "Sayntes begotten in whoredom"; a later paragraph calls monks "spirituall sodomytes and knaves"; other passages contain revisionist hagiographies meant to depict saints throughout history of being pimps, homosexuals, idol worshippers, and of bearing illegitimate children with their mistresses, who were often the wives of kings and noblemen.[9] In his play *Kynge Johan* (1539),[10] the villain Sedycyon claims to be able to absolve the fealty of the king's subjects with "a maggot of Moyses and a fart of Sainte Fandingo."[11] When it comes to tales and fables Bale uses precious few, except for the legends which had been granted verity by John Leland's propagandistic revisionism. Like his colleague Leland, Bale also used stories of Arthur and Brutus to promote the king's

5. Credibility Among Cynics

decree that England had always been an empire. In the *Apologie of Johan Bale* (1550), however, he added a sardonic element: St. Patrick, the papists' great liberator of Ireland, had been born as a result of a licentious union between a corrupt nun and the magician Merlin.[12] Derision rather than laughter is the point in Bale's use of cynicism in his work, and in *Yet a Course at the Romyshe Foxe* Edmund Bonner is depicted as its unfortunate, if not deserving, target for forcing William Tolwyn to recant his beliefs under pain of death.

Bale's ideas about the relationship of the individual to the state are inextricably linked to his ideas about reformed religion. Although he had been educated at Cambridge, Bale did not employ the methods of the humanists in his writing style. He preferred revisionism instead. As he composed *Yet a Course* he was in the process of developing an understanding of history, the state, and the individual, which he would later incorporate into more comprehensive treatises devoted to the subject. In 1555 he literally rewrote the history of the Christian church in *Acta Romanorum Pontificum*, in order to demonstrate that the Roman church had been a mere counterfeit of the true church. In conjunction with his revisionist effort was his establishment of the connection between corrupt monastic vows and a failed state.[13] This agenda is especially evident in *Actes of the Englyshe Votaryes*. Because of corrupt vows neither the church nor the government could function as proper guardians of the citizenry. In *Yet a Course at the Romyshe Foxe* Bale presents an abbreviated version of his revisionist history of the Church, attacking Edmund Bonner and the other English bishops on the ground that they have no credibility upon which to base their demand that William Tolwyn recant his reformist beliefs. They are the products of over fifteen hundred years of perjury and imposture. In Bale's view, the English church needed to be released from its false bonds, or vows, to the Roman church and be properly bound with the true church.[14] A national church purged of such corruption would produce strong bonds between itself and the state, which would eliminate the need for recantations. As it is, however, the state allows bishops such as Bonner to force recantations upon men like Tolwyn. Bale is a loyal subject, but he is adamant that the state has not gone far enough to ensure that the agents of Rome will not force papist vows upon the English people. Despite his criticisms of the state, Bale avoids discussion of the Royal Supremacy or the king's ecclesiastical policies. His concern lies mainly with his apocalyptic vision of London as the New Jerusalem, as part of his quest for an eschatological national self-awareness.[15]

John Harington's *A New Discourse on a Stale Subject* is literally packed with witty references, inside jokes, and puns, many of which Elizabeth Story Dunno, in her definitive edition of the work, admits are lost to history. Nevertheless, Harington's work, and especially its *Apologie*, makes skillful use of topical satire, which, although it is aimed at Harington's adversaries at court, nonetheless invites the reader to join in. Although Harington couches much of his humor in subtleties, the work is more than a collection of broad political statements and references to long-dead courtiers. It is an indictment of indictment, a criticism of the system by which an impudent nobleman might be dragged into court, presented with jurists, and forced to recant statements which, although they are insolent, are true. In this sense, Harington's overall effort bears similarities to both More's and Bale's: like More, Harington subtly ridicules the hypocrites who wish to advance themselves politically by using him as a sacrificial lamb; like Bale, Harington is not afraid to use rude, even outrageous, language. Unlike More and Bale, however, Harington's *Apologie* is overtly satirical in its portrayal of the contemporary legal system and the powerful men who control it. Despite its humor, at the heart of the *Apologie* is a potent cynicism for the whole culture of the Elizabethan court, of its privileges, honors, favors, and ambitions that approaches both the contempt of More's work and the outrage of Bale's. Nevertheless, Harington's piece, unlike that of Bale or More, is not meant for posterity. Where Bale writes for the benefit of future reformers, and More for the preservation of his family's legacy, Harington writes for the Elizabethan present.

Harington's background and education had assured him a place at court. He had been born into a well-connected family, was the Queen's godson, and had attended both Eton and Cambridge. He was, as Dunno states, "irresistibly attracted to the glitter of the Elizabethan court," although he was never awarded any position of consequence.[16] He developed a relationship to the Elizabethan state that revolved around the commonly-held view that devotion to letters was an appropriate means of advancement. His career as a courtier, therefore, is inseparable from his career as a writer. Like his contemporary Edmund Spenser, Harington

5. Credibility Among Cynics

believed that those two things worked together to produce a servant who could be appreciated for his devotion to his monarch by way of his talent. The full extent of the political references in *A New Discourse* cannot be fully understood because they have been lost to time; but the piece, and especially the *Apologie*, shows that Harington's imprudence, cheekiness, and even rudeness, reflects not a weakness but rather a strength of individual assertion, an awareness of self-fashioning.[17] This assertion, however, gave Harington as much trouble as it gave him security. He was a valuable member of the Queen's court, and his status as her godson allowed him more than a fair amount of comic transgression; but his refusal to sign the 1584 Bond of Association kept him from establishing a fully assured pledge to the Elizabethan state. The Bond, a "vow and promise" before God, sought to form "one firm and loyal society."[18] Harington also held poorly (or perhaps unwillingly) concealed Catholic sympathies, and as a result he was suspected by many of being ambivalent about his loyalty. Harington flirted with both humor and suspicion at once; and the *Apologie* serves as an affront to the idea that the self-fashioned courtier can be browbeaten into either professing or recanting his writings, and also his persona.

All three authors were aware of the fact that sworn bond was part of the discussion which surrounded adiaphorism, or moral neutrality concerning matters that were neither commanded nor forbidden by scripture.[19] During the sixteenth century, the establishment of the Royal Supremacy, changes in ecclesiastical policy, the creative explosion among artists and writers, and the cultivation of the self led to vast differences in the ways individuals made distinctions about their beliefs. Moreover, because it bridged theological and secular matters, sworn bond represented one of the few cases in which the subject of adiaphorism could be discussed outside theology. Sworn bond therefore became an important vehicle for how English Christians chose to exercise their political , personal, and spiritual liberties. More, Bale, and Harington knew that this issue was an important aspect of whether a person could be pressured to swear or made to recant, and it contributes to their cynical outlook of the practice.[20] Recantation in its most traditional form was a descendent of the old ordeal system. It called for a reconciliation between the swearer and the process of oath-swearing as the church defined it. For reformers like Bale, this system was no longer acceptable. When it came to sworn bond, Bale believed that spiritual liberty extended to reconciliation with God rather than with the church or its traditions. Although they did not share Bale's radical theology, More and Harington were equally skeptical about compulsion and sworn bond. There had been provisions against swearing under duress for centuries. More's attitude in the *Letter*, and Harington's attitude in the *Apologie*, are meant as an affront to those who would take liberties with time-honored legal traditions that were constructed to guarantee truth for the sake of the public weal.

It must be said that none of the three authors discussed here espoused adiaphorism *per se*. For More, conscience is exclusively determined by universal truths which are guaranteed by Christian tradition and which reflect God's will. In the *Letter*, the king's counselors represent those who have made adiaphoristic determinations about the ability of the Acts of Supremacy and Succession to describe universal truths which can be bound by oath. More's expression of conscience via the dialogue and fables in the *Letter* express his cynicism for the counselors' willingness to conform for the sake of political expedience. Bale's beliefs are almost identical in their reductionism, but are in complete opposition theologically to More's. Bale believes that universal truths indeed reflect divine will and guarantee conscience; but those truths stem from the revisionist view that traditionalism is a fallacy and must be eradicated. Bale will not tolerate the adiaphoristic view that a rite or ceremony can be tolerated as neither evil nor forbidden.[21] In *Yet a Course* Edmund Bonner is the adiaphorist, the parasitic bishop who, because he tolerates forced recantation, seeks to undermine reform and promote ritualism in order to subvert the king's government. Of the three authors, Harington appears to be the closest to accepting adiaphorism; but upon close examination, the *Apologie* expresses much cynicism for the concept. As he depicts (and lampoons) the court in which Misacmos is to be judged, Harington criticizes subjective ideas about the right of the individual to determine his own relationship to the truth. His humor masks the eloquence of his argument, but his point is clear: the accused is not the one whose morals are questionably undefined. The adiaphorists are the judges and jurors, who, steeped in tradition, ambition, and pretension, determine truths based on how far their careers will be advanced.

After More was committed to the Tower, he was shown a list of men who had already sworn the oath which accompanied the Act of Succession,

5. Credibility Among Cynics

and among them were the names of his sons-in-law: William Daunce, Giles Heron, Giles Alington, and William Roper. Unmoved, More still refused to swear, even after perusing the Act of Succession and its oath for upwards of an hour. Despite the efforts of his sons-in-law to distance themselves from him, More still felt that he was an emissary to the family, and that his words and actions would be of great value to the family's survival and posterity. In this sense he especially valued his visits with his daughter Margaret, who funneled messages to and from the family through her father. Together with Margaret, More devised a scheme to keep the king's commissioners away from the rest of the family while confounding their efforts to bully him into changing his mind about refusing the oath. Margaret sent her father a letter, folded but unsealed, knowing that it would be intercepted by Henry VIII's Lord Chancellor Thomas Cromwell. In the letter, she reported that she would be taking the oath, in obedience to her husband.[22] In the letter she implored her father to change his mind, claiming, albeit as a ruse, that the oath was not a cause worth dying for. Cromwell took the bait. He granted Margaret unlimited access to her father, and allowed her to visit him in the Tower as often as she liked.

As More remained in prison and continued to visit with Margaret, he began work on the *Dialogue of Comfort Against Tribulation*, which would emerge as one of his last, but most definitive, works. At the same time, however, More was presented with another letter by his daughter. Alice Alington, Margaret's stepsister, owned a country house not far from where Audley was staying while hunting with friends. Alice had attempted to intervene on behalf of her stepfather, but Audley had dismissed her with two fables, which Alice reported to Margaret. The first, Audley claimed, came from Aesop: There once was a country populated almost entirely by fools, with the exception of a few wise men. It was soon predicted that a great rain would come, and that all those caught in the rain would become fools themselves. The wise men hid away in caves as the rains came, and when it was dry they emerged, expecting to rule over the land of fools. What they found instead was that the fools had formed the majority, and that they ruled themselves as they pleased. Confounded, the wise men wished that they had been caught in the rain, and had become fools as well.[23]

After laughing at his own joke, Audley told a second fable to Alice Alington, about a lion, an ass, and a wolf, who come to give their confessions of gluttony to a priest: The lion confessed first, saying that he devoured all the beasts he could come by. The confessor absolved the lion because as king of the forest, it was the lion's nature to do so. The ass then confessed to having stolen a straw from his master's shoe because he was hungry, and he feared his master had taken cold because of the hole in the shoe. The priest refused to absolve him, and sent him to the bishop, who commanded him to fast. The ass did so, to his great suffering. Then the wolf confessed, and the priest commanded him not to spend more than sixpence at any meal. After a while of observing this diet, the hungry wolf observed a cow and her calf pass by. He conformed his conscience to his desire, and quickly determined that the cow and calf must be worth sixpence together, and thereafter ate them.[24]

More and Margaret were amused at Audley's attempt at wit, and in response they penned a return letter to Alice Alington. It was a letter on its face, at least, but its true function was as a dramatic interpretation meant to embarrass Audley, Cromwell, and Cranmer (whom they knew would intercept the letter). The dialogue imagined an exchange between Margaret and More in which she attempted to convince him to change his mind and take the oath. In reality the piece expressed More's contempt for Audley's pretension to wit, and as the character "More" listens lovingly to the character "Margaret," More begins to play a game with men he clearly despises.[25] More made clear his contempt for those he did not respect, and as he throws Audley's fables back at him he does so with the attitude that Audley, like Cranmer and Cromwell, held precious little credibility with him, and no sway over his conscience.

In the letter, Margaret appears before her father in order to attempt to persuade him to change his mind and take the oath. Because she had conformed to her husband's wishes and sworn for her own part, her attitude in the letter is meant to be taken as genuine by the king's counselors who she and More knew would intercept it. But the Margaret of the letter is not the Margaret known to the More family. She is a character within the letter's dialogue, which serves as a wider moral example illustrating why More should *not*, in fact, change his mind. She pleads, dutifully:

> I pray god good father that theyr prayers & ours & your owne therewith, maye purchase of God ye grace, that you may in this great matter (for which you stand in this trouble, and for your trouble all we also that love you) take such

5. Credibility Among Cynics

> a waye by time as standing with the pleasure of God, may content & please the king, whom ye have alwaye founded so singularly gracious unto you, that if ye should stiffly refuse to doe the thing that were his pleasure, which God not displeased you might do ... it wold both be a great blot in your worship in every wise mannes opinion, and as my selfe have heard some say (such as your selfe have always taken for well learned and good) a peril unto your soule also.[26]

The phrase, "which God not displeased" refers to a provision in one version of the Oath of Supremacy that permits the swearer to accept its terms as far as the law of God will allow. This provision had been permitted quietly by Cromwell for the benefit of some of the London Carthusians, but without the king's knowledge. Margaret had chosen to invoke this provision when she took the oath. Her reference to it in the *Letter* is meant to inform Cromwell that More is aware that Cromwell had acted without the king's knowledge. In presenting Margaret as a character useful to a man such as Cromwell, the *Letter* communicates More's misgivings about Cromwell's ability to serve the king as faithfully as More himself had. Margaret's plea also identifies that these same doubts extend to the credibility of the king's other counselors as well. To refuse the oath would be to blot More's respectability in "every wise mannes opinion." But More knows, as does his family, that the men he considers to be wise, and whose opinions he values, are not among those who will intercept the *Letter*. The backhanded tone of the *Letter* continues as Margaret points out that if her father does not change his mind, he will lose "al those frendes that are hable to do you any good."[27] Those who are able to More "good," in the case of the *Letter*, are men who More considers to be mere factional cohorts, and not his real friends. The phrase, spoken with full irony by the character Margaret, points to More's intolerance of expedient men who are good with words, but are not good to their word.

More then begins to depict Margaret as the "maistres Eve," who comes to tempt him with the oath after Alice Alington had "played the serpent" with her to make him swear against his conscience.[28] Here, the pressure to swear is depicted by More as a device meant to break down the family relationship between father and daughter. In constructing this allegory More reminds his adversaries that God is the paramount witness for a sworn bond, and not the king. If Margaret is to be seen as Eve, and if she has come on behalf of the serpent Alice (as an agent of Audley), then whose command does More break if he accepts the forbidden fruit? God's or the king's? As playful as More's suggestion might be, it shows how deeply cynical More is for the entire design of the king's legislation. Even as Margaret/Eve expresses her respect for Audley's position, More continues to denigrate the careerists for whom he had little regard. She protests, "For [Audley] saith, that where you say your conscience mooveth you to this, all ye nobles of this realme & almost all other men too, go boldly furth with hy contrary & sticke not thereat."[29] Anyone who knew More, and especially anyone who knew his true feelings about his position, knew that he considered his desire to preserve his family and defend his conscience to be completely different from the efforts of the aristocracy to maintain their estates and family dynasties.

More discards Audley's fables with sweeping dismissal, stating at the outset that "my lord Esops fables do not gretly move me."[30] About the first fable, he says, "I have heard oft ere this: it was a tale so often told among ye kinges counsel by my lorde Cardinall [Wolsey] when hys grace was chancellour, yet I canot lightlye forgeate it."[31] Such a statement is given with a grin by More, and points directly to Alice's statement that Audley had laughingly appreciated his own wit in telling it. Not only is the fable a stale, often-told adage; it had been favored by the famously fallen Wolsey, a man who had failed to serve the king well and who had lost everything his ambition had once earned him (including the magnificent Hampton Court Palace, which Henry VIII was currently, and triumphantly, living in). More then summarizes the tale as he claims Wolsey had told it. He widens the context to address the insinuation by Audley that More considered himself to be a sheltered, self-important wise man. He turns the tables on Audley, stating that the true meaning of the fable is that, in thinking themselves safe from the folly raining down upon others, the so-called wise men were even more foolish than those they sought to rule.[32] More's dismissive tone points to the fact that he had understood Wolsey's meaning better than Audley had.[33] Certainly, More was ten years older and had a more distinguished career, but he also wishes to point out Audley's lack of cleverness. Wolsey had used the fable to illustrate the folly of sitting aside during a "variance" between the Emperor and the French king. He had suggested that if England played the wise man while the fools fought, eventually the fools would achieve a concordance between

5. Credibility Among Cynics

them and fall upon England.[34] Despite his knowledge of this context, More pretends not to understand Audley's reference: "Howe be it daughter Roper," he says, "whome my Lorde here [Audley] taketh for the wyse menne, and whome he meaneth to be fooles, I cannot verye well geasse, I cannot reade will suche riddles."[35] In making such a statement More plays the fool, and thereby makes a fool of Audley. By "correcting" Audley's understanding of the fable, More makes it clear that Audley is an unsophisticated counselor, and More allows an important question to emerge from this subtlety: can a man such as Audley, who fails to comprehend one of Wolsey's old stories, truly understand the oath which he demands that More swear?

More pretends not to know the origin or meaning of the second fable, but he does presume, purposefully, that he is meant to be represented by the ass, "...signifying (as it seemeth by that similitude) that of oversight & folye, my scrupulous conscience taketh for a gret perilous thynge toward my soule, if I should sweare this othe, which thing as his lordship thinketh, wer in dede but a trifle."[36] Catching Audley in his own trap, More accuses him and the other counselors of diminishing the oath to a trifling matter. If this were indeed true, it would be a dangerous presumption for Audley to make; if it were not in fact true, it would expose Audley as a fool. In this case More slyly accepts the ass as an allegory for himself. He may be a simple and scrupulous creature, but he knows that the oath is not a mere straw in a shoe. More then takes the opportunity to illustrate how the conscience, when terribly misguided, produces sworn bonds terribly misunderstood:

> "Some may dooe for favour, & some may dooe for feare, & so might they carye my soule a wrong way. And some might hap to frame himselfe a conscience, and thinke that while he did it for feare, god would forgeve it. And some may peradventure thinke that they will repente & be shriven thereof & that so shall god remit it them."[37]

Although More comes compellingly close to criticizing sacramental abuses (albeit in the Erasmian mode), he nonetheless uses this statement to point out that only a fool would swear under such circumstances. Audley had not been able to perceive this aspect of the story as he told it, and he has made a fool of himself again. Happy to play the ass, More stands vindicated.

Margaret then tells a tale of her own, addressing Alice Alington rather than her father. The tale is apparently one of More's, and although Margaret assumes the character of dutiful daughter again she still functions as the temptress Eve. More had referred to Margaret as "Eve" in order to express his resentment at Audley's having told Alice Alington the fables, knowing that they wold be communicated to More in an effort to embarrass him for his obstinate stance. Now the *Letter* uses Margaret's voice to bring a similar apple to Audley. The tale tells of a man who, accused of being an outlaw, had been brought to the court at Bartholomew Faire. "And at the laste the matter came to a certayne ceremonye to be tried by a quest of xii men, a iury as I remember they call it, or elles a periurye," says Margaret, pretending to fetch the story from deep in her memory, and also pretending to barely understand the jury system.[38] Upon retiring, the jurors wished to dispense with the outlaw quickly, but one juror, named Cumpanye, did not deliberate, but sat and listened stoically. Margaret explains, "And because the felowe semed but a fowle, & sate still & sayde nothing, they made not rekoning of hym, but sayde we be agreed now, come let us go geve our verdit."[39] But Cumpanye refused to go along with the unanimous verdict until proper deliberation had taken place, saying that he wold only vote guilty if each juror gave his reason for wanting to convict the outlaw. The jurors reproved Cumpanye, exhorting him to go along with the majority. Cumpanye refused, saying that although God might very well send the other jurors to heaven for following their consciences, He might also send Cumpanye to hell for going against his own conscience and swearing to a verdict in which he did not believe.[40] Margaret concludes with a seemingly innocent plea: should not More spare himself, and his reputation, by doing as the majority of his fellowship do?[41]

In what is likely the strongest argument for the presence of Margaret Roper's literary voice in the *Letter*, the tale of Cumpanye sends Eve back to the serpent (here, redefined by More as Audley rather than Alice) with a temptation to reconsider his ideas about obedience, friendship, and servitude. Here, Margaret/Eve uses the pretense of a woman's folly to again make a fool of Audley. She listens obediently as More explains the story's simple moral — that one's conscience is answerable to God alone — and gently corrects her for her effort to attempt to change his mind. Margaret pretends to be disappointed, but her mock ignorance allows one of the

5. Credibility Among Cynics

most important points of the *Letter* to emerge: there is an important connection between theology and the law, which is provided by sworn bond. The king's counselors are forgetting, or perhaps ignoring, this connection. More believes that no man can swear to a law which has not been lawfully made, and that no legislative body can "commaunde and compel" a man to conform his conscience to acceptance of the matter.[42] Although More uses the rejection of Margaret's plea to explain that he does not answer to the king's counselors, he is careful not to suggest that he does not answer to the king himself. In fact, he states explicitly that only the king can command him.[43] Such caution, however, does not eclipse More's great cynicism for conformity presented by this simple tale of jaded and forsworn jurors.

The overall tone of the *Letter* is one of great irony, as More and Margaret both pretend to be puzzled and confused by the fables; and we must be very careful about how seriously we take More at times like these. Even in his most serious works, More has a habit of departing from matters of great consequence to lampoon someone or something with what was no doubt seen by friends and foes alike as a frustratingly deadpan wit. Many times he ridicules his enemies by pretending not to understand their arguments or ideas.[44] Many times he mocks the work of an adversary by asking him to restate his principle to the point of redundancy, as he does in his extended dialogue with Tyndale. Other times he simply satirizes an opponent's earnest work, as he does when he attacks Simon Fish's skill at arithmetic.[45] At the close of the *Letter* Margaret points out that even Harry Patenson, the family jester, has taken the oath, and this statement sets up More's conclusive assertion: it is apparent that Audley, along with the other counselors, bears an understanding of the oath no better than that of a jester. No credible counselor would trivialize such an oath, and no true servant of the king would demand that a man's conscience should be compelled to swear it. Audley had presented himself as a figure of influence, whose clout might offer More reprieve in the inner circle of power from which he was now excluded. In return More had stripped Audley of his credibility using Audley's own words, and replaced them with the credibility of the man of conscience whose great skepticism for the delusion of conformity identified him as the king's, and God's, better servant. The *Letter* bears a strong relationship to the *Dialogue of Comfort Against Tribulation* which followed it, and which employs many of its elements. Indeed, the *Letter,* even with its satirical tone, is meant to provide comfort, nominally to Alice Alington, but also to the More family and even More himself as he prepared for death.

John Bale wishes to provide no such assurance in *Yet a Course at the Romyshe Foxe.* Writing in exile in Zurich, Bale approaches his work with a pronounced bitterness that even if More felt, he was too understated a writer to express. Bale has no patience for such eloquence, and in his sardonic attack on Bishop Bonner Bale depicts a perverse view of sworn bond, which is used as a weapon to torture William Tolwyn into recanting his beliefs. When More discusses the pressure placed upon him to swear, he does so with the idea that violence will follow his refusal of the oath. When Bale discusses Tolwyn's forced recantation, he does so with the idea that a forced oath *is* an act of violence. It is, quite simply, blasphemy on the part of both Tolwyn and Bonner — albeit for different reasons — in which each man commits an act of violence upon the name of God by invoking it falsely. Where More had hoped that God would look mercifully upon the inward scruple upon which he based his actions, Bale maintains that God will punish the false swearer, both the reformer and the papist, for the act itself, regardless of the swearer's intent.

Attitudes toward the Royal Succession and Henrician ecclesiastical policies had changed by the mid-1540s when Bale wrote his treatise. Anne Boleyn had fallen, and her daughter had been declared illegitimate; Jane Seymour had provided a much-needed son, but she had died; the Cleves marriage had been an embarrassment, and the Howard marriage had been a disaster. By the time of the printing of *Yet a Course,* Henry VIII had married the thrice-wed but childless Katherine Parr. Like many radical reformers, Bale had much hope that the young Prince Edward would introduce further reforms that would be both more comprehensive and more speedy than his father's had been. Bale had been irked by the fact that Henry VIII had allowed the English bishops to retain a great deal of their power and privilege after the establishment of the Royal Supremacy. Bale was also enraged at the fact that because of the power of the bishops, those like himself, who preached *sola scriptura* and the teachings of Calvin, still had to write under pseudonyms and in exile, just as Tyndale had over a decade earlier. Bale believed that despite their sworn fealty to the king, the English bishops were engaged in seditious acts against Henry VIII. He

5. Credibility Among Cynics

believed that even as they enforced the king's ecclesiastical policies they sought to usurp the royal prerogative. In effect, Bale believed that the English bishops were agents of Rome who acted as the true rulers of England.[46] Despite their vocalized fealty to the king, their adherence to ceremonialism proved that their true motives lay elsewhere, and formal recantations of accused heretics were the perfect examples of their scheme. In Bale's unyielding view, ceremony led directly to superstition and allowed act to trump intent. Tolwyn's public recantation of his beliefs was therefore seen by Bale as a seditious attempt by Bonner to replace Tolwyn's fealty oath to the king with one to the pope.

Sworn bond occupies a prominent place in the mind of John Bale. He believes that it provides assurances and guarantees which will follow the English people into their nation's eschatological role as the events of Revelation unfold. The long standing implications that sworn bond has for England's spiritual destiny is expected to culminate in the vindication of the elect. Bale had spent a significant amount of spiritual and intellectual energy developing his view of sworn bond by rereading the Chronicles with the Apocalypse in mind in order to establish a new historical perspective. An intrepid state would be necessary; the state would have to purge itself of false vows to Rome and reestablish new bonds reflective of England's liberation from ceremonialism. In *Yet a Course* Bale criticizes the state for allowing Bonner to persecute Tolwyn because it does not possess the courage to embrace reforms wholeheartedly. In this sense Bale's exiled status protects him from the Roman Church and the Henrician government alike; but even when doubly threatened, Bale was undaunted. He had been a chronicler and bibliographer in his early career as a Carmelite monk, and he had complete confidence that his understanding of his sources reflected the truth — although he had no qualms about cherry-picking his evidence. He accepted completely Geoffrey of Monmouth's *History of the Kings of Britain*, complete with its legends of British kings and heroes and its effort to build a pseudo-biblical history of Britain. He quoted Polydore Vergil, John Capgrave, and Ranulf Higden when it suited him, and he relied on John Leland's work, when Leland's theology was not too traditionalist for him.[47] Bale, in short, knew how to conform data to his vision, and he defends it with a claim that since the history of the Roman church is equally contrived, his attack on their credibility is legitimate. Bale's cynicism for the history and traditions of monasticism is what drives *Yet a Course* in its charge that the ceremony of formal recantation is nothing more than an exercise in delusion. God, as deliverer of justice, would not excuse this delusion in either the compulsory figure or the swearer.

Bale's anger is accompanied by a ferocious use of alliteration to lend a satirical sense to the work: he calls Bonner a "satellite of Satan," and "a verye fearce furyouse angel of the bottomlesse pytt."[48] Bonner's motives are those of Pilate and Caiaphas, says Bale, "...And sens that tyme hath the byshoppes bene seldome without soche prodygyouse pykethankes and glaverynge glosers, to bringe men *coram nobis*."[49] The radical sympathizer who reads Bale's book is likely in exile himself, probably a member of a community of English reformists taking refuge in Zurich, Antwerp, Basel, or another city in which radical Protestants were welcomed and hidden from Henry VIII's agents. If caught, he would suffer the same fate as William Tolwyn: he would be arrested, presented to the king's ministers and bishops, and be either forced to recant or executed. The reader of Bale's work, therefore, comes to the piece with fear, outrage, and zeal. It is a potent mixture of emotions, and Bale takes that mixture and infuses it with derision. *Yet A Course* is meant to provoke righteous indignation, and to emphasize the absurdity of the bishops' efforts to compel intent with ceremonialism.

There is precious little wit in *Yet a Course*. Its ability to ridicule the credibility of the bishops lies in its capacity to sneer at them rather than to rile their intellects with subtleties. Upon reproducing, per the report he has been given by witnesses, the recantation presented to Tolwyn,[50] Bale claims, "...I have redde diverse recantacyons made in Iohan wycleves tyme ... but non siche as thys ys, neyther so folyshe nor yet so devylyshe."[51] Part of this "devilishness" is built into the language of the recantation itself, which Bale states is sophistical rather than sophisticated, and over the head of William Tolwyn, a parson of simple speech and simple faith. He says:

> Partly hath Tolwyn by his owne confession denounced hym selfe for a sedycyouse doer, deetested hymselfe for an heretique, and presented hymselfe for a grevouse offender for not observynge the popes holy tradycyons ... never coulde Tolwyn thoroughlye knowe that these rhetoryckes meant, as are denuncyacyon, deteccyon, and presentacyon, so long as he was in cambryge, neyther by hys art stodye, nor yet by hys scole dyvynyte, tyll he came to my lorde of Londons [Bonner's] howse.[52]

5. Credibility Among Cynics

Bale does not mean to denigrate Tolwyn's learning; he means instead to attack Bonner's profusion of terms, meant to confuse and perplex a man already terrified by the prospect of being burnt at the stake. Here, Bale's ridicule of the language of Bonner's recantation relegates it to the rhetorical exercises of the university. Neither Tolwyn (nor, presumably Bale) had heard such language since their Cambridge days. Bonner, the Oxford man, now seeks to impose it upon Tolwyn. Bale depicts Tolwyn as a man whose acceptance of the plainer language of reform is connected to his rejection of ceremonialism. The "glavering glosses" which Bonner is imposing upon Tolwyn are depicted as being equivalent to the profusion of words and procedures in papist rituals. Dismissing the words of the recantation as mere babble, Bale trivializes their credibility.

Bale has similar harsh words for the witnesses brought against Tolwyn, saying that their credibility lies only in their upholding of "the popes olde faythe," and nothing more.[53] Moreover, Tolwyn was forced to recant based on a *suspicion* of heresy, and Bale is quick to point out that Bonner means to procure a renunciation for an offense which may or may not have taken place. How then, can the witnesses act in accordance with the truth, as they are sworn to do? The "papysticall vowe," that authorizes the witnesses, says Bale, is nothing more than a sworn observance to an assortment of vices and abominations. To legitimize vice by way of a sacred oath is, in short, foul, as Bale states bluntly: "Sone yow may knowe wher of yowre holye prelates smelleth, yf ye way thys mater a right." Just in case the reader fails to perceive Bale's meaning, he repeats his statement even more bluntly in the margin, saying, "Smell here what yowre holye prelates are."[54] The reformer who has been able to obtain the book (a dangerous undertaking even on the continent) can congratulate himself for being able to identify the stink of papism, a stench which the Pope's agents have become accustomed to. Having cleansed himself of such offensive beliefs, the reformer can more easily sense the filthiness of others. To point out that one's opponents smell foul is an almost childish metaphor, but it is one that Bale uses to amuse his reader, even as he provokes outrage. The offense committed by the English bishops is both literal and metaphorical, both spiritual and olfactory.

Bale reserves his greatest cynicism for the manner in which Tolwyn's guilt was "evidenced" as he recanted: heretical books allegedly owned by

Tolwyn were presented to the crowd, but were concealed in a sack and were not seen by the witnesses, or by Tolwyn himself. Tolwyn was forced to condemn each book as Bonner named it, but Bale notes an interesting fact: Bonner recites the names of the authors of the books (John Frith, Martin Luther, John Oldcastle, William Thorp, and others), but not the titles of the books themselves. Bale says, for example, "Now cometh a boke on prayer made by Martyn Luther, yet nothynge ys seane but the bagge."[55] He continues to protest this scheme by Bonner as each book is named but not shown. Bale uses this fact to make a shocking accusation: that Bonner is simply lying. Because he does not open the bag and show the books to either Tolwyn or the witnesses, and because he does not name the titles or speak of the specific content of each book, Bale charges that Bonner does not in fact, have the books.[56] This charge is especially poignant considering that Tolwyn was accused of suspicion of heresy rather than its commission. Bale claims that Bonner does not name the titles of the books because he does not know what they are. He has never seen them because he does not have them; and he does not have them because Tolwyn never had them. Bale states, "We schall have the names of the bokes (ie, the authors' names) contayned, though we have nothinge else. And that ys Inough to make foles beleve the mone is made of a grene cheese."[57] Even amid the severity of the charge of blasphemy on Bonner's account, and even amid the gravity of Tolwyn's situation, Bale infuses his disgust with a snicker: anyone foolish enough to accept the absurdity of the recantation, from the overblown rhetoric of its oath, to its forsworn witnesses, to the spectacle of the trumped-up evidence, may as well believe that the moon is made of green cheese. Such is Bale's enemy, the papist: a gullible and superstitious fool, staring blankly at the moon. Equally laughable is the bishop, who believes that standing upon a moon made of cheese will bring him closer to heaven.

A large part of Bale's attack on Bonner's credibility has to do with Bale's condemnation of ceremonialism. Although the clergy had been defined by its vows, namely those of chastity, poverty, and humility, Bale maintains that the English bishops do not understand vows at all. Because they have no relationship with the truth, he argues, they have negated the genuine bonds found in Scripture, such as those made between Abraham and God, or among the Israelites in the name of God.[58] The papists have

5. Credibility Among Cynics

replaced them with bonds that do nothing more than bind themselves, and the ignorant masses, to the Roman Church.[59] These churchmen bring no offerings to the altar, as the Israelites had done; instead their vows refer only to themselves, to feed their desires for worldly power and wealth: "Vowe and performe," mocks Bale, "promyse and paye."[60] The performance of the recantation therefore stands as purely theatrical, an invention which can only pretend to be worship.[61] In Bale's view, Tolwyn's recantation is a mere theatrical performance which the public has "paid" to see. What emerges from this connection is the depiction of Tolwyn's recantation as a comic, farcical piece of theatre, with both Tolwyn and Bonner clowning in front of a rude audience which does not see the foolery in it. The reformer, however, perceives the absurdity. Interestingly, Bale connects this idea with his view of the monastic vow of celibacy as fraud. In doing so he is able to add a bit of bawdy humor to further attack Bonner's credibility: the bishops pretend to celibacy, but defile women who ought to have husbands.[62] When it suits them, the bishops accept vows of celibacy from their mistresses, and thereby transform common whores into nuns, who then pretend to be virgins. Referring to Bonner's mistress, he points out that Bonner has a "sawte bitch of hys owne,"[63] and that now he seeks to make a whore out of Tolwyn. True virginity, for Bonner's mistress and for Tolwyn, says, Bale, comes from being liberated from "the advoutry of your Romyshe lawes and customes."[64]

Bale demonizes Bonner as an utter villain, but he also refuses to grant Tolwyn the role of martyr. Bale sees Tolwyn as a willing participant in a farcical, and blasphemous performance. He derisively, and quite coldly, mocks Tolwyn for his fear of the stake, and he expects his reader to feel the same way.[65] Threatened only by a man, and facing only bodily harm, Tolwyn is blamed for his part in the miscarriage of God's justice, his own credibility doubted by Bale's unforgiving taunt: "Thy sute was not little with promes and othe to maynteyne all Romyshe poperye, to save thy syllye carcass from the fyre."[66] Bale's willingness to blame the victim of Bonner's tyranny gives *Yet a Course at the Romyshe Foxe* its most poignant demonstration of Bale's unyielding radicalism. He ends the piece with a disturbingly callous parody of Tolwyn's recantation:

> I Wyllyam Tolwyn make my newe profession to my lordes grace here in the popes stede, and promyse to observe these iniunccyons of myne ordynarye

without the grace of god and my kynges true obedience, unto my lyves ende. Myne owne hande wrytynge to wytnesse least anye thynge be layed to my lordes charge for yt an other daye. [Bale:] I dare saye yf hys good lorde of London [Bonner] schuld have sayd unto hym [Tolwyn] at that houre that Christ was a thefe and his father an hangemanne, he wolde have subscribed unto yt for the saveguard of hys lyfe.[67]

Bale's cynical outlook, and his unrelenting derision, extends to the entire practice of recantation of reformist beliefs, and to all parties who participate in it. No amount of self-preservation, no exception, no form of intent, lends credibility to the process or its participants — and Bale expects for the righteous to laugh them all to scorn.

It is difficult to tell whether Bale enjoys his cynical approach. He writes on a matter of life and death, as More does, but without More's gallows humor that, despite its mischievous tone, reveals a sense of peace which More has achieved concerning his destiny. Even though Bale himself is not the one threatened with death, he understands that the stakes are very high; but his mockery of the recantation nonetheless reveals a deeply troubled spirit in the bilious polemicist. Bale is confident in his beliefs, but he is not at peace with the course of providence. Cynics often express their scorn as a form of protest for being unable to change the course or state of things. More accepts the fact that he cannot change the careerism and ineptitude of men whom he does not respect, but who now control his fate. His wit in the face of death is the laughter of the man who goes to the scaffold as the intellectual superior of his executioners. Bale accepts that reform has taken place too slowly, and he believes that both Bonner and Tolwyn are his intellectual and spiritual inferiors, but his sneers of derision reflect an unyielding, steadfast rage.

John Harington, writing at the end of the Elizabethan era, was familiar with the dangers faced by a writer who displeased the monarch or who violated ecclesiastical policies. As a sympathetic friend to many English recusants, and as a writer of impish wit, Harington did both. Harington embraced controversy and even danger in his writing, and in the *Apologie* for *A New Discourse on a Stale Subject*, he illustrates his grudging willingness to accept a redundant, outdated, and hypocritical jury system by which an author is dragged into court and forced to disavow his own book. As he does so, he unleashes a volley of criticism at figures real and metaphorical,

5. Credibility Among Cynics

and dares his reader to see his cynical view of the Elizabethan legal system as its true representation. And he enjoys every minute of it.

Born into privilege, John Harington was close to the culture of the Elizabethan court. As a result, he had a lifetime of experience with the ironies and hypocrisies of court life. He found it difficult to stay out of trouble, whether it involved feuds with friends and family, such as with his brother-in-law Edward Rogers; or more serious quarrels involving his volatile temper and his eagerness to provoke others.[68] His sense of wit, when combined with his tendency for provocation, produced epigrams which commented on the court and those who moved within it. His epigrams were often appreciated for their cleverness and satire, but they were just as often disliked for their suggestive or offensive content. In 1591 he produced what Elizabeth Dunno calls "a spirited translation" of Ariosto's *Orlando Furioso*, which had allegedly been produced as an act of penance undertaken by the Queen's command. The story that circulated the court was that Harington had translated the ribald twenty-eighth canto to amuse Elizabeth's maids of honor, but that the Queen had been offended by the canto's theme.[69] It was an attractive theory in 1591, and it continues to appeal to readers of Harington, but there is only limited evidence that the story is true, even though Harington himself referred to the incident in the *Apologie*.[70] What is true is that Harington had a lifelong interest in translation, and in Ariosto in particular. He did, apparently, enjoy the rumor for his own part, as it lent credibility to his art and promoted him as a keen, albeit affected wit among Elizabeth's courtiers.

He therefore used his next project to cultivate his fame. The *New Discourse of a Stale Subject, Called the Metamorphosis of Ajax* is an unapologetic impeachment of Elizabethan society, in which the troubles of the world are likened to excrement. The comparison does not come without its irony, especially as Harington describes how the unavoidable duality of society's ills require that one praise excrement even as one is disgusted by it. In Part II, called the *Anatomie*, Harington proposes the construction of a machine — essentially a flushing toilet — that will facilitate the riddance of the sewage which the wealthy, beautiful, and powerful of the court continually dump in their own midst. Writing under the thinly-veiled pseudonym of Misacmos (hater of filthiness), Harington adopts the character of the wise fool, but again, with his own unique adaptation. Nodding to

More and Erasmus but forgoing Plato and Socrates completely, Harington's wise fool functions as a figure of hilarity in his own right. In this sense his work on Ariosto, and his appreciation of Castiglione, show that he is willing to use contemporary traditions of wit to play the clown among those he intends to ridicule. Although More had played the ass, he had made sure to point out that the ass was the wiser figure, correct in his simplicity of faith and eagerness to obey out of purity of heart. Harington is not afraid to play as a jester does, using himself to propel his own comic agenda.[71] Harington knew that not everyone would appreciate such a joke. Rick Bowers and Paul Smith acknowledge that Harington's education "had prepared him fully for a career in foolery," and that he knew trouble would almost always follow, giving him "a critical power of merriment"; but Bowers and Smith also acknowledge how dangerous this power could be, stating that Harington developed an ability to use wit as a coping strategy for the consequences of his comedic cynicism.[72] Jason Scott-Warren is a bit more critical, stating that Harington's indiscretion could be dangerously short-sighted, and that although the *New Discourse* provides a scathing depiction of a world literally full of its own shit, the effort was one more mistake "in a whole lifetime of miscalculation and predictable disappointment."[73]

In an effort that is partly derived from his imagination, and partly derived from real disgust on the part of his critics concerning the *New Discourse*, Harington penned the *Apologie*. It was published separately at least once, in 1596, but it was soon included in the *New Discourse* as Part III. In it, Harington professes his cynicism for the disavowal of a writer's work, made under duress, from the very title of the piece. It is called:

> *An Apologie: 1. Or Rather a Retraction, 2. Or Rather a Recantation, 3. Or Rather a Recapitulation, 4. Or Rather a Replication, 5. Or Rather an Examination, 6. Or Rather an Accusation, 7. Or Rather an Explication, 8. Or Rather an Exhortation, 9. Or Rather a Consideration, 10. Or Rather a Confirmation, 11. Or Rather all of Them, 12. Or Rather None of Them.*[74]

Playing upon the twelve jurors of the legal system, Harington provides twelve possible definitions of his disavowal. It might be a simple retraction of his statements, or a formal recantation of the beliefs on which those statements are based. The material may be considered or examined; but such an exhortation may require Harington to recapitulate, replicate, or explicate what he has written, which would of course require the sensitive ears of his accusers to hear the material all over again. Harington admits that as the victim of sworn testimony under duress he may have to accuse himself, but he warns that the disavowal might be all-encompassing, and that it might also be completely futile. Either of the last two options threatens to overwhelm the system and render the verdict meaningless. In its entirety, the title provides a series of the quasi-sincere words that talk all around the issues of court testimony.

In the *Apologie*, Harington states that, during a late-morning sleep, he dreamed, or perhaps fantasized, that a "nimble dapper fellow" came to him, telling him of certain learned men, among them two scholars named Zoylus and Momus, who had read the *New Discourse* and had taken offense.[75] The young fellow, it is revealed, is Harington's attorney; and as he informs Harington that he is to appear in court, amusing details emerge regarding the aptitude and integrity of Harington's accusers. Revealing themselves to be of sub par education and intelligence, but convinced of their superiority in both, they have sworn that the name Misacmos "signified myse in a sack of mosse."[76] Confident that they understand the book and its author fully (having taken it at face value as a genuine praise of excrement) they vow to destroy Harington. The lawyer reports: "And soon after, swearing over a Pater Noster or two, and cursing two or three Credoes ... they vowed a solemn revenge, and taking pen and inke, they fell to quoting of it, meeting with some matter almost in everie page..."[77] Their disgust at the subject matter has apparently required them to take the Lord's name in vain, curse, vow revenge, and then reiterate on paper specific passages that have offended them most. Here Harington is having much fun with the hypocritical self-righteousness of black-cloaked Puritan ministers and parliamentarians.

As he is brought before the judges, Harington willingly admits that he is both guilty and not guilty. To the charge that he has "taken a laughing libertie to grace som that have favored me, and grate against some that had galled me," he says, "*guilty my lord.*"[78] To the charge that he has scoffed at "some gentlemen that have served in some honorable services," he claims he is not guilty, except for his criticism of those who have neither worth, wealth, nor wit — which turns out to be most of them.[79] Threatened with having a hole bored into his ear if he is found guilty,[80] Harington is told to select "xii free holders" to serve as his jurors; he agrees, tossing in the remark that a good knight of England is never one to forswear hanging, and that for the sake of his family's prestige, he had better go along with the trial. Here, Harington jabs at the idea that a gentleman's credibility at court was often tied to the extent to which he, or his relatives, had been suspected of knavery, roguery, or slander.[81] Although he agrees to participate in the trial, he insists that his book be shown to those outside the court. He wishes that it be shown to "a housekeeper," a "builder," "all manner of ladies," and to those both "wise and sober ... [and] wanton and waggish."[82] In one of his most provocative suggestions, Harington remarks that the book should be kept away from fools, superstitious folk, and beggars; because of their poverty, false notions, and poor diets, they have irregular bowels and are therefore incapable of ingesting the material properly. Only those who defecate well, and often, are worthy of judging his book, and are good for their word in court.[83]

Harington then separates John Harington the man from Misacmos, the author of the *New Discourse* in much the same way More had done in separating Margaret Roper, the apparent author of the *Letter*, from the temptress Eve, a character within the *Letter*. Harington is to act as foreman of the jury and select the jurors who will judge Misacmos. There is a problem, however: Misacmos asks that Harington not be sworn in as foreman. As the lawyer explains, "your worde will be taken for a greater matter then this, by ten thousand pounds without oth."[84] In order to protect the protagonist of his book, the artist, although he may sit in judgment, cannot be sworn as a jurist. The writer must judge himself, but to the satisfaction of others. Harington here produces a ironic double entendre, aimed at the ability of the Elizabethan court to create personages out of its culture, habits, and intrigues, only to protect itself as an institution by disavowing its own creation as a pretense for defending justice.

Several of the twelve jurors are men who were either admitted or suspected recusants, and almost all come from noble families. Many of the jurors, although they have attained prestige, are of dubious honor, and some of them are known for high-profile litigations against them. As he lists each one and approves him for his jury, Harington comments cynically upon the willful overconfidence the Elizabethan jury system has in its noblemen and their ability to function as sworn jurors. Each of these men are Sir John Harington's peers, and many are known to his family. But is

5. Credibility Among Cynics

it enough to be well-connected and prestigious? Harington uses their reputations as recusants or Catholic sympathizers to put a fine point on this question and to drive home his cynical view of such trials. He especially calls attention to what he sees as the jury trial's failure to reflect justice; first, because charges are brought against the accused by way of rumors, secondhand information and misinterpreted "facts," which the accused is forced to disavow; and second, because it cannot assure that each juror is good for his word. Deeply mistrusted in Elizabethan society, recusants were presumed to be sworn to Rome first, and therefore of questionable loyalty to Queen and country. Hardline reformers accused them of outright treason.[85] Presented here as approved jurors for the trial of Misacmos, recusants function as antagonists to the state in an unexpected way. Instead of depicting them as spies for the king of Spain or as agents of the pope, as Bale had, Harington employs recusants as sworn jurors to criticize the legitimacy of the English courts. How might justice be perceived if the jury is made up of men presumed to be disloyal? Could each man's word be valued? Did they serve the Queen's government, Harington himself (who was a personal friend to many of them), or their own aristocratic traditions?

Harington wishes to draw out such questions as he profiles each juror. He demonstrates that much, perhaps too much, of a nobleman's worth is placed not upon his ability to keep his word, but his ability to maintain his estate. Whether or not a man's word is his bond is less relevant than whether he is a good "builder" or "maintainer" of his estate and family heritage. Sir John Peeter of Stonden had Catholic sympathies, and his wife was listed as a recusant in 1587.[86] Sir John Spenser, of the Althorp Spensers, was conspicuously wealthy, and had improved his family's pedigree by tracing his descent to the ancient house of Despenser, the earls of Gloucester and Winchester.[87] Harington means to accuse Spenser of currying favor with the College of Arms to be awarded with this family history. Here, Harington's cynicism for aristocratic pretension is evident: by improving his pedigree, Spenser boosted his family's credibility. Although Spenser was not suspected of recusancy, Harington suspects him of artificiality. Thomas Stanhope had been accused of being in league with Scottish Catholics. He had served in several Parliaments as a knight of the shire and had been sheriff of both Nottinghamshire and Derby; he was also plagued with what Elizabeth Dunno calls "almost incessant litigation" between 1591 and 1596.[88] Could a man sued so often, and by so many, put up his word as a juror? Harington the foreman accepts him without hesitation. Matthew Arundel was a recusant; Francis Willoughby died with his estate in chaos, with his relations fighting over their rights to the fortune he made in coal mining, iron smelting, and glass making.[89] John Berin had been sheriff and justice of the peace in Nottinghamshire and Lancashire; Sir Edward Baynton and George Sampoole were of well-established families; Ralph Horsey had been an MP for Dorset in 1596; and Sir Hugh Portman had been sheriff in 1590. Despite the prestige of their careers, Harington judges each man by whether or not he wears velvet or satin, has well-married sisters, or a well-built house. Baynton's house was indeed well built. In fact, it was huge, nearly as large as Whitehall Palace, with outrageously expensive accoutrements. Harington admits that at least one of his jurors is a good man in his own right: Hugh Portman is the kind of man who, essentially good, is "kept in store for a dead lift," in case he is needed.[90] Of the first ten jurors, Portman is the only one who is determined by Harington to be good for his word apart from his wealth, family history, or political career.

The lawyer reports that at ten jurors, they've run out of knights. Harington therefore chooses two gentlemen: Ralph Sheldon and Thomas Markham. Sheldon is a good housekeeper (meaning that he maintains his estate well); although he is a Catholic, and unthrifty to boot, he will do.[91] Sheldon is actually a more consequential figure than Harington makes out in the text: he had been imprisoned for "obstinacy in religion" in 1580, and was implicated in an alleged plot to kill the Queen in favor of the Earl of Derby. Upon being questioned, Sheldon had promised to conform, to the scorn of his fellow recusants. For Harington, Sheldon is the perfect juror: for the sake of his "oves and boves," as he says, Sheldon had renounced his very faith. What better man to give his word?[92] Here, Harington is no less forgiving about Sheldon's opportunistic recantation than Bale is about Tolwyn's. Harington may condemn Sheldon with a wink, but admitting him to his jury places expediency, careerism, and self-preservation at the heart of the legal system. It allows Harington to express profound cynicism at the ability of a trial by jury to deliver justice when the system is based on expedience and reputation. Markham, Harington's

5. Credibility Among Cynics

last juror, is both lame and a Stoic.[93] Markham was married to an admitted Catholic, but was suspected of being a recusant himself. Harington would rather not have a Stoic on his jury because of Markham's inability to see either the humor in the *New Discourse* or the absurdity of the jury itself. He was, in fact called "blacke Markham," both for his cloak and his temperament.[94] Harington would rather have an Epicurean. But the lawyer assures Harington that not only does Markham say his prayers upon the commode, he swears he has heard Markham thank God for having made a good stool.[95] In the end, Markham will do.

As the list of jurors is presented, Harington is asked to approve or disapprove of their credibility, so that they will be able to judge the credibility of Misacmos in turn. Harington's narrative reveals a redundant and reciprocal process in which the manner of accusation, and of the attestation of the accused to his innocence, has not progressed since the days when William Tolwyn was bullied by Bishop Bonner or when Thomas More was double-crossed by Thomas Audley and Richard Rich. In this vein Harington worries aloud:

> Now began I to have a good hope, nay rather a firme assurance of my acquittall; having got a jurie of so good sufficiency, so great integritie so sound ability: but it is commonly seene that in matters depending controversy, the greatest danger is bred by too much securities: For the accusation was so hard followed, that some of the Jury began to be doubtfull of their verdict, the witnesses were so manie, their allegations so shrowd,[96] & the evidence so pregnant. And not onelie the faults of this present Pamphlet but my former offenses which were before the pardon (contrarie to the due course of all Courts) were inforced against me.[97]

Although Misacmos is eventually pardoned, Harington notes that after the jury is discharged, two "formal fellows," wearing black cloaks (Zoilus and Momus again), review the case and its outcome and charge Harington with being "in hart a Papist."[98] Of all the cynical and witty statements Harington makes in his *Apologie* regarding the absurdities of the jury system, this one is the most consequential. No matter what the original charge or the tone of the trial, no matter who the witnesses are or what the outcome, all suits ultimately prioritize one subject: is the accused a papist?[99] Harington maintains that he never defended any opinion of religion that has conflated with the "Communion booke,"[100] but this protestation is not enough. All the jurors then demand that he confess his religion. Here, Harington allows his "trial" to reach the very apex of absurdity, as many of the jurors themselves are either recusants, married to recusants, or who have no objection to serving on a jury with recusants. Harington responds to their demand by confessing himself to be "a *protesting Catholicke Puritan*."[101] He then explains to his dumbfounded questioners that good thoughts, words, and deeds are what make good religion, and are what make a man good to his word. The court pronounces him to be a Puritan on the grounds of his pure view of virtue — not a subversive Catholic, but not a conformist, either. Just as Harington entertains the idea of suing them for a pardon, he awakens from his dream.

Harington has a great skepticism for what qualifies as evidence, and how that qualification evidences that one's sworn testimony is true. Aristocratic privilege capitalizes on its connections, and on its ability to capitalize economically. As Jason Scott-Warren states, Harington is aware that the English aristocracy "confect" their aristocratic histories for money, privilege and worth — and he notes that Harington was keen to serve up the Althorp Spensers as archetypal examples of this tradition.[102] Scott-Warren suspects that Harington does not know quite where he stands, being that he himself enjoyed similar privileges, which included having his word accepted without question. It seems, however, that Harington does have a stance in the *Apologie* concerning its function as thematic aftermath of the *New Discourse*. Harington is reacting to an almost daily reality of Tudor politics: the pressing need for aristocrats to reiterate their histories and ancestries; the continuous bestowal of privileges and rewards for services both real and imagined; and the constant suspicion that Catholics sought to subvert the whole system, destroy it, and replace it with the Spanish model. Harington knows that an important part of this reality was the coerced sworn bond, whether it came in the form of recantation in a bishop's chamber, or disavowal in a jury trial. Harington knew that retraction under duress was at the core of the Elizabethan government's ability to secure itself against authorities, histories, beliefs, and opinions that dissidents did not accept. And he knew that the Elizabethan government believed that dissidents were everywhere. Harington's effort is lightened by his humor — at one point he protests that he is loathe to fight for the "jestification" of his wit.[103] It is just as painfully dull for Harington to explain a joke as it is for More. But as with More, Harington's ability to

5. Credibility Among Cynics

point out the stupidity of his enemies and the absurdity of their procedure against him allows him to make profound charges against the institutional hypocrisy among the inner circles of privilege in England. Bale is far more blunt and far less witty, but he is every bit as calculated as the other two. Sworn bond, and especially recantation under duress, is far too closely allied with men of great power but little credibility.

All three authors possess the ability to detach themselves from the corruption they witness, even as they admit, grudgingly, that corruption is a reality. This detachment is essential in the cynic, because it allows him or her to decode society's symbols it has constructed for itself. Careerism, expedience, ceremonialism, and traditionalism are all deeply encoded symbols of Englishness in the sixteenth century; and More, Bale, and Harington are all engaged in efforts to take apart those symbols. By way of their writing, they wish to rewrite Englishness, in terms of what loyalty, faith, and family history mean. They do so in the face of great danger, but opportunistic counselors, corrupt bishops, and half-educated lawyers and judges must be confronted so that they might no longer be able to control sworn bond to the extent they do. More, Bale, and Harington each choose to use overstatement as a means by which their messages will be delivered. More's underhanded animal fables, Bale's alliterative insults, and Harington's cheekiness serve to assist their cynical views far beyond amusement, double-entendre, or ridicule. The use of overstatement as a rhetorical device speaks to the idea that coercive sworn bond is itself a form of rhetorical overstatement. The compulsion to swear, the forced recantation, or the disavowal under duress establishes an absurd set of preconditions for an oath. These preconditions amount to an attack on a speech act which takes place between the swearer and God, no matter how many human witnesses are present. Even as they confront the authority of counselors, ministers, judges, and noblemen, More, Bale, and Harington assert authority by creating what they see as an appropriate perspective for the discussion of sworn bond. Because of the presence of coercion, however, the context of that discussion must be expressed in the language of the cynic. As their integrity, loyalty, and faith are attacked, each author maintains, in his own way, that the cynic is the man whose credibility cannot be impeached.

Chapter 6

Oath, Obligation, and Obedience
Fealty and Service in Three Plays About King John

Sixteenth-century England was a nation engaged in a dialogue with itself. Part of that dialogue involved a discussion of the past, as a means of determining whether the figures and events of previous generations were worthy of the discourse of the present. King John (1199–1216) is one such figure. Notorious throughout the Late Middle Ages as cruel, unjust, and responsible for the excommunication of England from the Catholic Church, King John was known as the king who had brought on his own deposition at the hands of the Pope, and who had been deservedly forced to sign the Magna Carta by his nobles. During the sixteenth century however, King John achieved a new relevance: promoters of the Reformation saw him as a king who dared to defy Rome and assert his royal prerogative in the face of the Pope's spiritual authority. His reign was seen to prefigure that of Henry VIII, his defiance of Innocent III a precursor to Henry's (and later Elizabeth's) Royal Supremacy. Moreover, John's reign was reinterpreted, and his reputation reconsidered, because many of the other problems that vexed Tudor England appeared to have a connection to those of John's day. The threat of invasion was omnipresent; sedition was feared to permeate the realm; and there were deep disagreements between the monarch and his or her nobles and bishops. Like John, both Henry VIII and Elizabeth I had been excommunicated as a result of their disputes with

6. Oath, Obligation, and Obedience

Rome.[1] The two Tudor monarchs and their predecessor had shared the indignity of having their subjects' fealty absolved by the Pope, and they also shared the uneasy allegiance of an opportunistic aristocracy. Sworn fealty — of subjects to their king and of the king to his subjects — had been the traditional bond which lay behind the ideal of the three estates through the ages. That bond had been dissolved amid King John's downfall, and part of the dialogue in which Tudor England was engaged with itself revolved around the idea that once again that bond was threatened.

Polemicists and politicians were of course embroiled in the issue, but so were the playwrights. Between 1539 and 1596 three plays about King John appeared on the English stage, and all of them explored the issue of sworn fealty between the King, and the clergy, aristocracy, and commons. John Bale wrote *Kynge Johan* some time after his conversion in 1533, and performed it before Cromwell's household during Christmas 1539. He then revised the play and perhaps prepared it for a performance before Elizabeth at Ipswich in 1561, although the play was not performed at that time. *The Troublesome Raigne of King John* appeared anonymously in 1591, and is proclaimed by its author to have been performed "sundry times" by the Queen's Men in London.[2] In 1596 came Shakespeare's *King John*, a play which is claimed by many to be based on *The Troublesome Raigne*, or to be a revised version of it, at least in part. In all three plays service and loyalty are profoundly affected by appropriately placed sworn bonds. The relationships between the plays' characters and their respective obligations to the king and to each other, stem from their abilities to swear proper fealty, by the proper faculties. In each play, an important dichotomy emerges between these oaths and the responsibilities that bind the swearers to them. Interestingly, service emerges as a social issue rather than a political one. Sworn fealty, reflected by proper service, is identified as a concept that preserves society's ideals and binds the three estates together precisely *because* it transcends politics. All three plays, whether they are allegorical or historical, didactic or dramatic, depict a culture re-envisioning itself by taking a long look at how sworn fealty is connected to loyalty and service outside the politics of expedience. The plays do so with great irony, in depicting that connection as stemming from the breakdown of the three estates, as King John fails his subjects — clergy, aristocracy, and commons — and they fail him. As each play demonstrates, the ceremonial rite describing an oath or vow has little to do with the bond guaranteed by truly sworn fealty. A true bond, it would appear, has more to do with Right than rite.

Earlier chroniclers had been hostile towards John in their accounts of his reign. He had been more than a failure — he had been a villain. Roger of Wendover famously justified Innocent III's excommunication and deposition of John, by claiming that John had waged "...a most severe persecution against the clergy, as some of the laity, and had entirely destroyed all kind of hope in every one of any improvement or satisfaction, and pope Innocent could no longer put off the punishment."[3] Others, such as John Capgrave and Henry Knighton, emphasized John's submission to Rome over the loss of his lands or the signing of Magna Carta as the key event in his reign.[4] As Chris Given-Wilson states, "what the national humiliation of 1215 came to represent was the transformation of historic liberty into servitude."[5] In the sixteenth century, however, John became a heroic figure. William Tyndale, in *The Obedience of a Christian Man* (1528) justifies John's defiance as reflective of his Divine Right, and accuses earlier chroniclers of having a papist agenda:

> Consider the story of King John, where I doubt not but they [earlier chroniclers] have put the best and fairest for themselves, and the worst of king John: for I suppose they make the chronicles themselves. Compare the doings of their holy church (as they ever call it) unto the learning of Christ and of his apostles. Did not the legate of Rome assoil all the lords of the realm of their due obedience, which they ought to the king by the ordinance of God? ... was not King John fain to deliver his crown unto the legate, and to yield up his realm unto the pope, wherefore we pay Peter-pence? They might be called the polling-pence of false prophets well enough.[6]

A generation later, Raphael Holinshed makes a similar statement. In his *Chronicle* (1577), Holinshed promotes King John as a victim of circumstance, an underdog standing up to the bullying injustice of Innocent III, with the king's cruelties interpreted as acts of retribution for the Pope's wrongdoing:

> Many [other] reasons the Pope alledged in his letters to King John to have persuaded him to the allowing of the election of Stephen Langton. But King John was so farre from giving care to the popes admonitions, that he with more crueltie handled all such, not only of the spiritualitie but also of the temporalty, which by any maner meanes had aided the forementioned Stephen.[7]

6. Oath, Obligation, and Obedience

The revisionism of Holinshed and Tyndale, among others, was influential. King John was transformed into a Protestant martyr whose death (long rumored to be a result of poisoning) was seen as an assassination.[8] John Bale (d. 1563) was heavily influenced by both Tyndale and Holinshed, and was an experienced chronicler himself. Much of his work had been completed when he was a Carmelite monk, before his conversion to Protestantism in 1533; but after his conversion he set out to publish a revisionist view of English history. He did so, primarily in two books: *Actes of the English Votaryes,* and *A Mystery of Iniquitye*. In addition to these efforts, however, Bale engaged in historical revisionism in almost all his works, including his own autobiography, *The Vocacyon of Johan Bale*.[9] *Kynge Johan*, one of Bale's several morality plays, is unapologetically polemical and revisionist. Using allegorical characters, Bale makes a direct comparison between King John's struggle with Innocent III and Henry VIII's with Clement VII. Bale's efforts are meant to fortify the Royal Supremacy by demonstrating that sworn bond is essential to its preservation. His patron, Thomas Cromwell, concurred; as Lord Chancellor Cromwell had embarked on his own campaign to rescue King John from the Chroniclers.[10] For a play that was conceived during the time when the Act of Supremacy was drafted and an oath devised to confirm it, *Kynge Johan* is a well-timed (and nearly state-sanctioned) piece of propaganda.

It is not known whether the anonymous author of *The Troublesome Raigne of King John* knew of Bale's play, although as a playwright with reformist sensibilities it is likely that he had heard of it, and he most likely knew of John Bale's polemical works. Bale had been a major influence on John Foxe, whose *Acts and Monuments* was undoubtedly known to the playwright of *Troublesome Raigne*. Bale had been appointed Bishop of Ossory by Edward VI, and his polemical tracts enjoyed reprintings well into the Elizabethan era. *Troublesome Raigne* adopts the didactic attitude of the morality play, yet establishes itself as undoubtedly Elizabethan in terms of plot and character development. It comments upon and validates Tudor historiography, and moves beyond polemic to introduce The Bastard, a character who transforms historiography into his own historical experience, and confirms it with an oath.

Many have argued that Shakespeare revised *Troublesome Raigne* (perhaps around 1595) to produce *King John* in 1596. Indeed, a comparison of the two plays shows great similarity between the two, but this issue lies outside the scope of my discussion here. Nor do I wish to discuss whether *Troublesome Raigne* or *King John* is based in whole or in part on Bale's *Kynge Johan*. Rather than examining whether, or to what extent, any of these plays is derived from either or both of the others I intend to discuss the fact that these three plays demonstrate the extent to which sixteenth-century England is a culture revising and re-envisioning itself. I do not intend to discuss whether Shakespeare revised *Troublesome Raigne* as it was written by someone else (Robert Southwell and Christopher Marlowe have been suggested), or whether it is his own work in an early form. What I do find important to discuss here is that in *King John,* as in his other histories, Shakespeare displays a knowledge of the historiographical process of his day. As Marsha Robinson points out in her discussion of Shakespeare's use of historiography in *King John*, "His aim in the play is not merely to recreate the past but to dramatize the process by which historical experience is translated into historiographic meaning."[11] Shakespeare, like the anonymous author of *Troublesome Raigne*, witnessed revisionist history-making and understood that the past was presented to the public as fiction. He, like his anonymous colleague, sought to dramatize this phenomenon and generate new meaning from it. Unlike the author of *Troublesome Raigne*, however, Shakespeare is not playing to the past. Shakespeare is playing toward attitudes that his audience has about revisionism itself, in their own time. This fact makes Shakespeare's version markedly different from *Troublesome Raigne*; the two plays may bear similarities in their lines, but they differ greatly in terms of sense. *Troublesome Raigne* reproduces the format and issues of the morality play. In *King John* Shakespeare adapts the format of the morality play so that its issues will be contemporary rather than retrospective.

In *King John* Shakespeare illustrates, with great poignancy, the difficulties that arise when sworn fealty collides with sentiment. It would be very difficult to suggest that Shakespeare knew of Bale's *Kynge Johan*; but he did know that the historical figure of King John had been undergoing a steady reinterpretation for most of the century. And he very likely did know that *Troublesome Raigne* was not the first piece on the subject. In any case, many members of Shakespeare's audience would have known of Bale's work, although most of them were too young to have heard Bale preach during his career. Bale died a scant six months before Shakespeare

6. Oath, Obligation, and Obedience

was born, but his work left a lasting influence on many polemicists, including one of the most notable propagandists of the Elizabethan era — John Foxe. Indeed, the audience who came to see *King John* in the 1590s was well acquainted with the legend of Bad King John and its reinterpretation by reformists earlier in the century.[12]

Re-textualized as a martyred figure, King John was nonetheless given an ironic portrayal. Even as a prefigured hero of the Reformation, King John was still known best for his failures as a monarch. In each play King John falls far short of the medieval ideals of kingship, and in each play those shortcomings are illustrated by the uses and abuses of sworn bond. Oaths, as they are used by King John himself and against him by his enemies, dictate the progression of his downfall. King John is unable to uphold his sworn duties to the three estates, and the estates are unwilling to uphold their sworn fealty to him. All three plays make suggestions about which party is the most responsible, but in the end they all employ sworn bond as a means by which the three estates redeem themselves, the nation, and the king, after his death.

The ideals upon which the relationship between the king and the three estates are built avoid the which-came-first argument about whose obligations come before the others. The clergy, aristocracy, and commons are bound to each other, and to the king; and he is bound to them. The relationship is based on continuous reciprocation: the clergy are to defend the realm and its inhabitants spiritually, providing a strong and stable institution which gives the people comfort; the aristocracy is charged with defending the realm and its inhabitants from invasion, and with defending the king in his actions and policies; and the commons is charged with providing labor, and tax and tithe revenues, to support the other two systems. The commonalty must also remain righteous for the sake of the monarch, and in the name of the Church.

All three estates owe their fealty to the king, and in turn he bears several obligations to them. An English king is sworn to his subjects and owes his subjects his loyalty to them.[13] The ways in which he performs his duties therefore affects the allegiance of his people because it affects their trust. If he performs his duties poorly, or not at all, he cannot count on the fealty and service of his subjects. The king must be true to God, to his alliances, and to himself. This is a moral obligation rather than a political one, and a good king was expected to know how to determine these truths. A king must be willing to receive counsel, and must be able to listen well to his counselors, taking heed to dissent for the good of his kingdom.[14] He must preserve the trust of his subjects and uphold the principle of Divine Ordination to justify his kingship. If he fails, he risks earning the label of tyrant, and he will lose the fealty of his subjects. In this sense the duties of the king transcend his humanity. He is expected to make distinctions between his will and his moral obligations, between justified, albeit austere actions, and tyranny.[15] It was well known over the centuries that not every king would live up to this task, and kings that failed to do so suffered in the chronicles. Roger of Wendover, writing after King John's death, associated his inadequacies with an inherent unworthiness to serve his country as king. He points to King John's own coronation, in which the Archbishop of Canterbury "added a solemn personal adjuration to John in heaven's name warning him not to venture upon accepting the regal office unless he truly purposed in his own mind to perform his oath."[16] King John had assented to this adjuration, and Wendover, when interpreting the events of John's reign in hindsight, saw the event as prophetic. He adds:

> Archbishop Hubert was afterwards asked why he acted in this manner, to which he replied that he knew John would one day or other bring the kingdom into great confusion, wherefore he determined that he should owe his elevation to election and not to hereditary right.[17]

It had been Archbishop Hubert Walter whose death had provoked King John's rejection of Stephen Langton, the Pope's own candidate for the position. The ensuing dispute had, in the popular view, led to John's excommunication, and eventually to his being forced to sign Magna Carta. For Wendover, the connections were clear: King John had sworn an oath which he was ill-prepared to keep. The result had been a catastrophic reign.

All three plays are deeply affected by the Tudor dynasty's development, and all three playwrights were familiar with the degrees of successes and failures to which a monarch could be subject. In each play King John enjoys a brief period of success in which he is shown preserving relationships between himself and the three estates, as he secures loyalties and provides remedies for ills and quarrels. In Bale's play one such bond is established between Kynge Johan and Englande, a widow who appeals to the king for protection against an exploitive clergy:

6. Oath, Obligation, and Obedience

> ENG. That I trust yowr grace wyll waye a poore wedowes cause,
>   Vngodly vsyd, as ye shall know in short clavse.
> K. JOHN. Yea, that I wyll swer, yf yt be trewe and iust.[18]

Here Kynge Johan establishes a sworn bond between himself and Englande, who embodies all three estates. Although Clergye has been abusing Englande, he is nonetheless a part of her, and Kynge Johan recognizes his duty to defend the whole of the realm from destructive elements both inside and outside of it. The bond between Kynge Johan and Englande is confirmed in the form of a loyalty oath to which Clergye must assent. Although Clergye resists, he submits to the king "bothe body and goodes," (I.506). Even as he does so, Clergye tries to subvert the king's bond by attempting to substitute the Pope for the king in his oath:

> K.JOHAN. Aryse, Clargy, aryse, and ever be obedient
>   And as God commaundeth yow, take us for yowre govnere.
> CLERGYE. By the Grace of God, the Pope shall be my rulare.
> K.JOHAN. What say ye Clargy? Who ys yowre governer?
> CLERGYE. Ha, ded I stumble? I says my prynce ys my ruler.[19]

Satisfied that he has secured Clergye's fealty, Kynge Johan prays for the endurance of his obedience. Clergye in turn assures the king that he will not break his oath. Bale's cynicism here points to his distrust of the Submission of the Clergy, in which the convocation had promised not to enact any ecclesiastical policies without the king's permission.[20] As a polemicist dedicated to exposing what he saw as centuries of feigned loyalty, Bale doubted that the English clergy could be trusted to obey that piece of legislation, which was first passed by the convocation of Canterbury in 1532, adapted and passed by the Reformation Parliament in 1534, and then renewed in 1536.[21] The 1534 version of the three articles did not bear an expiration date, and so the renewal of the articles two years later suggests that neither Parliament nor the king trusted the clergy to keep their promise. A reiteration was clearly in order. In *Kynge Johan's* thinly veiled parallel to the Submission, Clergye's oath to take the king as his sole governor, is flawed, but Kynge Johan does not demand a full reiteration of the oath. After a brief correction, Kynge Johan overlooks Clergye's attempt to circumvent his oath and determines Clergye's submission to be a success.

Having also summoned Nobylyte and Cyvyle Order, Kynge Johan requires them to swear allegiance as well:

> K. JOHAN. Ye shall first be sworne to God and to the crowne
> To be trewe and just in every cetye and towne
> And this to perfourme set hands and kysse the bocke.²²

Cyvyle Order responds:

> C. ORDER. With the wife of Loth we wyll not backeward loke
> Nor turne from owre oth, but ever obeye yowre grace.²³

For Kynge Johan and Englande this is a comforting moment in the play: things are functioning the way they should. What Bale, and his audience, is aware of is the false sense of security generated by Kynge Johan's trust in the ancient rite of the fealty oath to maintain good relationships between the three estates. For Bale, this relationship had fallen apart in Henry VIII's reign just as it had in King John's. Henry VIII had responded with innovations in sworn fealty; the oaths that accompanied the Acts of Supremacy and Succession, for example, sought to redefine this damaged relationship and establish an adapted and modernized bond between the king and his subjects.²⁴ Unlike Henry VIII, John had required no further iterations or adaptations.

In *Kynge Johan* Bale presents allegorical characters who stand in for the groups that contribute to John's false sense of success; in *Troublesome Raigne* and *King John*, the anonymous playwright and Shakespeare both use the Faulconbridge dispute to demonstrate John's brief success with long-established conventions of fealty and submission. As he pronounces his judgment against Robert Faulconbridge in *Troublesome Raigne*, the king seeks to resolve the issue by using his own word as his bond. Robert protests, stating that although the agreement of the lords present would confirm his brother Philip as the son of Richard Cordelion, such a judgment would damage the reputation of his family. He says:

> ROBERT: The proofe so plaine, the argument so strong
> As that your Highnes and these noble Lords
> And all (save those that have no eyes to see)
> Shall sweare him to be Bastard to the King.²⁵

Here Robert Faulconbridge literally begs King John to see the whole picture. Undeterred, the king makes his pronouncement, noting that his word is paramount in his kingdom. He responds:

> K. JOHN. This is my doome, and this my doome shall stand
> Irrevocable, as I am King of England.²⁶

6. Oath, Obligation, and Obedience

King John seeks to put an end to the issue by requiring a threefold vow from both Robert and his mother, and he will accept the outcome as a truth thrice sworn. King John calls for the threefold vow "for fashions sake,"[27] connecting his judgment to a longstanding tradition of taking vows in this manner. In doing so, King John seeks to get at the truth by challenging Philip and Margaret to swear falsely. Although it seems unlikely that Philip will admit to being illegitimate and Margaret to being an adulteress, the King's plan works, and the truth comes out. Although King John uses sworn bond as an underhanded way to get at the truth, he earns the obedience of Robert and Margaret Faulconbridge, and the loyalty of Philip Faulconbridge.

Here, the King makes the judgment and The Bastard must accept the outcome. In Shakespeare's version, King John allows The Bastard to choose to renounce his inheritance, and The Bastard swears of his own accord. Proud of his newly-sworn knighthood, he reports to his disappointed mother after the fact: "What! I am dubbed; I have it on my shoulder."[28] Beatrice Groves, in her article comparing *Troublesome Raigne* to *King John*, notes an important aspect of The Bastard's change of status as it pertains to sworn bond. She states,

> As the Bastard discovers his nobility, the difference between the inescapable power of the thrice reiterated vow and the voluntary decision of a self-made man marks the divergence between a traditional dramaturgy based on folk structures and ritual and an emerging dramaturgy structured around psychological realism.[29]

It is an interesting distinction between the observance of tradition on the one hand and psychological realism on the other; yet, in both cases, the outcome is the same: King John uses the situation to affirm his ability to resolve issues of descendancy and inheritance by way of his word. Whether The Bastard is required to comply with the King's decision, or whether he chooses his own identity, the fact remains that the King's word is paramount in the situation. In both plays King John determines that the Faulconbridge issue is resolved, and that his authority is at the heart of the success. The king's privilege to determine the validity of another man's pedigree is effectual whether ancient tradition or "self-fashioning" is at the source of the bond.[30] But just as Bale's Kynge Johan overlooks Clergye's insincerity and chooses to herald the oath of submission as a success, the

King John of *Troublesome Raigne* and *King John* also overlooks problems that lurk beneath the surface. In *Troublesome Raigne* King John disregards Margaret's defeated acceptance of his decree. Indeed, he is not there when The Bastard threatens to murder her if she does not support his claim:

> And here by heavens eternall lampes I sweare,
> As cursed Nero with his mother did,
> So I with you, if you resolve me not.[31]

Nor is Shakespeare's King John present when The Bastard delivers a soliloquy in which he fantasizes about the privileges he will enjoy as a nobleman. His word will be supported by the king whenever necessity arises. His word will also be worth more on the aristocratic marriage market. He boasts, "Well, now I can make any Joan a lady."[32] Although King John is satisfied, his early successes in each of the three plays are shaky at best. By refusing to look hard at the whole picture, John has been remiss in his obligations as king, and other characters in the plays take notice.

Soon enough, each play turns to the subject of John's downfall, and in each case sworn bond is linked to the degeneration of the relationship between the king and the three estates. In Shakespeare's version John's faults are depicted not long after the investment of The Bastard. In II.i Philip, King of France contests John's claim to the throne. He asserts Prince Arthur's right and vows to protect the boy's claim:

> Lo! In this right hand, whose protection
> Is most divinely vowed upon the right
> Of him it holds, stands young Plantagenet,
> Son to the elder brother of this man [John]
> And king o'er him and all that he enjoys.[33]

Referring to the Divine Right of Kings, Philip holds Arthur with his right hand and simultaneously vows with it. Just as Kynge Johan had demanded that his Nobles and Civil Lawyers "kisse the bocke" when swearing their fealty, King Philip uses Arthur as a divine object which can guarantee the coronation oath of a king. In this sense, Arthur's claim allows him to validate himself; this equivocal paradox is only possible when Divine Right supports the candidate. Indeed, King John had relied upon this principle when he had resolved the Faulconbridge issue. But the introduction of Arthur into the play raises the question of King John's claim to the kingship, and whether he indeed is God's agent on earth.

6. Oath, Obligation, and Obedience

Much has been said about whether or not the people and government of Tudor England believed (or wanted to believe) the historical John to be a usurper. For Bale, the issue is settled: John was the rightful king because Richard had decreed it. Bale had argued that John's defiance of Rome and his establishment of rights for the English Church via Magna Carta proved that he had been destined to be God's representative for England. As a result, the succession issue does not appear in *Kynge Johan*.[34] Nevertheless, the issue of Richard's will, and the Divine Will that stems from it, is important to Bale as an historiographer. The issue was not lost on the author of *Troublesome Raigne*; as Eleanor and Constance argue over the alleged will that disinherits Arthur in favor of John, Constance likens the document to a demonic pact:

> CONSTANCE: A will indeede, a crabbed Womans will
> Wherein the Divell is an overseer,
> And proud dame Elnor sole Executresse:
> More wills that so on peril of my soule,
> Were never made to hinder Arthurs right.[35]
> ARTHUR: But say there was, as sure there can be none,
> The law intends such testaments as voyd,
> Where right dissent can no way be impeacht.[36]

Although the issue of succession revolves around documentary support in *Troublesome Raigne*, it nonetheless points to the utmost value of a king's word. A king's word reached out to the public by way of documentary evidence, such as injunctions, decrees, and statutes. There were in fact few times when the public could witness a king's vow: they could do so by witnessing his coronation if they were present, or they could do so by witnessing his marriage, but again, only if they were present. In such cases the vast majority of those present were nobles and elite members of the clergy. The king's word therefore was almost inextricably linked to documentary support in the minds of most people. In *Troublesome Raigne*, Constance rejects Richard's last will and testament as having been illegally influenced by Eleanor; although she had been the queen of Henry II, and the mother of Richard I, Eleanor's will is that of a woman, and her word is therefore not legally binding in the face of the authority of her deceased son. Constance therefore accuses Eleanor of trying to circumvent the law by citing a conveniently missing document that grants the throne to the candidate of her choice, her will. Rather than representing legal validation of King John's claim, Richard's last will, as influenced by Eleanor's will, is simply a wish for fulfillment of Eleanor's ambitions. For Constance, such a flagrant interference with Divine Right is practically satanic. Rather than being a contract with God, "Eleanor's will" is a pact with the devil, an adversarial plot to stand in the way of God's Will. As young Arthur himself states, dubious legal documents can be impeached, but Divine Right cannot. Shakespeare's Constance simply refuses to believe the report of Lewis' marriage to Blanche, protesting, "I have a king's oath to the contrary."[37] In this case Constance will not entertain the unthinkable — that the authors of the truce would violate a king's will. But the will of a dead king soon proves to be lost amid the professed claims of live ones, and in the face of Eleanor's accusation of II.i.122–3 that Arthur is illegitimate, King John remains on the throne, but his legitimacy is not untainted.

Constance also rages against King Philip in *Troublesome Raigne*, as an opportunistic and dishonest king who is willing to disenfranchise her son in favor of John. Although he had promised to protect Arthur, Philip had abandoned that promise when faced with the benefits offered by the fruitful partnership of Lewes and Blanche — benefits offered, and engineered, by John and Eleanor. In her estimation, Philip's perjury is an extension of John's dishonesty:

> He promised Arthur, and he sware it too,
> To fence thy right, and check thy foemans pride:
> But now black-spotted Perjure as he is,
> He takes a truce with Elinors damned brat,
> And marries Lewes to her lovely neece.[38]

A friendship between England and France is anathema to Shakespeare's Constance as well, as she cries, "France is a bawd to Fortune and King John/That strumpet Fortune, that usurping King John!"[39] Although she curses both kings, Constance lays much of the blame upon John, calling to heaven for avengement on behalf of God's true anointed — Arthur, by way of his uncle Richard I. She cries: "Arm, arm, you heavens, against these perjured kings!"[40]

All three plays depict King John's tragic, but nonetheless utter, failure: abandoned by his nobles, betrayed by his clergy, and forsaken by his commons, King John dies, or is murdered. The three depictions of John's failure all stem from his shortsightedness concerning his reliance upon his suc-

6. Oath, Obligation, and Obedience

cesses, albeit in different ways, and to different degrees. In each case the rites of the past, which by tradition secure loyalties and obligations via sworn bonds, are affected by changes in circumstances, intent, and sincerity on the part of the king's clergy, nobles, and commons. This is nothing new — but King John's relationship to the tradition of sworn bond prevents him from using the important instincts and discernments that a good king is supposed to have. King John becomes a tragic figure in each play because he cannot adapt and maintain control over the uncertain or changing circumstances that accompany sworn bonds. This factor makes King John's failure complex, and each play questions, to varying degrees, John's overall worthiness as a historical figure because of it.

A king's success is connected to the extent to which his nobility, clergy, and commons obey and serve him. An oath may be sworn, but its obligation must be performed, and service is the means by which loyal subjects demonstrate the validity of their bonds. In each of the three plays the subjects of King John fail to support their fealty with the proper performance of service. Although Bale uses allegorical characters and expository speeches rather than individual characters and dramatic narrative, ultimately, he makes the same point that the other two playwrights do: a king cannot live up to the ideals of kingship if he is not supported by proper service. The system works by reciprocation, and the idea that the king and his subjects are obligated to each other is what allows all three plays to promote a figure of a tragic king rather than a "bad" one.

In this way the plays each emphasize a rejection of ceremonial oath-swearing, even as they continually depict it. Ritual expression of sworn bond is the very thing which continually comes between King John and his subjects; and yet the three plays are filled with characters who believe they are acting in deference to their duty.[41] Both *Kynge Johan* and *Troublesome Raigne* at first depict formal oaths sworn in the traditional manner, then invalidate them by associating them with the exploitive, material practices of the Roman Church. Shakespeare takes a different approach and omits the formal action of swearing from most of the play. The effect is more subtle, but the message is clear: it is human faith and trustworthiness, not ritual, that is crucial in the interactions between subjects and their king. As Guy Hamel points out, Shakespeare uses the absence of formal action to illustrate its futility. He says, "The theatrical equivalent of the purging of verbal forms is the rejection of ceremony. Even without comparing *King John* to *The Troublesome Raigne* one might notice that *King John* is unusually lacking in formal action for a history play."[42] Shakespeare is more critical of Catholicism in *King John* than he is in most of his other plays, and he uses sworn bond as a channel for his criticism of religious faith and its potential to interrupt human loyalties rather than to secure them. Shakespeare is therefore doing the same thing Bale and the author of *Troublesome Raigne* are doing: he is rejecting the ritual expression and materiality of sworn bond as an archaic principle that does not assure true worth or true service.

In Bale's play, Clergye begins planning Kynge Johan's downfall immediately after taking his oath. In "stumbling" Clergye reveals his intent to be less than sincere, and he uses this loophole to absolve himself of his allegiance. He reveals his subversive plan to Nobylyte, and instantly corrupts him:

NOB. But how wyll ye do for the othe that ye take?
CLERGYE. The keyes of the Church can all soche materes of shake.
NOB. What call ye those keyes? I pray yow, tell me!
CLERGYE. Owre Holy Fathers power and hys high autoryte.
NOB. Well, I can no more say, ye are to well lerned for me.[43]

Nobylyte immediately craves the materiality of the Church's power: the keys (or what he thinks to be real keys) that can absolve sworn fealty and disassociate Nobylyte from an excommunicated king. Soon after, Sedycyon, Bale's Vice Figure, gives Nobylyte the absolution Clergye had promised, saying, "I assoyle the here from the kynges obedience/By the auctorite of the Popys magnificence."[44] He then produces a long list of relics and invokes a veritable litany of saints which he will use to absolve the fealty oaths of Nobylyte, and also Clergye and Cyvyle Order. The rite is filled with vulgarity. The relics he produces to assure the absolution of his allies include "A dram of the tord of Seynte Barnabe," and "A Maggot of Moyses with a fart of Saynte Fandingo."[45] Sedycyon's absolution is a travesty, an absurd external act which does not describe true obedience or service. Instead, it describes an oath as an asset, an act which is a product of opportunity rather than something which stems from true sentiment. Clergye and Sedycyon show how a false sense of security is created when a focus on ceremony replaces a focus on divinity. In Bale's view, the clergy was

6. Oath, Obligation, and Obedience

sworn not to God's service, but to the Pope's, as part of an institution of salvation, an enterprise that used ceremonial oaths to validate its own principles and advance its own agendas. What Kynge Johan's subjects do not realize is that the absolution of their fealty by the Church actually deprives them of their liberty. Although Bale does not discuss Magna Carta in his play, his depiction of obedience to the Church as representing a loss of liberty provides a strong connection to the issues of the document King John was most famous for signing. In being absolved, Kynge Johan's subjects are bound to the Church of Rome and deprived of their right to a God-given ruler, since the Pope, as Bale tirelessly pointed out in his polemical writings, was elected by men, while the king was chosen and ordained by God.

When it is evident that Kynge Johan stands alone, Cardinall (Pandulphus) presents the king with a final compulsion to submission: the threat of foreign invasion from France. In his own defense Kynge Johan abandons his resistance and adopts an alternative sense of duty. He pleads with Cardinall for his vow that if he submits his crown to the Pope there will be no invasion, and Cardinall offers it:

> CARDINALL. Yea, they shulde go backe indeede
> And ther gret armyse to some other quarters leede
> Or elles they have not so many good blessynges now
> But as many cursinges they shall have, I make God avowe
> I promise yow, sir, ye shall have specyall faver
> Yf ye wyll submit yowre sylfe to Holy Chyrch here.[46]

Kynge Johan is then presented with an "oblygacyon," a written contract which is confirmed by oath. The "oblygacyon" requires the king to make great monetary compensation to the Church and to grant the clergy free license across the realm. Moreover, the contract binds not only Kynge Johan but also his future heirs.[47] An oath of compulsion such as this uses both public and personal humiliation to secure its bond, a process identified by Bale as being as far from true sentiment as one can get. Still, Kynge Johan surrenders his kingdom, pays restitution to the English clergy, and delivers his crown to Cardinall. Wistfully, the king recalls his own role in the Biblical covenant to King David, now supplanted by the machinations of the Roman Church. He laments, "As David sayeth, Lorde, thu dost not leave thy servaunt/That wyll trust in the and in thy blessyd covenaunt."[48]

However futile in the moment, Kynge Johan makes a proclamation of his Divine Right of Kingship.

In *Troublesome Raigne* and Shakespeare's *King John*, the relationship between King John and Pandulph is more legalistic, as Pandulph protests in *Troublesome Raigne* that King John has disallowed the election of Stephen Langton "...contrarie to the lawes of our holy mother the Church..."[49] Accused of violating Church law, King John cites his legal obligation to serve England as the basis for his right as king to make his own appointment. In a direct reference to the Royal Supremacy (and to the statutory punishment for its violation), *Troublesome Raigne's* King John states, "...as I am king, so wil I raigne under God, supreme head both over spirituall and temprall: and he that contradicts me in this, Ile make him hoppe headlesse."[50] Shakespeare's King John also cites statutory law to protect a king's word, and lashes out with even more resentment, saying, "What earthly name to interrogatories/Can test the free breath of a sacred king?"[51] Pandulph responds menacingly in both plays by asserting his own performative power: with a word rather than a ritual he excommunicates King John, absolving his subjects of their fealty to him. For a while, it works, but ultimately it is the king's word that serves the nation best, as Pandulph's word fails to serve the nation at all. Both kings cite their duty to defend and protect their subjects, and see Pandulph's interference as the Church's man-made attempt to subvert royal authority. Although it is supported by legislative documents, a king's word supersedes words on paper. In both Elizabethan plays Pandulph is referred to continually as a mere man in a mere appointment, rather than as a vocational figure, and Elizabethan audiences were able to perceive the gist of these references. By the 1590s clergymen were largely seen as career public servants rather than mystic sacerdotal figures. Rather than fearing the Roman Church, English men and women feared those who, either on the Continent or in England, were still controlled by it. What was portrayed radically in Bale's day could therefore be stated plainly in Shakespeare's; instead of using comical scenes featuring bell, book and candle, the Elizabethan plays depict Pandulph as a poor public servant.[52]

Because he wishes to focus on Kynge Johan as a tragic figure, Bale seeks to show John's ineffective but heartfelt protest at having to surrender his crown. When Kynge Johan perceives that he is about to be deposed, he calls on his subjects for help, according to their sworn duty. They deny him, prompting the king to demand an explanation:

> K. JOHAN. Why leve ye yowre prynce and cleve to the Pope so sore?
> NOB. For I toke an othe to defende the Chyrche ever more....
> CLERGYE. I am professyd to the ryghtes ecclesiasticall....
> C. ORDER. I am hyr feed man; who shuld defend her but I?[53]

The king upbraids the three characters for their misplaced allegiance, but still adheres to his own sworn duty, as much as he can. Considering Englande's best interests, Kynge Johan condemns the oaths of the three characters, but does not demand that they recant.

> K. Johan. Of all thre parties yt is spokyn reasonably;
> Ye may not obeye becawse of the othe ye mad,
> Yowre strong profession maketh yow of that same trad,
> Yowre fee provokyth yow to do as thes men do.
> Grett thynges to cawse men from God to the devuyll to go!
> Yowre othe is groundyd first upon folyshnes,
> And yowre profession upon moche pevyshnes;
> Yowre fee, last of all ryseth owt of covetousness,
> And thes are the cawses of yowre rebelyousnes.[54]

Kynge Johan had relied upon ritual swearing to secure the obedience of Clergye, Nobylyte, and Cyvyle Order, and now he must accept the consequences of his mistake. He dies defeated, but knowing the truth — and is therefore granted the status of martyr and prophet of the Reformation by Bale.

In *Kynge Johan* Bale makes a distinction between the Church and the faith, between ecclesiastical authority and the authority of scripture. He makes it clear that Nobylyte's greatest shortcoming is that he should have known that his duty is to defend not the church, but the *faith* from oppression. As such, Nobylyte has fallen short of proper service. *Troublesome Raigne* and *King John* also make much of the idea that noblemen must be able to identify and fulfill their true obligations without the interference of opportunity or ambition. In both plays, the nobles validate each other's fealty with assent rather than with an appropriate sense of duty. Although they give the Church due quarter, the nobles of *Troublesome Raigne* and *King John* base the validity of their fealty on what they want. In *Troublesome Raigne* a formal oath is sworn among the nobles at the Abbey of St.

Edmundsbury, in which they recant their fealty oaths to King John and swear new fealty to Lewes, the Dauphin. Their newly-sworn fealty comes in the form of a warrant, identified by the play's anti-materialist subtext as a man-made symbol of mere statutory law. Lewes appreciates their loyalty and praises "...this religious league/A holy knot of Catholique consent," and insists that the formula be followed to the letter. He states:

> My eyes must witness, and these eares must heare
> Your oath upon the holy Altar sworne,
> And after march to end our comings cause.[55]

Salisbury is the one who swears first, "...upon the Altar and by the holy Armie of Saints, homage and alleagance to the right Christian Prince Lewes of Fraunce..."[56] The other nobles follow suit, and the effect of the scene is striking. The simplicity of the stage direction, "All the Eng. Lords swear," precedes the simple response of the lords themselves as they state with one voice, "As the noble Earle hath sworne, so sweare we all."[57] Following this action, Lewes swears his own oath on the altar, but in a different manner. Although he prefaces his oath with complementary language, he does not swear in the manner of the English nobles with him. Rather, he states that he swears "in like sort," and the stage direction does not call for him to place his hand on the altar. In this scene three parties have sworn the same oath in three different manners. Salisbury, as leader, swears formally, taking care to identify himself, the person to whom he wishes to swear (Lewes), and the faculties by which he swears (the holy army of saints and the altar itself). The other nobles simply assent to Salisbury's oath without performing the same ritual. Finally, Lewes acknowledges their bond and offers his "recompense" to them as their king. These inconsistencies only seem to be minor; rather, they point to the deficiencies of the process of the Catholic oath, and to the faults of assent among an opportunistic nobility. Just as Bale had grouped the English nobles together as the allegorical character Nobylyte, so does the author of *Troublesome Raigne*, in showing their collective assent without each man having to be responsible for his own oath. As their current leader says, so say they all. They can each therefore defend their actions by the fact that the others have all assented to it. Although Bale is more blunt, the author of *Troublesome Raigne* also illustrates that where true fealty and service are concerned, such action on the part of the nobility is ill-conceived.

6. Oath, Obligation, and Obedience

The altar oath of *Troublesome Raigne* in which King John's nobles recant their fealty is depicted in a manner which emphasizes its realism; i.e., it looks and sounds like a traditional formal oath, in contrast to the comical depiction of Sedycyon's recantation of the fealty of Kynge Johan's subjects in Bale's play. The plot of *Troublesome Raigne* pauses so that the ritual can take place onstage as a dramatic interpretation of an historical event.[58] Although it is a "true" depiction of a formal oath (to perhaps use a sixteenth-century term) it is, ironically, definitively false. The nobles swear falsely because they abandon their true fealty to King John, and Lewes swears falsely because he intends to use the English nobles until they are of no more use to him, at which time he will have them executed. Furthermore, as Salisbury later points out, Lewes' oath is doubly false because he has forsworn his own fealty to King Philip in the process.[59]

The play's anti–Catholic sentiment makes it clear that the oath upon the altar of St. Edmund is an extension of the English clergy's betrayal of King John. Just as Bale had used Sedycyon as an allegory for the continual presence of the clergy's treachery, *Troublesome Raigne* uses St. Edmund's shrine as an ominous backdrop. The sedition of the Roman Church is a present and active element in the false fealty of the English nobles, in terms of both the place and the manner in which the false oath is sworn. The fealty oath to Lewes at the Altar of St Edmund relies upon the shrine of a saint to legitimize the bond. It is therefore no accident that a false oath should take place there; the trappings of idolatry, which identify the clergy's betrayal of King John, are what secure the oath and allow all present to assent to its terms. Indeed, the oath is sworn in the name of the altar itself, an act that by 1591 was considered to be deplorable, and even treasonous to Elizabeth I. The fact that Salisbury swears in the name of the army of saints only drives the point home: it is the Pope's figurative army, an army nonetheless made up of symbols now disenfranchised from English fealty and faith, that guide the nobles' bad intentions. *Troublesome Raigne* uses the formal oath to illustrate the dangers of assent, of expediency, and opportunity. Wishing to be allied with a stronger leader, and believing the rumors that John has murdered Arthur, the English nobles deploy distinctively Catholic means to help them get what they want. Although their cause is not justified by the play, their actions do reflect their deep resentments of John: he has ransacked the monasteries, called for the death of

Arthur, and brought on the excommunication of England from the Church. Although their grievances against John are identified as erroneous, *Troublesome Raigne* nonetheless demonstrates the fact that John's nobles do not feel that he has lived up to his sworn duty to them.

In Shakespeare's *King John*, the reenactment of a formal oath is absent from the play's action. Shakespeare omits a setting which would immediately identify the intentions and bonds of the swearers to be false; but he nonetheless depicts Salisbury's allegiance to Lewis as being guided by man-made, and Papist, influence. Like the Salisbury character of *Troublesome Raigne*, Shakespeare's Salisbury also has a written warrant upon which his oath and that of the others is based. Shakespeare, however, makes further use of the issue that the nobles' oath is based on their human desires rather than on true fealty: Salisbury wishes that the warrant be copied out in order to disseminate, and further validate, its terms among men.[60] He reports to Lewis, who, after reviewing their written document, has taken the Sacrament, by which he accepts their new fealty.[61] Salisbury responds by relating their oath to Lewis in person:

> And, noble Dauphin, albeit we swear
> A voluntary zeal and an unurged faith
> To your proceedings, yet believe me, prince,
> I am not glad that such a sore of time
> Should seek a plaster by contemned revolt,
> And heal the inveterate canker of one wound
> By making many.[62]

Just as The Bastard's sworn investiture takes place offstage but is described by him afterward, this scene describes sworn bond rather than depicts it. In both scenes, Shakespeare uses the description of oathtaking to emphasize the psychological realism of personal relationships over relationships which are dictated by ritual. The effect is surprisingly iconoclastic, and unexpectedly similar to that produced by Bale and *Troublesome Raigne*. Shakespeare removes the backdrop of the saint's shrine, but still allows anti–Catholic sentiment to remain. He references the Sacrament, which could only be administered by a priest, thereby reminding his audience that a clergyman had been at the center of the treasonous rite. John Klause, in his discussion of *King John*'s possible sources in Elizabethan recusant writing, notes that in taking the Sacrament the nobles have

6. Oath, Obligation, and Obedience

"confirmed their faiths."[63] Here, Shakespeare allows a double-entendre: the nobles have pledged their faith falsely, and their pledge is made upon a false faith. Even Salisbury's much-copied warrant is idolatrous in this construction: the trappings of man, influenced by the treacheries of the Roman Church, are behind the false fealties of Salisbury and the other nobles. Bale's vulgarities are nowhere to be seen, but Shakespeare's audience is expected to be disgusted. The audience can hardly be surprised that behind the scenes Pandulphus has been driving even Philip and Lewis apart.[64] The audience might, however, be surprised at Salisbury's faint, but very real, pangs of guilt. Even as he swears, he feels he has done wrong. Still, like the Salisbury of *Troublesome Raigne*, he feels betrayed.

The commons is, interestingly, the most difficult group for each of the three playwrights to depict. What they all make clear, however, is that the fealty of the commoners is directly related to the amount of faith they have in King John to uphold his duty to support and defend them. Outraged by the ransacking of the monasteries and disturbed by rumors of the murder of Arthur, they lose faith in John's ability to maintain control over difficult circumstances. When they perceive that King John has failed to protect them from exploitation by the Church, or invasion from France, they are prepared to take their loyalty elsewhere. Although withdrawing fealty from the king did not necessarily fall within the rights of the commons, it was a well-known and inevitable consequence of negligent leadership in both the thirteenth and sixteenth centuries. The commons has the least amount of power in society, and yet without the support of the commons a king loses the fealty of the majority of the populace. Although they do not swear as individuals in their own right, commoners assure the strength of their fealty with sheer numbers. Theirs is a fealty unsworn, but subject to similar obligations as the clergy and nobility who take fealty oaths. They take on these obligations as a whole people, and thus they are able to assert what power they have to ensure that their king will keep their best interests in his mind.

The citizens of Angiers are a prime example of how fealty in numbers allows the commoners of *Troublesome Raigne* and *King John* to assert control over their circumstances when they determine kings to be unwilling or unable to do so. As their spokesman states, they are ready to profess their loyalty to the king, but it is not up to them to determine who the king is. In both plays King John demands that the citizens determine who their king is, and in both plays this demand is reversed, thrown back to John with an odd mixture of loyalty and defiance. *Troublesome Raigne* shows:

> K. JOHN. Acknowledge then the king, and let me in.
> CITIZEN. That we cannot; but he that proves the king,
> To him will we prove loyal. Till that time
> Have we rammed up our gates against the world.[65]

Despite the fact that King John points to his crown, and promises to provide witnesses for support,[66] the citizens of Angiers, via their representative, make the correct estimation of their obligation: it is not up to them to decide who the king is. Divine Right makes that decision, and not the people themselves. Here, both King John and King Philip are in error for placing that responsibility onto the wrong parties. They err further in deciding to lay waste to the town and then determine who will reign over the ruins. In their uncertainty they threaten to batter more than the walls of Angiers: they threaten to tear down a protective wall between the king and his commons, a "wall" which actually protects them both.

To save themselves and to save the role of kingship, the citizens of Angiers propose the marriage between Lewes and Blanche. This union will allow them to be loyal to both England and France. With the two bound by espousal, the citizens will be free to bind themselves to the two of them. But this isn't simply a marriage; it is a coronation, which will assure the fealty of Angiers. This coronation works in reverse to the traditional model: upon his coronation a king is bound to his nation, and they enter into a partly paternal, partly filial relationship with him. In *Troublesome Raigne*, and in *King John*, the bond comes in the form of an espousal. The espousal comes first ("For at Saint Mary's chapel presently/The rites of marriage shall be solemnized"),[67] and is to be followed by the coronation, presumably much later, after Philip's death. This "premature coronation" nevertheless allows the people of Angiers to give both John and Philip their loyalty immediately, and so the marriage between Blanche and Lewes is also a pseudo-coronation for King John and King Philip. It is no wonder why, in both plays, Constance rails against the act. Aside from disenfranchising her son from the royal succession, the proposition shows King John's willingness to manipulate the reciprocal relationship between himself and his commons for his own personal gain. Although she accuses King Philip as

6. Oath, Obligation, and Obedience

well, Constance places the majority of the blame on King John. As Arthur's uncle, John's fault is greater than Philip's because John's assent to the espousal is destructive to England's succession, whereas Philip's is constructive to France's.

Peter of Pomphret is another example of how *Troublesome Raigne* and *King John* use a representative of the people to bring their issue of the peoples' fealty to the attention of the king. In Shakespeare's play, Peter is brought to King John by The Bastard, who reports on the deteriorating confidence of the populace, which he perceived as the monasteries were ransacked:

> BASTARD: How I have sped among the clergymen
> The sums I have collected shall express.
> But as I traveled hither through the land,
> I find the people strangely fantasied,
> Possessed with rumors, full of idle dreams,
> Not knowing what they fear, but full of fear.
> And here's a prophet that I brought with me
> From forth the streets of Pomfret, whom I found
> With many hundreds treading on his heels,
> To whom he sung, in ride harsh-sounding rhymes,
> That ere the next Ascension Day at noon,
> Your Highness should deliver up your crown.[68]

Despite The Bastard's dismissal of the people's fears as irrational and fantastic, his presentation of Peter of Pomphret to the king is a message: the prophet bears witness to the mood of the commoners, whose voices cannot reach King John in any other way. In V.i.22ff, Shakespeare's Pandulph demands King John's oath of submission to Rome on Ascension Day, the very day on which Peter of Pomphret predicted King John would give up his crown. Distressed, King John tries to talk himself into accepting the event as a coincidence:

> KING JOHN: Is this Ascension Day? Did not the Prophet
> Say that before Ascension Day at noon
> My crown I should give off? Even so I have.
> I did suppose it should be on constraint,
> But, heaven be thanked, it is but voluntary.

The "idle dreams" of the people have become a self-fulfilling prophecy, and yet King John is right to downplay the mysticism of the event. The

Sworn Bond in Tudor England

English people have been disturbed by King John's weakness and indecision; he has allowed himself to be bullied by Rome and to be threatened by Prince Arthur; he has lost the lands won by Richard Cordelion; and he is rumored to have called for a second coronation.[69] Such an act would not, as Salisbury claims, reinforce the king's majesty "with double pomp"[70]; instead, it would stand as a form of sacrilege, a way for King John to prove that he had never been properly invested in his kingship.[71] The people's loss of confidence, and their loss of fealty, is represented by their increased faith in signs and portents; but those omens are not the causes of the people's loss of fealty, they are the effects. In *Troublesome Raigne* King John simply demands that Peter of Pomphret "unsay" his prophecy to restore his people's faith in him:

> K. JOHN. Peter, unsay thy foolish doting dreame,
> And by the Crowne of England here I sweare,
> To make thee great, and greatest of thy kin.[72]

But this is an oath which King John cannot fulfill. When he swears "by the Crowne of England" to make Peter a great man, he swears by a crown which is already in the process of being taken from him. What's worse, Peter cannot "unsay" the prophecy. Prophecies are instruments of fate, and fate is guided by Divine Providence. What Peter prophesizes, therefore, he has not really said, because the voice behind Divine Providence is God's. King John therefore cannot decree that the prophecy be unsaid, nor can he swear that which cannot be sworn. The bond between king and God is revealed to be tragically broken, as the voice of Providence speaks through the mystic representative of the people instead of through the king's mystic relationship with the Divine.

The second coronation of King John is dealt with subtly in all three plays. *Troublesome Raigne* is the only play that depicts it onstage, but no oath is spoken and the crown is simply placed upon King John's head. The second coronation in Shakespeare's version takes place offstage, in a consistent effort to keep ritual and rite away from the action of the play. An oath is implied, just as the absence of ritual in the St. Edmundsbury oath implies its presence. Guy Hamel is certainly right to remark that both plays suggest that more is going on. About *Troublesome Raigne* he says, "One cannot know how elaborate the business on stage may have been, but it obviously involved more than clapping a coronet on John's head."[73] To what extent

6. Oath, Obligation, and Obedience

the author of *Troublesome Raigne* chose to depict the second coronation will never be known. Bale does not deal with the issue where Kynge Johan himself is concerned; rather, he attaches the issue cautiously to the figure Imperyall Majestie instead. Appearing after Kynge Johan's death, Imperyall Majestie combines a resurrected King John, Henry VIII, and an allegorical figure for Divine Right. He represents a continuing kingship that transcends death and is therefore perpetually legitimate. In him, Kynge Johan is metaphorically, but very subtly recrowned. In any case, the putative second coronation of King John was only a legend. He had been rumored to have wanted one, but there is no record that the event took place.

In *Troublesome Raigne* and *King John* Hubert is the character through which the playwrights can communicate individual conscience and its relationship to the bond of fealty between a man and his king. Hubert becomes uncomfortable with his loyalty when he is ordered to kill Arthur, and is ultimately unable to blind the boy. Later, when King John tries to disavow the order he gave, Hubert becomes even more disillusioned with his fealty, and he uses that disillusionment to validate his disobedience. Rather than looking for someone to absolve him of his fealty to King John, Hubert decides for himself that disobeying the king had been the right thing to do. It was a longstanding convention, stemming from the chivalric tradition, that a king could not require a subject to commit an unlawful deed. Suspicious that Prince Arthur may indeed by the rightful heir, and affected by the boy's youth, Hubert hesitates, despite his protest that he must ultimately obey and burn out Arthur's eyes. In Shakespeare's version he binds himself to the specific act of blinding Arthur, and explains, "I have sworn to do it/And with hot irons must I burn them out."[74] In *Troublesome Raigne* Hubert is even more pragmatic, binding himself to the king's authority generally, and reminding Arthur that as a subject Hubert is obligated to obey the king. He says, "My lord, a subject dwelling in the land/ Is tied to execute the king's command."[75] Arthur's references to statutory law are subsequently dismissed by Hubert: statutory law is not his responsibility. Hubert tries to tie his obedience to the sacredness of kingship, and reminds Arthur that in deferring to the king's command, he obeys God, even if that command is unjust.[76] Although Bale does not include the issue of Prince Arthur's claim in his play, his character Englande nonetheless iterates the same principle: that obedience to the king's command is a duty of faith, saying, "For be he good or bade, he is of Godes apoyntyng: / The good for the good, the bade ys for yll doing."⁷⁷ In Shakespeare's day, that premise was still considered to be true, in all quarters of society.

Appealing to Arthur's chivalric common sense has little effect on the reality of the situation, though, and Hubert decides to reinterpret his obligation. Ultimately, Hubert is not being truthful with himself, and conscience requires that his intent trump his obedience. Hubert determines that it is wrong to kill Arthur, even if it is the king's wish. *Troublesome Raigne* and *King John* both use this scene to present a cautious commentary on the role of sworn fealty in the light of a king's rashness. King John's denial of the command, and his placement of the blame on Hubert, drives the point home. King John, mistakenly thinking the boy to be dead, tells Hubert in Shakespeare's version that Hubert should have defied him. He says, "It is the curse of kings to be attended / By slaves that take their humors for a warrant," and "Hadst thou but shook thy head or made a pause.... Deep shame had struck me dumb, made me break off / And those fears might have wrought fears in me."⁷⁸ This episode appears almost immediately after John becomes distraught at the news of the death of his mother, and in rearranging historical events, Shakespeare achieves a point where he can make an unexpected historiographical comment: that perhaps John is too human to be king. Kingship, in John's era as in Elizabeth I's, was believed to transcend the humanity of the monarch. In being too strongly affected by his humanity, King John cannot uphold his duties the way he should. Instead, he wavers, decides, then un-decides, vows, recants, then blames and despairs.

John Bale blames Commynalte, his allegory for the peasantry, the least of all for his participation in the breakdown of Kynge Johan's relationship with the three estates. Cyvyle Order had borne the brunt of Bale's criticism of the civil lawyers as members of the commons; in his tract *A Disclosynge or Openynge of the Manne of Synne* he calls lawyers "the Popes sworne benefactors."⁷⁹ Bale reserves no such criticism for the peasantry, the largest part of the commons, and in *Kynge Johan* Commynalte is deliberately and conspicuously excluded from the interaction between Kynge Johan and his three estates. Blind and poverty-stricken, Commynalte is absent from the circle of power that seeks to supplant Kynge Johan, and therefore he is excused from any of the blame. Yet, Bale makes it clear that

6. Oath, Obligation, and Obedience

his status is less than enviable; although he has an active role in society, he is not permitted to express fealty of his own or swear to it in his own name. Throughout the play, Commynalte is continually forced to comply with the policies of both Church and Crown at once. His blindness, therefore, is depicted as an effect of that intimidation, as the consequence of an uneducated society driven into xenophobia. As a result, Commynalte escapes blame for his misplaced fealty. Despite his innocence, however, Commynalte will continue to be exploited. Things will change little for him, even after his relationship to his mother, Englande, is restored and he is saved. Ultimately, his fealty to the king will be sworn for him by someone else. Indeed, in 1539, when Kynge Johan was staged, the Oaths of Supremacy and Succession were imposed only upon clergy and magistrates, while leaving out the general public. Still, members of the commonalty could be punished for being disloyal or disobedient. In that sense they are obligated to that which they have never sworn. It is an odd parallel with their king, who as God's anointed owes his nation an obligation he never promised—an assertion made eloquently by Shakespeare's Prince Hal, later, in Henry IV, part I.

The death of King John in each play is depicted alongside the redemption of his tragic, defeated, and martyred figure. Each play depicts the poisoning of King John by a monk, and in *Troublesome Raigne* and *Kynge Johan* the murderer is absolved of his crime in advance, on the grounds that the murder of a tyrant is not regicide. In *Kynge Johan* the murderer is Dissymulacyon (doubled as Simon of Swinsett), and he is absolved by Sedycyon (doubled as Stephen Langton); in *Troublesome Raigne* the murderer is Thomas the Monke, who is absolved by the Abbot of Swinsett. In *King John*, the murder takes place offstage, and is committed by a monk. This aspect of the plays is also based on legend. Although rumors persisted that he had been poisoned, by peaches in some versions and ale in others, and although those rumors proved convenient to sixteenth-century dramatists, King John nonetheless died of dysentery in 1216.

As John Klause states in his discussion of King John's murder, the absolution of the murderers in *Troublesome Raigne* and *Kynge Johan* raises an uncomfortable issue. If the loyalty of King John's people has been absolved, and if King John has indeed been excommunicated, then there is no regicide, no interference with Divine Right. Although Shakespeare does not depict the absolution of the murderer, the extenuating circumstances of King John's death suggests the same thing as the other two plays: that John has been so thoroughly humanized that his death no longer bears grave consequence. Shakespeare's King John admits that he has been reduced to a statutory version of himself. His word is an edict issued by a man's physical body rather than a performance of the divinely-ordained Body of the King. He laments, "I am a scribbled form, drawn with a pen / Upon a parchment, and against this fire / Do I shrink up."[80] In *Troublesome Raigne* the scene is made poignant by King John's futile vow to go on Crusade. He pledges, "To take on me the holy crosse of Christ / And cary Armes in holy Christian warres."[81] This vow comes too little, too late, and after the bursting of the bowels of Thomas the Monke, King John realizes that he too has been poisoned. As he dies, he questions the value of his word, asking, "When have I vowd, and not infringd mine oath? / Where have I done a deed deserving well?"[82] In King John's last moment, Pandulph attempts one last papal subversion of what remains of the king's power: he tries to extract from him a deathbed vow to the Church:

> PANDULPH. King John farewell: in token of thy faith,
>   And sign thou dyest the servant of the Lord,
>   Life up thy hand, that we may witness here
>   Thou dyedst the servant of our Saviour Christ.[83]

But King John does not raise his hand — not because he is no longer a servant of Christ, but because he is no longer a servant of the Pope.

Both *Troublesome Raigne* and *King John* are Elizabethan plays being performed after the succession issues of the 1530s and 40s were long over; but in the 1590s the question of Elizabeth's succession persisted among her enemies. The two Elizabethan plays recall the nearly century-long effort by the Tudors to emphasize that kingship never really dies, but lives from age to age through the succession. In 1591 and 1598 Elizabeth I was old, and both playwrights were familiar with the idea that the body of the monarch never really died, even after the physical body of the person did.[84] Although King John dies defeated, he does not die unredeemed. For the Elizabethan audience of *King John* and *Troublesome Raigne*, King John becomes a remembered hero. Robert Jones acknowledges the figure of the remembered hero as one that appears throughout Shakespeare's histories. He is a "true hero of the past, and can be revived, phoenixlike and undi-

6. Oath, Obligation, and Obedience

minished to bear his nation's standard in a new age."⁸⁵ Throughout the two Elizabethan plays, the memory of Richard I had functioned in this way. Upon his death, King John is redeemed in both plays by the reestablishment of the sworn fealty of his nobles. As King John lays dying in *Troublesome Raigne*, the forsworn barons enter and swear their loyalty anew.⁸⁶ Having discovered that Lewes' loyalty had been an exploitation, the barons realize their error.⁸⁷ They enter the scene of John's deathbed with daggers in their hands, offering to kill themselves for King John's sake. Even as Lewes reminds the barons that they risk forswearing themselves, Salisbury reminds the Dauphin that the oath he took at the Altar of St Edmund was also false, because he forswore his own fealty to King Philip of France.⁸⁸ As he dies, therefore, King John is granted the fealty owed to him, and after his death that loyalty becomes part of the extended fealty that the nobles owe to the monarch, whomever he (or, in Elizabeth's case, she) may be.⁸⁹ John now enjoys the privilege of being a remembered hero, just like Richard.

A similar episode of forswearing occurs in Shakespeare's *King John*, but in Shakespeare's play the reestablishment of proper fealty is a more personal issue, with Shakespeare's Salisbury expressing regret on behalf of the others to a penitent Melun:

> SALISBURY: We do believe thee, and beshrew my soul
> But I do love the favor and the form
> Of this most fair occasion by the which
> We will untread the steps of damned flight,
> And like a bated and retired flood,
> Leaving our rankness and irregular course,
> Stoop low within those bounds we have o'erlooked
> And calmly run on in obedience
> Even to out ocean, to our great King John.⁹⁰

In both Elizabethan versions the first person to swear fealty to the new Henry III is The Bastard. In both cases it is fitting that even after the reestablishment of true fealty by King John's nobles, the person who most closely embodies Richard Cordelion should be the one to set a new precedent. The Bastard therefore becomes the one figure who unites Richard, John, and Henry within the legacy of the remembered hero. This act serves as a model for the guidance of the nobility as a group as to where their fealty should be placed: they are to be loyal to Richard, John, and Henry in the same fashion. At this point in both plays The Bastard does not have to argue for his own authority to do so, for his unwillingness to follow the English lords into treachery has given him the upper hand. In Shakespeare's play his true fealty allows him to speak for kingship when no one else will: "Now hear our English king, / For thus his royalty doth speak in me."[91]

John Bale continues his pattern of allegory and polemic in *Kynge Johan* with the use of two characters who accomplish the single task of establishing Kynge Johan as a remembered hero, a dynastic legacy who connects King John with Henry VIII. Imperyall Majestie stands as a semi-resurrected figure of kingship, a symbol for the stability of lasting reforms.[92] He is at once Kynge Johan and Henry VIII, yet he also stands apart from both figures as an allegory for the everlasting, indeed, undying principles of Divine Right. *Kynge Johan* was first performed in 1539, in the wake of the Acts of Supremacy and Succession, after the execution of Thomas More, and just before the fall of Bale's benefactor, Thomas Cromwell. Bale was well aware that the issue of the King's privilege and right extended beyond the King's person and, by way of the Act of Succession and the fealty oaths that accompanied it, into future generations of the Tudor dynasty.

Imperyall Majestie is accompanied by Veritas, the unadulterated Truth. Veritas chides Clergye, Cyvyle Order, and Nobylyte for their misplaced loyalty, and attacks the disparagement of Johan's name, which, he states, has been taken up by the chroniclers:

> Ye were never wele tyll ye had hym cruelly slayne,
> And now, beynge dead, ye have hym styll in disdayne.
> Ye have raysed up of hym most shamelesse lyes,
> Both by your reportes and by your written storyes.[93]

What offends Veritas most is that an untruthful historical record taints the verity of Divine Right. It is so odious he can hardly bear to show the villains the ugly reality of their deeds. He says, "In your glasse wyndowes ye whyppe your naturall kynges / As I sayde afore, I abhorre to shewe your doynges."[94] Clergye, Cyvyle Order and Nobylyte recant their oaths to Rome immediately:

> VER. But are ye sorye for thys ungodly worke?
> NOB. I praye to God! Els I be dampned lyke a Turke!
> VER. And make true promise ye wyll never more do so?
> CLER. Sir, never more shall I from true obedience goo.

6. Oath, Obligation, and Obedience

VER. What say yow brother? I must also have your sentence.
C. ORD. I wyll ever gyve to my prynce due reverence.[95]

Veritas concedes that perhaps the three might be forgiven by God, but Bale is hardly finished with his penitent Three Estates. Their recantations are depicted as fearful reactions to the terrifying presence of the Truth. Although no ritual accompanies their recantations, the fact remains that the lack of formality in the scene casts doubt upon the sincerity of Clergye, Cyvyle Order, and Nobylyte. Their spontaneous recantations may suggest epiphany, but they also suggest changeability concerning the fealty of English subjects. Although Shakespeare and the author of *Troublesome Raigne* allow such ironies to remain in their plays' endings, John Bale does not. Because he wishes for a completely didactic accomplishment for his play, Bale intercepts the repentance of the three villains and depicts a second, but necessary iteration of their intent to remain loyal.

The complete redemption of Clergye, Cyvyle Order, and Nobylyte comes in the form of a reconciliation between the three villains and Imperyall Majestie. In the reconciliation scene, the three wayward characters are made to swear a new oath to Imperyall Majestie. Unlike the oaths administered to them earlier by the play's papal villains, the new sworn fealty of Clergye, Cyvyle Order, and Nobylyte is devoid of ritual. Imperyall Majestie simply requires their truthful pledge as they kneel and ask pardon, saying, "Than must ye be sworne to take me for your heade."[96] Despite the simplicity of the oath itself, the scene is actually quite long, with each character giving his own speech in which he explains himself and asks for forgiveness. Here, the speeches appear as professions of conscience that accompany their new oath. They are descriptions of the terms to which the three will swear, praise for the faculties by which they will swear, and declarations of their true intent, with Truth as their witness. Although there are no relics and no altar, the scene establishes a new bond and also makes an objection to the rite of oath-swearing in its Catholic form. This depiction is somewhat similar to Shakespeare's omission of ritual swearing in *King John*. Both playwrights seek to drain performative power from the Catholic ritual oath: Shakespeare does so by excluding it from the action of his play, and therefore interrupting its performance, both literally and figuratively; Bale does so by including it in a new form, and thereby transforming the performance of the rite of oath-swearing, both literally and figuratively. Although Shakespeare did not know Bale's play, it is clear that by the 1590s there were attitudes about ritual swearing and performative power that were still as provocative as they had been in the 1530s.

There is to be no redemption for Sedycyon, since as an allegory of pure evil he cannot be reformed. Imperyall Majestie does, however, offer Sedycyon a pardon, in response to the villain's demand for sanctuary, "...so that thu tell the trewthe."[97] Sedycyon then gives his own speech describing his crimes and those of the Church of Rome. Where the speeches of Clergye, Cyvyle Order, and Nobylyte serve to parallel ritual swearing and establish grounds for their redemption, Sedycyon's speech (within which Imperyall Majestie provides continuous interjections) produces no such effect. Instead, Sedycyon's speech is depicted as an admittance of guilt that will pave the way to his execution.[98] As he does so, Sedycyon becomes the victim of his own device: the cleverly worded promise, which is more beneficial to its maker than its receiver. Imperyall Majestie uses the word "pardon" antonymously, just as Christ uses the word "reward" in reference to the hypocrites in Mat. 6: 2 and 4. Sedycyon will be hung, drawn, and quartered at Tyburn, with his head placed on a pike at London Bridge. Bale was of course aware of the way Sedycyon's death reflected ironically upon the recent deaths of reformers at Tyburn. Elizabeth Barton (The Holy Maid of Kent) had been executed for objecting to the King's marriage to Anne Boleyn in 1534; and John Houghton, the Prior of the Charterhouse, had been executed for refusing to swear an oath condoning the King's divorce from Katherine of Aragon, in 1535. Bale does not mean to suggest that Sedycyon is their confederate; rather, he means to suggest that although sedition must be purged from the land, it is to be found among the Catholic clergy rather than among the reformers.

All three plays bring together the medieval and Tudor worlds, and then move into what Barbara Hogdon calls "a specifically Elizabethan configuration, in which the need for security in the matter of the succession breeds a unity called "England to itself.""[99] Even Bale, in his 1560 rewrite of the play, cites England's "quene" as a figure who stands as a living representation of Imperyall Majestie. Each playwright was aware of the cliché of ideas surrounding legendary historical figures, and each was aware of the power such myths could generate. Each of the plays asks its audience whether it believes the old myth of King John, even as they ask whether

6. Oath, Obligation, and Obedience

that same audience believes the new myth of Henry VIII, or the emerging myth of Elizabeth I. As a group the plays present a significant critique of medieval chronicle-writing, whether via Shakespeare's clever scorn of unquestioned official sources, the author of *Troublesome Raigne's* disparagement of rumor and reaction, or Bale's radical reinterpretation of his former monkhood. In all three plays King John is not the John of the Chronicles, nor the John of popular imagination, as the process of historicism is reevaluated in terms of its value to the dialogue Elizabethan England is having with its past.

The reversals of allegiance at the end of Bale's play at first suggest that such exposition is a cliché of the first half of the century; but the same reversals appear in the other two plays. This fact shows that playwrights late in the century relied upon a similar dramatic illustration of the moral and spiritual struggle of sworn allegiance and service as their Henrician predecessors had. The same can be said for the mythologizing of history, of depicting the Chroniclers as tacticians who shaped history to their wills; although Bale's work is more blatant, the Elizabethan playwrights question historical methods, judgments, and rationalizations in much the same way. They were all aware of the efforts of their own generations to produce competing explanations for past events and representations of past figures. They were especially aware of the role played by sworn allegiance and its relationship to ceremony. Bale understood that the Oaths of Supremacy and Succession were conceived as constructions of assent with the express purpose of demythologizing the investment of historical events with ceremonialism. More agenda-driven than Shakespeare, the author of *Troublesome Raigne* uses the fictive persona of The Bastard to suggest to his audience that unexpected (and at times intrusive and unwelcome) voices mattered in the dialogue surrounding history, service, and ritual. Midway between the periods that span the three plays came the coronation of Edward VI. At the coronation, Cranmer had stated, "Neither could your ancestors lawfully resign up their crowns to the bishop of Rome or to his legates, according to the ancient oaths taken upon this ceremony."[100] It was a public statement asserting true intent over custom, of anointing over election, of God's word over man's; and moreso, it was a public staging, a depiction of a realizable truth, that English playwrights and theatergoers wished to see over and over again.

Chapter 7

Virtue by Degrees
Espousal in Spenser's Faerie Queene, *Books III–IV*

As he seeks to fashion the virtue of his reader, Spenser uses the method of the Poet Historical to create characters that emerge as archetypes representing varying degrees of chivalric and courtly excellence. Since his reader is identified as a gentleman, much of the exemplary behavior depicted in *The Faerie Queene* is directed at the knights who are presumed to embody the transition of ancient chivalric principles to Elizabethan patriotic values. Book III, however, examines that transition in an unexpected way: it uses the experiences of key female characters to promote aspects of *gentilesse* and worth that reflect good service to the queen. The stories of Britomart, Amoret, and Florimell connect Britain's ancient past and its Tudor present by illustrating how these characters make and are affected by sworn bonds in their respective roles. These bonds ultimately revolve around the concepts of betrothal and espousal. In Books III, and continuing into Book IV, sworn bond and espousal cooperate with the chivalric ideal, to promote the view that Elizabeth was a complete monarch, rather than a queen who had yet to be completed by marriage.[1]

Britomart is the model figure that combines both chivalric excellence and ideal royal marriage; her ability to fuse the two encompasses her own experience with her vision of Arthegall and her subsequent rescue of Amoret. As a symbol of modernity Britomart develops a profound understanding of sworn bond and imposes order upon situations which exhibit discord. Amoret stands as a symbol of the traditions of espousal among

7. Virtue by Degrees

the aristocracy in Elizabethan England. Her rescue sets Britomart apart as the exception to the rule. Florimell, however, represents the dysfunction of the ancient courtly love system. Her quest to find Marinell is based on an impetuous and careless vow, and the increasing danger in which she finds herself emphasizes the archaism of the medieval romance as a vehicle for the illustration of courtly virtue. For Spenser, characters like Britomart and Amoret demonstrate self-awareness by relating the bonds of espousal to chivalric worth and *gentilesse* (although Amoret does so to a lesser extent). Even though she is reunited with Marinell in Book IV, Florimell fails overall as she demonstrates the aspects of espousal and courtly love that Spenser feels represents social deterioration for the Elizabethan age. These depictions demonstrate Spenser's understanding of his nation's cultural history. *The Faerie Queene* is rife with archaic images from the medieval past, and yet Spenser resists an unqualified acceptance of that supposedly Golden Age. Even as he praises its successes, he does so in conjunction with a condemnation of its failures.

Part of Spenser's unique understanding of the Chivalric Age is rooted in the influence of Richard Mulcaster, who had been instructor to Spenser in his youth at the Merchant Tailors' School. Mulcaster had been a member of the Society of Archers, also called "The London Round Table." The group enjoyed much success in London society, and promoted the romantic legend of Camelot in both reimagination and reenactment of the events of the romances.[2] Although there had been similar groups since the time of Edward III, the Elizabethan interpretation of Arthurianism was unique. Namely, it revolved around the primary figure of a queen rather than a king. Elizabeth I was seen as a constructive force, a figure of power and stability, as Arthur had been; the queen's role stood in opposition to the traditional depictions of Guinevere and Morgan Le Fay as manipulative, destabilizing figures.[3] Moreover, the Elizabethan imagination concerning the Arthurian legend was affected by the events of the Reformation. As early as the 1530s polemicists had used the Arthurian legend to encourage a nationalist view of the past, which served to legitimate the Royal Supremacy. They were led by John Leland, whose work established a precedent for Henry VIII's claim that England had always been an empire.[4] Leland then published his *Assertio Inclytissimi Arturii Regis Brittaniae* in 1544, which claimed Arthur to be head of this empire. In 1578 Elizabeth

Sworn Bond in Tudor England

I gave her approval to a report by Dr. John Dee called "Her Majesty's Title Royal." The report claimed that Arthur had been a conqueror of those countries named in the queen's title. Moreover, William Lambard's *APXAIONOMIA* (1568) claimed that Arthur had been Christian. He attributes to Arthur the ancient custom of "folcmote," or feudal swearing of allegiance in the presence of the king's bishop. Such a fact supported a claim of Arthur's Christianity, and therefore justified Elizabeth as Supreme Governor of the Church of England. Mulcaster's group had experienced a hiatus during Mary's reign, but its reestablishment after Elizabeth's succession encouraged its members and other enthusiasts to connect a romantic view of the Arthurian legend with the optimism of Elizabethan nationalism and Protestantism.[5] In 1590, as Books I–III of *The Faerie Queene* were published, Elizabeth I stood as the living symbol of her dynasty's ancient right of sovereignty and its present right of governance over the English church. The successes of Spenser's female characters in Books III–IV therefore reflect the progressivism of Elizabeth's reign; their failures reflect the destructive elements of an archaic and deteriorated past. This outlook effectively divorces the Arthurian legend from the Catholicism and Continentalism of the medieval period and attaches it to the Elizabethan present.

Spenser's use of bonds of espousal in Book III provides an innovative view of chastity, because of the way the concept reflects on Elizabeth I. Essentially, chastity is defined not by an absence of sexual behavior, but by a ritual legitimization of it. As Spenser would later show in *Prothalamion*, Elizabethan society was familiar with ritualized betrothal, which had been traditional practice since at least the twelfth century. Ritualized betrothal allows chastity and espousal to act together; the two participants are linked by their promise to marry, but they cannot consummate the relationship until a later date. Ritual betrothal allows chastity to remain an important quality after the wedding as well, for the pair is now defined by their restraint, and the couple is limited to sexual contact only with one another. Although this concept is almost completely mythic, it had nonetheless been defended by proponents of married clergy since the 1530s. Britomart, Amoret, and Florimell must all seek or return to their betrothed or espoused partners. They are bound to Arthegall, Scudamore, and Marinell by the aspiration for spiritual benefit that characterizes an oath or vow; moreover, they are bound to the very act of swearing as well. The

7. Virtue by Degrees

irrevocable act of swearing produces the swearer's resolve to perform the bond; in the case of Book III, Britomart, Amoret, and Florimell must embark upon quests by which they will be united with their prospective husbands. Bonds of this type indicate a permanent objective that can only be discharged by the performance of the bond's original obligation: marriage. Spenser's characters can therefore only be released from their quests by performing the espousals to which they are bound. On that occasion, more vows will be sworn.[6] Although they are motivated by different reasons, each woman becomes characterized by how her bond of betrothal or espousal shapes her persona.

This is not to suggest that the three characters discussed in this chapter are connected. Britomart and Amoret are connected insomuch as Britomart must rescue her amidst her own quest to find Arthegall; Amoret, although she is rescued by Britomart, emerges from the House of Busyrane to find Scudamore gone[7]; and Florimell seeks Marinell on her own, without contact with the other two characters. This apparent disjointedness nonetheless corresponds to Spenser's use of extended metaphor and continued allegory in his poem, as a "darke conceit." Unlike common metaphors, a "conceit" relies on resemblances between seemingly unrelated, or obscurely related, vehicles and tenors. In creating a "conceit" a poet must cause his reader to see similarities which are more subtle than in other works. In *The Faerie Queene* this association happens as both story and characters develop within the intricate pattern of Spenser's structure. Spenser employs the method of *entrelacement*, in which he braids together several different plots and moves among them without directly referring to connections between them. Paul Alpers rightly suggests that the reader is responsible for generating meaning within the "darke conceit," since a comprehensive meaning is unlikely to be generated by the poem itself.[8] I do not mean to suggest that sworn bond cannot be traced through the plots of Book III by itself. It certainly can, but with much difficulty. I agree with Alpers that an analysis which seeks to overcome the problems of structure and/or organization within the cantos produces the best result. It facilitates and clarifies the reader's understanding of how the "darke conceit" works regarding what happens when, where, and to whom. Sworn bond, as it relates to espousal and betrothal, connects Britomart, Amoret, and Florimell by way of a manifold depiction. The forms of these bonds vary, as do their effects. These variances and differences, however, cause the characters and their stories to refer to each other precisely because of the many levels on which Spenser causes the concept of sworn bond to operate.

Following the models provided by Middle English and French romances, Spenser uses Britomart as the model for the worthy knight in Book III. Loyal to both church and monarch, the ideal knight is chaste, protects the weak and the poor, and condemns evil in all its forms. Upon his investiture, a knight swears to adhere to a high standard of nobility in both word and deed. He further swears to maintain a disposition of courtesy, to keep his word, and to respect all oaths.[9] In Book III, Britomart's bond of espousal governs the sense of worth with which she can be rewarded as she embarks on her quest to seek Arthegall. If she succeeds, she will justify the Elizabethan view that the Tudors are the bearers of Arthurian ancestry; she will at once represent Elizabeth I, and the queen's own ancestor. Spenser knew, however, that in order for Britomart to achieve her goals she must accomplish what Elizabeth I did not: she must be defined by espousal. Without this aspect of her character, Britomart threatens to stand for the end of a dynasty rather than for its beginning. In 1590 that idea was dangerously close to the truth, but it was a truth which Spenser chose to coat with optimism. The idea of Elizabeth was that of a youthful, marriageable, progenitor of a continuing dynasty, even if the real queen was not.

Book III therefore presents a unique harmony of desire and honor through Britomart. The harmony she embodies establishes a separation of love from lust early on in the Book, pairing her budding chivalry with the cultivation of her chastity. Rather than being in love with the man Arthegall, she is in love with the idea of Arthegall, represented by the phantom vision she sees in Merlin's mirror. Her perception of sworn bond relies heavily on her understanding of how chastity and chivalry relate to her destiny as Arthegall's betrothed. As she develops a sense of purpose and resolves to embark on her quest, Britomart learns to unify expressions of love, sex, and chastity with martial behavior. Although Britomart herself does not swear for Arthegall's sake,[10] she develops a profound understanding of the concept as she reacts to and is affected by the oaths and vows of others where espousal is concerned. She becomes devoted to it, employing her strong impressions as ways to augment her own virtues for the sake of others, and for Arthegall as well.

7. Virtue by Degrees

In III.ii she relates the story of her quest to the Redcrosse Knight with an acute sense of self-awareness, revealing that she has already learned much about what her quest means and why her own sense of virtue is so important. As she looks back on her discovery of Arthegall, and on her resulting love-sickness, she illustrates how Glauce's devotion and Merlin's wisdom have taught her about the virtues of espousal and sworn bond. When Cupid's arrow renders her love-sick she learns her first lesson in human resolve. Glauce vows to heal her ailment, professing, "...I avow by this most sacred hand / Of my deare foster child, to ease thy griefe / And win thy will..."[11] Britomart learns that love is the cause of her apparent malady, and she forms an appreciation for the power of love by way of Glauce's vow to solve the problem of a destiny unfulfilled. Glauce's response to Britomart's further plaints of illness is another vow to help seek her destiny, as she says, "Then I avow to thee, by wrong or right / To compass thy desire and find that loved knight."[12] Glauce's two vows make a great impression upon Britomart, and Britomart soon agrees to consult Merlin about the effects of the mirror. These experiences allow Britomart to combine the devotion of Glauce with the foresight of Merlin in her own persona. Britomart resolves to fulfill her nurse's vows herself; although well-meaning, Glauce has no capacity to make good on her vows. Britomart takes on the obligation to fulfill them, and subsequently takes on knighthood. Although the chivalric tradition mandates an investiture with an oath, Spenser does not depict this ritual. Instead, Britomart's virtue and destiny provide the authority to invest her into "advent'rous knighthood."[13] Spenser can therefore avoid an uncomfortable depiction of oath-taking in the Catholic tradition. To emphasize this point, as soon as she resolves to take on knighthood Britomart transforms from a heart-sick girl to a fearless knight dedicated to her quest. She stands as an improved figure, one who is characterized by reason, wisdom, and temperance.[14] She interprets her experiences, accepts Glauce's devotion, and hears Merlin out completely before declaring that she must fulfill her destiny. She resolves to change the direction of her life without rashness or impetuosity, and without misconceptions about the importance of her duty.

Although she does not marry Arthegall within the scope of Spenser's poem, Britomart's commitment to her journey points to her acceptance of her search for Arthegall as a form of betrothal. As she seeks her destiny,

Britomart develops a conceptual understanding of espousal as it relates to her identity. Britomart sees her quest as a precursor to marriage, and thereby places the importance of who she will be over who she presently is. One of the defining aspects of betrothal is that the parties agree to adapt their identities in this very way. Interestingly, Britomart becomes betrothed to Arthegall without a ritual of betrothal, or even a proposal of marriage on his part. Here, Spenser uses the episode of Merlin's mirror to turn the Elizabethan convention of betrothal on its head: although Glauce is Britomart's guardian, she is not in control of the betrothal; Britomart is. Such an idea was controversial in Spenser's day, when private betrothals were rare, and sometimes punishable without the consent of parents or guardians. Nevertheless, young people during the Elizabethan era often contracted private betrothals, in defiance of parental authority. In these cases, the contracts were difficult to undo: as T.G.A Nelson points out, "Once the spousal *per verba de praesenti* had been effected, parents or guardians would be (theoretically) unable to force either party into a marriage with another partner, since each would be, though in a limited sense, married already."[15] This is why Glauce acts the way she does when Britomart becomes lovesick. She knows that Britomart has become betrothed to Arthegall in so many words (or perhaps without any), and she cannot undo it. Merlin later validates the betrothal as divinely ordained, saying, "The man whom heavens have ordaynd to bee / The spouse of Britomart is Arthegall."[16]

Britomart's betrothal to Arthegall is given further validation because there is a love token involved. The presentation of love tokens could strengthen an Elizabethan betrothal agreement, and in some cases, could override parental protest of the bond. With Britomart the concept of the love token is made mystic, as it takes place via Merlin's mirror. Britomart does not exchange anything physically with Arthegall, but they are joined by way of the pneumatic gaze, with the mirror itself as the binding token.[17] Here Spenser inverts the Petrarchan metaphor of the lady at her mirror, which had been well adapted by his contemporaries, such as Shakespeare and Sidney, in their respective sonnet sequences. Elizabethan poet-lovers and their beloved subjects look into the mirrors of each other's eyes, to see themselves reflected there.[18] In this construction, English Renaissance poets use the metaphor of the mirror to define the moment in which the lovers' self-images come into contact with each other.[19] Spenser redefines this

7. Virtue by Degrees

model, ironically bringing it closer to Petrarch's vision: the lover cannot see his reflection in his beloved's eyes, just as Petrarch cannot see himself in Laura's eyes. Although Arthegall cannot see Britomart, her gaze is joined with his image, and they are bound by the mirror as love token between them. Glauce is the guardian who witnesses the event, but it is only after Merlin's proclamation that the vision is divinely ordained that the betrothal is validated. In this case, Britomart again defies Elizabethan conventions of betrothal — she alone determines the betrothal, without consent from Arthegall. As Lesel Dawson interestingly points out, Britomart then dresses as a knight to become the mirror image of her betrothed, thus taking him with her on her quest.[20] The betrothal is now complete, as both parties are represented.

In order to emphasize the connection between her betrothal to Arthegall and her sense of chivalric duty, Spenser shows Britomart entering into sworn bonds with other knights. These encounters demonstrate her understanding of chivalry and her ability to embody its principles ideally. By the time she meets Guyon in III.i, Britomart has already been searching for Arthegall for an undetermined amount of time.[21] It is clear, however, that her understanding of her duty has led to a sublime perception of sworn leagues among knights. She contests Guyon, and beats him fairly. The two then reconcile and make allies of each other:

> Thus reconcilement was betweene them knit,
> Through goodly temperance, and affection chaste,
> And either vowd with all their power and wit,
> To let not others honour be defaste,
> Of friend or foe, who ever it embaste,
> Ne armes to beare against the others side:
> And with that golden chaine of concorde tyde.
> So goodly they all agreed, they forth yfere did ryde.[22]

Britomart's persona combines both chastity and chivalry, a mixture of what Dame Juliana Berners had called "temporall" and "ghostly" virtues.[23] The reconciliation of Britomart and Guyon is marked by Britomart's respect for her adversary's talent, by her own restraint in the fight, and by her recognition of his honor. The result of such chivalrous behavior is Britomart's ability to overcome the sexual tensions that exist between her and Guyon. They make a chaste vow of allegiance and accept each other on equal terms. Spenser notes that the bond created by the vow represents a "golden chaine of concord tyde." Unlike a commonplace bond which binds two knights of the same sex, or a man and woman on the grounds of betrothal alone, the bond between Britomart and Guyon represents a harmonious, and ultimately ideal, synthesis of chivalry and chastity that is essential to Britomart's development. Spenser must address this issue even though Guyon does not yet know that Britomart is a woman. Britomart must maintain a continual affirmation of her chastity for her own sake; to overlook chastity in her sworn allegiance with a male knight would be to compromise her devotion to her betrothal.

As Britomart travels alone she must expand her understanding of sworn bond by imposing it upon others. She must especially do so for the sake of a helpless victim. At Castle Joyeous she is called upon by her duty to defend the Redcrosse Knight from Malacasta's six champions. Within the scope of the episode, Britomart defends Redcrosse because his cause is just. In a larger sense, Spenser demonstrates to the reader that Britomart must preserve the overall value of espoused chastity by defending his marriage to Una, even if only the reader knows of his marriage.[24] The six knights who assault Redcrosse are in the sworn service of their own Lady, Malacasta, who has compelled them to force others into her service.[25] Upon hearing this story, Britomart contemplates it, saying, "Perdy ... the choise is hard."[26] Hesitating to react, Britomart does not fight until she comes to a satisfactory moral conclusion.[27] The "hard choice" she must make is between Redcrosse's bond with his lady, and the bonds Malacasta's knights have sworn. As the six knights attempt to justify Malacasta's law, Britomart listens to their misconceived notions about chivalry and courtly love. Finally, she applies Redcrosse's dilemma to her own situation and invalidates Malacasta's injunction:

> Love have I sure (quoth she) but Lady none;
> Yet I will not fro mine owne love remove,
> Ne to your Lady will I service done,
> But wreake your wrongs wrought to this knight alone,
> And prove his cause.[28]

Britomart chooses to fight for Redcrosse because Malacasta's law is offensive to her own situation: she, presumably, would not forswear her betrothal to Arthegall for Malacasta's — or anyone's sake. Although Malacasta's knights

7. Virtue by Degrees

are sworn to her service, the fact that their courtly love vow demands that they force others to forswear their own lovers makes their devotion to Malacasta a travesty of courtliness. The Redcrosse Knight's vow is therefore the valid one, in Britomart's correct estimation. She is more correct than she knows: although she does not realize it, Redcrosse is married to Una.[29] Britomart has defended espousal, a bond whose virtue surpasses that of the premarital (and extramarital) courtly love vow. Here, the courtly tradition is identified as outdated, irrelevant, and unworthy of a place in the heart of a true monarch. Its relation to Britomart's situation is therefore appropriate: as the knight of chastity, Britomart's virtue is Providential, and she is destined to make the right choice. Although she is an Arthurian figure, she bears no trace of the destructive courtly love system that had undermined and destroyed Camelot. That element is left at Malacasta's castle. To represent progressivism, Britomart must leave behind problems which are too ingrained in the errors of the past to resolve.

Britomart swears a platonic league with The Redcrosse Knight when they part ways. Having told him the story of the birth of her knighthood, and having learned more about Arthegall from him, the two profess their friendship "with unfeigned heart" at the end of Canto iii.[30] Spenser describes it as "A friendly league of love perpetuall,"[31] and relates it to the character of Queen Elizabeth herself:

> Well worthy stock, from which the branches sprong,
> That in late yeares so faire a blossome bare,
> As thee o Queene, the matter of my song,
> Whose lignage from this Lady I derive along.[32]

The two episodes of Britiomart's platonic leagues with other knights function together to illustrate her development as a knight of ever-increasing conviction. She emerges as an ideal example of worth as she swears leagues with two different knights, and gives both men the same regard. As a result of her experiences, Britomart becomes even more fully dramatized that she had been at the beginning of her quest. She learns to fight for just and worthy causes, yet she learns that a total defeat of false devotion and devalued espousal cannot always be effected.

Spenser recalls this very idea, when, in III.xi and xii, Britomart saves Amoret from a coerced denial of her husband Scudamore by the sorcerer Busyrane. In this episode, Britomart repeats her effort of Canto i to defend sworn espousal in anticipation of her own marriage to Arthegall. Busyrane has abducted Amoret at her wedding "before the bride was bedded."[33] Because the marriage has not been consummated, Busyrane believes he can compel Amoret to deny her marriage vows to Scudamore. Here Spenser depicts another situation reflective of marriage laws of the period: marriages could not be considered valid unless consummation had taken place. In the 1590s, a couple who had married in secret could be considered lawfully married if they testified to have had "carnal dole."[34] Amoret's moral resistance to Busyrane's coercion, however, provides the extent of the protest on behalf of her marriage. Defeated, emasculated, and debilitated, Scudamore lies wallowing on the ground outside Busyrane's house, unable to defend his marriage. Scudamore's failure to restore his espousal is rooted in the way his marriage to Amoret was established: having defeated "twentie knights" in a single battle, Scudamore took Amoret away as his prize, and wedded her "as did him behove."[35] Unlike Britomart's one-sided, but virtuous, betrothal to Arthegall, Amoret's espousal is characterized by objectification and seizure. Amoret is able to resist Busyrane's tortures out of devotion to her marriage vows, but she cannot escape. Scudamore's sense of loss after Amoret's capture, therefore, is a form of self-punishment. It is tied closely to the concept of *acedia*, or self-absorbed suffering that is distinct from other forms of love-melancholy, namely Britomart's.[36]

Acedia, as Marion Wells points out, is "an agonized desire that presumptuously forestalls its own progress toward the desired object."[37] It stems from the Petrarchan tradition and describes a situation in which the lover feeds on his own tears in an act of autoerotic self-wounding.[38] In Scudamore's case, the suffering arises from emasculation: having taken Amoret as a prize, he now must tolerate the violent seizure of his bride by another man. His loss is depicted as the loss of an object rather than that of a phantasmic idea, which the beloved ideally represents. Busyrane's disruption of the wedding ceremony and abduction of Amoret stalls the consummation of the marriage and transforms Scudamore into an emasculated servant of Cupid, a degraded antithesis of both a knight and a husband.[39] Only the restoration of the espousal will cure Scudamore's melancholy, but this goal lies outside Scudamore's capacity. Scudamore's acquisition of Amoret is represented by the hypermasculine tradition of winning a woman in battle; but his objectification of Amoret causes her to be coveted by

7. Virtue by Degrees

Busyrane, who sees her as a mere addition to his temple dedicated to Cupid's objectified conquests. The only thing that stands between Busyrane and his total possession of Amoret is her refusal to recant her marriage vow. Scudamore all but abandons his bond and wallows in near-despair. He continually feeds his melancholy with self-pity, while the phallic symbol of his knighthood — his sword — lies on the ground.

Unlike Scudamore, Britomart does not suffer from *acedia*; although she is lovesick for Arthegall, her melancholy is not characterized by self-absorption or degradation of her martial prowess. Indeed, her lovesickness has caused her to pursue chivalry, and to excel in knightly virtues. As she observes Scudamore's debilitation and hears his story, she assumes the fulfillment of his espousal. Moreover, she corrects his disavowal of his chivalric duty and restores to him "his armes, which he had vowed to disprofesse."[40] She literally *re*-masculates Scudamore by negating that vow: she dresses him in his armor, helps him to stand erect, and returns his sword to him.[41] Scudamore cannot endure the flames that surround Busyrane's house, however; and Britomart must leave him outside while she enters the house to restore his espousal to Amoret. In doing so, Britomart defends her own impending espousal to Arthegall. Although the marriage of Scudamore and Amoret has not been consummated, vows taken must be fulfilled; and object and phantasm must be united to effect true espousal. Here, Britomart's attitude toward unconsummated nuptials mirrors that of Elizabethan judges, who hesitated to force eloped couples apart if their parents or guardians disapproved of the match. Even if the marriage had not been consummated, the exchange of vows and tokens was often enough to uphold the bond; the mutual understanding that the couple considered themselves to be man and wife could also be enough to secure it.[42] Insofar as Britomart restores the espousal of Scudamore and Amoret, she validates her own betrothal to Arthegall.

This time Britomart's victory is marked by destruction. She forces Busyrane to submit to her and destroys his enchanted house.[43] In doing so, she preserves the exclusivity that exists between spouses, and by extension, between betrothed lovers. The destruction of the House of Busyrane at the end of Canto xii recalls the dilemmas of Canto i, but provides a greater sense of satisfaction for the knight of chastity than her victory over Malacasta does. The similarity of these events reflects upon Britomart's ability to make distinctions between battles she can immediately win and battles which must be continually fought. Battles in the name of espousal are winnable because they are supported by formal vows, and are validated institutionally. Battles for the sake of the courtly love system, however, are more complex, and victories can be as ambiguous as the courtly love vow itself.[44] Ironically, this issue is made more complex by the alternative endings of Book III. In the 1590 version, Amoret and Scudamore are united by "that faire Hermaphrodite," who, although she is moved in spirit, nonetheless half-envies their bliss when she views them as a unified pair, "as grown together quite."[45] For now, her feminine vulnerability and Arthegall's martial prowess are fused in her, betrothed but unfulfilled; she must observe, and perhaps envy, the fulfillment of espousal in Amoret and Scudamore. In the 1596 version, Britomart leaves the House of Busyrane with the rescued Amoret to find Scudamore gone:

> But he, sad man, when he had long in drede
> Awayted there for Britomarts returne,
> Yet saw her not nor signe of her good speed,
> His expectation to despaire did turne.[46]

Her efforts have preserved the couple's marriage vows, but they have failed to provide either security for Amoret or perseverance for Scudamore. The Knight Britomart now possesses the still-objectified Amoret as her *de facto* lady. Both scenarios present a paradox of winnability that serves to remind Britomart that even when sworn bond is successfully defended, triumph is not always clearly defined.

The ability to make such distinctions and to perceive the importance of the role of the love vow in Faeryland (however problematic it may be) is precisely what causes Florimell to fall well behind Britomart or even Amoret as a model of chastity. Florimell emerges as a figure who embodies the ironies of *gentilesse*, and its relation to chastity as a virtue. In Florimell, Spenser presents an essentially good, but deeply flawed character; although he credits her with goodness of intent, and acknowledges that Marinell is her one true love, Spenser allows her choices to lead to seemingly endless dangers and troubles. These choices revolve around her use, and abuse, of the courtly love vow. Despite her beauty and virtue, Florimell does not possess the chivalric qualities that Britomart does; nor is she endowed with the legitimacy of purpose that Amoret's marriage vows allow her. Instead,

7. Virtue by Degrees

Florimell possesses qualities of gentility attributed to ladies of the court in English and French Romances. One of these qualities is the courtly love vow that binds her to Marinell. Unfortunately, problems within this stereotyped pairing arise when Florimell abandons her *gentilesse* to seek Marinell. In doing so she creates a dysfunctional form of espousal that belongs to the past.

Fearing her knight to be dead, Florimell makes her first mistake: she departs the court and sets out on a quest to find him on her own. In doing so she vows "never to returne againe" until she finds him.[47] Pursuing her is a Dwarf, who sees in Prince Arthur an opportunity to remedy the situation. The Dwarf begs Prince Arthur to set out after Florimell and return her to Gloriana's court:

> Therefore, faire Sir, for love of knighthood gent,
> And honour of trew Ladies, if ye may
> By your good counsel, or bold hardiment,
> Or succour her, or me direct the way;
> Do one, or other good, I you most humbly pray.[48]

Here the Dwarf asks Prince Arthur to negate Florimell's vow. Since the making of the vow is a bond which can only be released by the performance of its original obligation, Florimell disenfranchises herself from returning to court until she finds Marinell. Both the Dwarf and Prince Arthur desire a nullification of this vow because of its terms and the circumstances under which it is made. Because the vow is hasty and because Florimell is not capable of protecting herself on her quest, Prince Arthur is justified in embarking on his own quest to nullify Florimell's effort. In doing so he will become a character who seeks to restore order to Faeryland, just as Florimell, however unwittingly, undermines that order.

Florimell's vow to find Marinell is more than a mere description of her intentions; it binds her to him and identifies the two as exclusive to each other in the courtly love tradition. Romances in the Arthurian tradition had for centuries promoted the view that the courtly love vow bound the knight and his lady in a manner that suggested betrothal, even in the event that the lady was already married, as in the case of Guinevere or Iseult. The courtly love vow demands complete devotion of the lovers to each other: a knight must go to the ends of the earth to search out his beloved should she be imprisoned; and a lady must wait for many years until her knight returns from a quest.[49] In most cases, however, the lovers are prisoners of fate: if the lady is married, she and her knight must tryst in secret. They cannot enjoy institutional validation of their relationship: in the case of Tristan and Iseult, they must die in order to be together. In the case of Florimell and Marinell, their espousal stands in direct opposition to that of Britomart and Arthegall. Britomart and Arthegall are instruments of Providence, and not prisoners of fate. Their espousal is meant to build a dynastic empire, and not to undermine a kingdom.

Florimell swears in a state of near hysteria. She leaves the court of the Faerie Queene without an escort, desperate to find the man who is now bound to her by her vow. Through Florimell, Spenser dismisses the courtly tradition as archaic because its rashness undermines individual choice and empowerment in espousal. At the heart of the issue is the tradition of espousal *per verba de praesenti* — a means by which lovers could become espoused by simply declaring themselves to be married. Between the twelfth and seventeenth centuries, couples in both Catholic and Protestant Europe could do just that.[50] Espousals of this type function much the same way in real life as they do in literature: they stand as a protest against arranged marriages, and especially forced unions. Verbal assent was the strongest evidence that the two parties indeed considered themselves to be married, regardless of the existence of a marriage contract, dowry, witnesses, or exchange of tokens. Church courts, when asked to rule on the validity of such an espousal, asked both parties whether they regarded themselves as man and wife. If the two assented, the espousal could be, and often was, considered to be legitimate.[51] In the last quarter of the sixteenth century marriage laws gave more liberty to couples concerning this tradition, especially to brides. Young women were allowed more control over the legal validity of their espousals, and therefore more of a choice over who they would marry than they had been given before. This development in Elizabethan marriage laws proved to be compelling to writers of the time. As T.G.A. Nelson observes, Renaissance writers acknowledged "the alluring presence within that law of recognition of the integrity of the speaking subject, the "I" that performed — or sought to perform — a change of civil status by means of a verbal utterance."[52] Writers like Spenser, who were aware of the challenges to espousal *per verba de praesenti* by outraged parents and greedy guardians, noted the romanticism apparent in the subject.[53]

7. Virtue by Degrees

They also noted that the granting of more rights for espoused couples was directly related to the fashioning of the self. Florimell's vow conflates with this view. It represents neither an assertion of her individuality nor her freedom of choice; rather, it stands as a testament to her lack of control. Florimell is a figure of and for the past, running aimlessly, and in constant peril, through Faeryland. In 1590 London the practice of espousal *per verba de praesenti* was legal and undergoing reform; Catholic Europe, however, had banned the practice through a decree of the Council of Trent nearly thirty years before. This coincidence allows Spenser to depict a practice whose ideals speak directly to the bygone romance of the Arthurian past while outliving the conventions of Catholicism at the same time. Britomart's performative espousal with Arthegall represents the type of progressivism Spenser wishes for his poem to reflect, and for his queen to see.

Florimell's choices represent an abandonment of *gentilesse*: when she leaves the court she also leaves behind the "debonair" self-restraint for which she is well-known.[54] Moreover, she turns her back on the attitude of deferment expected from courtly ladies: ideally, she is to enlist a knight into her service to accomplish such a task for her. Florimell's actions result in her assumption of the role of victim for the rest of Book III, as she becomes fugitive, helpless, and constantly threatened by male attackers. Eventually, she finds herself the prisoner of Proteus, unable to escape on her own and fulfill her vow. She becomes a hapless object of lust rather than a subject of desire, as Britomart is. Just as Britomart challenges threats to chastity and fidelity, Florimell flees from them. Florimell's chastity is attacked violently and brutally, as Spenser denies her the privilege he gives to Amoret: the ability to refuse her attacker and withstand painful, but nonsexual torture designed to cause her to relent. By Canto viii, more knights have agreed to set out to save Florimell. Because of her "ungentle" behavior — represented by her rash vow — it will take a whole group of worthy knights to remedy the situation. Britomart, however, will not be among them. In keeping her in a close parallel with effective sworn bond, functional espousal, and the queen's own virtue, Spenser keeps Britomart well away from Florimell's dilemma.

In an ironic nod to Florimell's problematic espousal-by-declaration, Spenser resolves her situation much later, in Book IV. A six-year gap separates the compositions of Books III and IV, and the resolution of

Florimell's situation can be taken in the light of other matters, such as the revision of the end of Book III, to suggest that Spenser was not entirely satisfied with Book III's unresolved issues. At the very least, the issues of sworn bond and espousal did not leave his mind. The reunion of Florimell and Marinell relies almost completely upon the appropriation of Florimell's bond by others. The performance of the bond relies upon two authority figures who validate and institutionalize the espousal of the lovers: Cymodoce, Marinell's mother, and Neptune. Cymodoce, unable to rescue Florimell herself, makes "humble suit" to Neptune to procure her release.[55] The sea god drafts a warrant, "Under the sea-gods seale autenticall," which calls for Florimell's immediate freedom.[56] Proteus is bound to the warrant by his sworn allegiance to Neptune, and Florimell is officially betrothed to Marinell. Interestingly, once the bond is validated by appropriate authority figures, the relationship between Florimell and Marinell becomes retroactive. They become officially betrothed, but must wait until Book V, Canto ii for their wedding. They are not permitted to live as a married couple immediately. Unlike Britomart, who develops a stronger understanding of sworn bond with each experience, and unlike Amoret, who displays a complete understanding of marital fidelity, Florimell comes no closer to understanding the implications of her vow than she had been when she made it. Although her situation is resolved, she must wait for the completion of the performance of her bond.

Britomart's union with Arthegall in Book IV also reflects Elizabethan betrothal traditions; but here, Spenser emphasizes Britomart as a modern figure, with a fully realized persona. Rather than being passive while her issues are resolved by others, as Florimell is, Britomart "sets things right" herself. Arthegall bests her on the field of battle, and almost immediately begins a suit for her hand.[57] As these events unfold, Britomart changes certain aspects of her behavior, namely those which identify her as a pseudo-masculine figure. Arthegall takes on the role of the chivalric lover, wooing his lady with a volley of oaths and vows, per the custom of courtly devotion:

> At last through many vowes which forth he pour'd,
> And many othes, she yeeled her consent
> To be his love, and take him for her Lord,
> Til they with marriage meet might finish that accord.[58]

7. Virtue by Degrees

In doing so Spenser reestablishes Arthegall as the man in the relationship; part of this role is for Arthegall to pledge his love to his lady, and await her acceptance of the bond. Britomart relinquishes her chivalric role willingly: she listens to his suit for days, content "To lend an eare and softly to relent," and finally accepts his hand.[59] Effectively emasculated, Britomart is thrust back into an exclusively female role so that a more customary, and institutionally validated, image of betrothal emerges. In the traditional model, the gentleman establishes the bond, and the lady affirms it; here, Britomart and Arthegall create a bond that is the antithesis of Florimell's bond with Marinell. It employs elements of the chivalric tradition that give it its romantic charm; but then it moves beyond those elements to become a progressive act. As such, theirs is very much a betrothal of the 1590s: it nods at tradition, but there is no need for the involvement (or interference) of parents, ancient sacred traditions, or outdated institutions. Because part of Britomart's quest involved learning experiences by which she developed a profound understanding of sworn bond, Britomart is able to make a prudent and sound decision about her betrothal. Their inevitable separation, therefore, does not signify unresolved issues, but rather points to the couple's uninterrupted virtues. Upon marrying Arthegall, she will reassume her customary role in the espousal as bride, wife, and queen. In this way Spenser honors the chivalric tradition while overcoming it, in a way which is satisfactory to him as a poet, a patriot, and a reformer.

It is perhaps appropriate then, that Britomart leaves Arthegall accompanied by Scudamore. As she parts Arthegall with "right heavy mind,"[60] she joins Scudamore in his search for Amoret, once again taking on responsibility for the sworn bond of another to guarantee the validity of espousal. In helping Scudamore fulfill the terms of his betrothal, Britomart will lend even more validation to her bond with Arthegall. Britomart will not make hasty, uncourtly mistakes as Florimell has, nor will she become a victim characterized by loss, as Amoret has. She, like these characters, is identified by separation from her beloved; but hers is at first defined by Providence, and then by chivalric duty. Unlike the others, the separation of Britomart from Arthegall reflects the strength of her betrothal and eventual espousal rather than its weakness. This depiction is part of Spenser's overall motive to connect Britomart to Elizabeth I as an allegorical representation rather than solely as an ancestor.

Sworn Bond in Tudor England

Ultimately, all of the situations in which these betrothed/espoused couples find themselves reflect upon the marriage issues that revolved around the queen. At issue here is the manner in which Elizabeth I empowered her unmarried state. As Anne McLaren points out in her study of monarchy and gender, the politics of succession had at first fantasized about ideal physical unions for the queen. She states, "In the early years of Elizabeth's reign ... marriage promised a solution to the problem posed by female rule. It offered a means by which Protestant rectitude and Tudor royal blood could be conjoined ... and a king constituted, ambiguously through the marriage itself or through issue."[61] After the queen was no longer of childbearing age, and after the questions of marriage had long been given up on, the fantasy changed: it evolved into a desire for an espoused political union between England and Scotland, between international Protestantism and the English imperial crown. Since Elizabeth's accession in 1559, the idea of an Anglo-Scottish alliance dressed up as espousal had been reinterpreted regularly, but with difficulty. Unlike her rivals Lady Catherine Grey and Lady Jane Grey, Elizabeth had not been espoused before her accession; both Grey sisters had, as McLaren states, "been subsumed in and constrained by noble English Protestant males [Dudley and Hertford] when their claims to the throne were under consideration."[62]

Spenser was attracted to a literary version of this fantasy marriage construction. In his hands the marriage between Britomart and Arthegall represents a new espousal between Protestant rectitude (Britomart) and Tudor Arthurian ancestry (Arthegall). Their espousal is continually reaffirmed and legitimated even though it is characterized by separation and looks forward to a distant, uncertain fulfillment. Although the dysfunction of the other two couples is meant to contrast with Britomart's success, it nonetheless reflects upon the difficulties experienced by the Elizabethan law courts as judges struggled to reconcile ancient traditions with contemporary practicalities. There were challenges to traditional ideas of espousal and betrothal, of inheritance and guardianship, which came from beneficiaries and wards, and also from the queen herself. As he illustrates his complex visions of chastity and friendship in Books III and IV, Spenser illustrates a dynamic fashioning of his nation's virtues in response to a society in continuous flux and adjustment.

Appendix A.
The French Version of the Anomalous Form of the Oath of Edward II

Sire, volez vous graunter et garder et par vostre serment confirmer, au people d'Engleterre les leys et les custumes a eux grauntees par les auntienes rois d'Engleterre vos predecessours, droitures et devotz a Dieu, et nomement les lois, les custumes, et les franchises grauntez au clergie et au people par les glorieus roi Seint Edward vostre predecessour?

— Respons. Jeo les graunte et promette.

Sire, garderez vous a Dieu et Seint Eglise, et au clerge et au people, paeis et accord en Dieu entierment, solenc vostre poer?

— Respons. Jeo les garderai.

Sire, freez vois faire en touz voiz jugemens ovele et droit justice et discretionm en misericordie et verite a vostre poer?

— Respons. Jeo le frai.

Sire, grauntez vois a tenir et garder les loys et les custumes droitureles les quiels la communate de vostre roiaume aura esleu, et les defendrez et afforterez al honur de Dieu, a vostre poer?

— Respons. Jeo les graunte et promette.

Reprinted in Jones, *Crowns and Coronations*, p. 275 n.

Appendix B.
The Recantation of William Tolwyn, Recorded by Alexander Seton, and Reprinted by John Bale

NOTE: Spelling is Bale's; there are minor spelling discrepancies between Bale's version and Seton's. Ellipses represent Bale's breakup of the recantation into smaller sections, so that he can insert commentary. Reprinted by Bale in *Yet a Course at the Romyshe Foxe*, pps. 14v; 17r; 20r; 25r; 27r; 30r; 31v; 34v; 37r; and 39r.

> Good peple, so yt is/that I William Tolwyn master of artes and persone of saynt Antonynes within thys cyte and diocese of London have bene lawfully denounced detected/and presented to my lorde byshopp of London/that I have bene and am a manne vehementlye suspected/noted/and enfamed of hereticall and sedicyouse opynyons ageynst the catholicke faythe of oure holye mother churche.... And also that I have bene a great favourer/defender/maintainer/and receptour of heretyques, accustomed also to have in my custodye bokes of heresye and other unlawfull workes forbidden by the kynges magestees proclamacyon and ordinaunces and also contrarye to the decree and inhybycyon of myne ordynarie ... and more over that I am not accustomed to observe and keep the laudable ceremonyes/rytes/and customes of thys catholycke churche of englande comonlye observed and kepte by other/that is to saye neyther in goynge procession upon saturdayes at evensonge, not in the usage and maner of makynge of holye water and holy brede, nor in makynge my confession or saynge of masse, mattens or evensonge as I schuld or ought to have.... Whych denuncyacion/deteccion/and

The Recantation of William Tolwyn

presentacyon/hath bene partlye by suffycyent witnesse and recorde in that behalf suffycyentlye proved.... And al it be for my offense in so doynge/I knowledge to have deserved no small ponyshment/yet I have founde soche charitable goodnesse and mercie in my lorde bisshopp of London/upon my submission and sute unto hym.... That upon onlye thys declaracyon/here made of myne offence unto you/with promise that I wyll indever my selfe to the best of my power to lyve as a catholicke mann ought/and schuld do here after.... And that I do not here after preache or teache anye heresyes/errours/ or noughtye opinions contrarye and ageynst the catholike faythe of owre holie mother the church/but as mocke as can lye in my power to mayntayne/defende/and advaunce the seyd catholycke fayth ... and utterlye to detest/abhorre/and avoyde all/and all maner of heresyes/errours/and noughtye opynyons/with the favourers/maynteyners/defenders/or anye of them durynge my life ... hys lordeshypp ys content to respite the rest of my penaunce/and upon my good deservynge and doynge accordynge to my seyd promyse/to forgeve all togyther ... besechynge therefore you that be my fryndes/to geve hym most hartye thankes for the same/and to take example by me to avoyde the lyfe daunger. Amen.

Chapter Notes

Preface

1. Canfield, J. Douglas. *Word as Bond in English Literature from the Middle Ages to the Restoration*. Pennsylvania: University of Pennsylvania Press, 1989.

2. Shirley, Frances. *Swearing and Perjury in Shakespeare's Plays*. Sydney: Allen & Unwin, 1979; and Kerrigan, William. *Shakespeare's Promises*. Baltimore: Johns Hopkins University Press, 1999.

3. Condren, Conal. *Argument and Authority in Early Modern England: The Presupposition of Oaths and Offices*. Cambridge: Cambridge University Press, 2006; and Vallance, Edward. *Revolutionary England and the National Covenant*. Woodbridge, Suffolk, UK: Boydell Press, 2005.

4. Bartlett, Robert. *Trial by Fire and Water: The Medieval Judicial Ordeal*. Oxford: Clarendon Press, 1986; and Duffy, Eamon. *The Stripping of the Altars*. New Haven: Yale University Press, 1992.

Introduction

1. See Austin, *How to Do Things with Words*. The lectures provide Austin's comprehensive definition of sworn bond and a complete breakdown as to how it works in both "felicitous" and "infelicitous" situations.

2. The dangerous ironies of oath-swearing provided sixteenth- and seventeenth-century Puritans with reasons for why they chose to follow Matthew 5:34 and reject sworn bonds completely.

3. Elton, G.R. *Reform and Reformation: England 1509–1558*. Cambridge, MA: Harvard University Press, 1979, p. 24.

4. See Bernard, G.W. *The King's Reformation: Henry VIII and the Remaking of the English Church*. New Haven: Yale University Press, 2005.

5. See *Henry VIII and His Afterlives*, ed. Mark Rankin, Christopher Haighley, and John N. King. Cambridge: Cambridge University Press, 2009; Walker, Greg. *Writing Under Tyranny*. Oxford: Oxford University Press, 2005; and Lipscomb, Susannah. *1536: The Year That Changed Henry VIII*. London: Lion Publishers, 2009.

6. For an expanded discussion of this subject, see Shuger, Deborah. *Habits of Thought in the English Renaissance*. Berkeley: University of California Press, 1990, p. 9.

7. Especially the Stoics, who believed that moral good was the only good, and that it was therefore also expedient. Cicero in particular rejected this idea. Cicero, M. Tullius. *De Officiis*, trans. Walter Miller, ed. T.E. Page. Loeb Classical Library Series. New York: Macmillan, 1913, III.iii.11.

8. Cicero, *De Officiis*, III.xvii.70, xxiv.92, xxix.104, and xxxi.111; and *De Legibus*, trans. Clinton Walker Keyes. Loeb Classical Library Series. New York: Putnam, 1928, II.viii.19, and ix.22.

9. Shelton, Jo Anne. *As the Romans Did: A Sourcebook in Roman Social History*, 2nd ed. Oxford: Oxford University Press, 1998, pps. 332, 370n, 374, and 376.

10. Shelton, *As the Romans Did*, p. 370.

11. Shelton, *As The Romans Did*, pps. 369–70.

12. Here the identity of Mars is blended with that of two gods of the Britons, who appear elsewhere as separate deities. Both of these inscriptions, among others, can be found in *Corpus Inscriptionum Latinarum*, editione altera. Berolini: Apud. G. Reimerum and W. de Gruyter, 1893, 7.36, 84, and 176; and in *Inscriptiones Latinae Selectae*, ed. Hermann

Notes — Chapter 1

Dessau. Berolini: Apud. Weidmannos, 1892–1916, 4586a and 4540.

13. This concept applies only to free men. Nobles could clear themselves with unsupported oaths, but *ceorls* could only do so with three witnesses from their peers.

14. See especially *English Historical Documents*, ed. Dorothy Whitelock. New York: Oxford University Press, 1979.

15. I Ine 54.

16. At the time of the Anglo-Saxon invasions in Kent, the word of a bishop was also considered to be incontrovertible. Sawyer, P.H. *Anglo-Saxon Charters: An Annotated List and Bibliography*. London: Royal Historical Society, 1968, p. 236.

17. The Franks and Saxons had made contact somewhat earlier. Robert Bartlett theorizes that perhaps the Franks brought their customs, including that of the ordeal, to the upper Thames valley in the fifth century. The legend that St. Patrick introduced the ordeal of the cauldron to Britain is most likely a myth. Bartlett, *Trial by Fire and Water*, pps. 5, 7n, and 8.

18. Bartlett, *Trial by Fire and Water*, pps. 1, 4, 8, and 9.

19. Shelton, *As the Romans Did*, pps. 371–73.

20. Augustine's philosophical and doctrinal influence is especially important to the assumption of the culture of Divine performativity by the Britons. See his discussion of the relation of human speech to the concept of the Word made flesh in *De Doctrina Christiana*, especially I.xiii:

> It is as when we speak ... but our thought is not transformed into sounds; it remains entire in itself and assumes the form of words by means of which it may reach the ears without suffering any deterioration.... In the same way the Word of God was made flesh without change that He might dwell among us.

21. I Alfred 1–12.

22. V Ethelred 24–25.

23. II Cnut 30.2–3.

24. Bartlett, *Trial by Fire and Water*, p. 13.

25. Cicero had argued that no material gain could compensate for moral law. *De Officiis*, III.xx.81.

26. British Library Manuscripts Catalogue descriptions for MS Cotton Tiberius E viii, fol. 100a.

Chapter 1

1. Tite, Colin G. *The Early Records of Sir Robert Cotton's Library*. London: The British Library, 2003, p. 113.

2. Ratcliffe, Edward C. *The English Coronation Service*. London: Skeffington and Son, Ltd., 1936, p. 53; also Jones, William. *Crowns and Coronations: A History of Regalia*. London: Chatto & Windus, 1902, p. 275; and Ellis, Henry. *Original Letters, Illustrative of English History*. London: Harding, Triphook, & Lepard, 1824 (front leaf reproduction).

3. For a full and varied discussion of the rituals of the English coronation service, and their roots in English law, tradition, and religion, see Ellis, *Original Letters*, and Jones, *Crowns and Coronations*; also Strong, Roy. *Coronation: A History of Kingship and the British Monarchy*. London: HarperCollins, 2005, Schramm, Percy. *A History of the English Coronation*, trans. Leopold G, Wickham-Legge. Oxford: Clarendon Press, 1937; and *English Coronation Records*, ed. Leopold G. Wickham-Legge. Westminster: A. Constable & Co., Ltd., 1901.

4. The coronation ceremony was abbreviated for the sake of the young Edward VI's youth, as recorded by William Prynne much later; the young king's oath was altered by the Lord Protector and the King's council, to read as follows: "Do you grant to make no new laws, but such as shall be to the honor and glory of God, and to the good of the Commonwealth, and that the same shall be made by consent of your people as hath been accustomed?" This distinction bears less controversy than would appear. It asserts that laws are necessarily made by the people according to ancient tradition, and that the king is bound to confirm and uphold them. Prynne, William. *The Signal Loyalty and Devotion of God's True Saints and Pious Christians Towards Their Kings*. 2 vols. London: T. Childs, Printer, 1660, vol. ii, pps. 250–51; also Jones, *Crowns and Coronations*, p. 276 (quoting Jeremy Taylor, in an incited reference).

5. Jones, *Crowns and Coronations*, p. 276.

6. Scanlon, Larry. *Narrative, Authority, and Power: The Medieval Exemplum and the Chaucerian Tradition*. Cambridge: Cambridge University Press, 1994, p. 311.

7. The French version is found in Appendix A of this volume.

8. Schramm, *History of the English Coronation*, p. 215.

Notes — Chapter 1

9. Loach, Jennifer. "The Function of Ceremonial in the Reign of Henry VIII," *Past and Present* no. 142 (Feb. 1994), p. 53.
10. Schramm, *History of the English Coronation*, p. 216.
11. BL MS Add. 19398, f. 44.
12. Several examples of the king's handwriting in letters during the 1530s are found in MS Cotton Cleopatra E vi; some earlier examples, showing the development of his handwriting between 1513 and 1534 are found in BL MS Harley 6986 f. 8 (letter to the Earl of Shrewsbury) and also in BL MS Kings 9 f. 231b (notes to Anne Boleyn in a psalter), and BL MS Kings 2 A xvi (autograph notes in a psalter).
13. A few examples are BL MS Cotton Vespasian C vii f. 71 (additions to instructions for Imperial Ambassadors Sir Philip Hoby and Sir Thomas Wyatt), and BL MS Autograph 32, 654 f. 58 (addition to Lord Metford's proclamation on invading Scotland).
14. 25 Henry VIII, c. 19 (Act in Restraint of Appeals).
15. Great Britain, Public Record Office. *Letters and Papers, Foreign and Domestic, of the Reign of Henry VIII*. London: Longman, Green, Longman & Roberts, 1862–1910: Vaduz, Kraus Reprint, 1965–1976, vol. v, item 721 and vol. vii, items 2 and 57.
16. Guy, John. *Tudor England*. Oxford: Oxford University Press, 1988, p. 198.
17. BL MS Cotton Cleopatra E vi, f. 185 (Draft of the Act in Restraint of Appeals).
18. BL MS Cotton Tiberius E viii, f. 100a (Coronation Oath, anomalous form, with emendations by Henry VIII).
19. 25 Henry VIII, c. 19 (Act in Restraint of Appeals, Preamble).
20. In an irony of document emendation, birth announcements which had been prepared heralding the arrival of a prince had to be corrected by hand to read "princess" for the newborn Elizabeth — although these additions were not made by the king himself. BL MS Harley 283, f. 75a.
21. Saul, Nigel. *The Three Richards*. New York: Hambledon & London, 2005, pps. 169–70.
22. By the end of the 1530s the saint at the forefront of this distinction would be Thomas Becket. Henry's desire to distance reformed kingship from the Becket tradition was so strong that he had Becket's shrine destroyed and the bones burned.
23. Hillam, David. *Crown, Orb, and Sceptre: True Stories of English Coronations*. Gloucestershire: Sutton Publishing, 2001, pps. 24–25.
24. Hillam, *Crown, Orb, and Sceptre*, pps. 4–9.
25. Loach, "The Function of Ceremonial," p. 53.
26. Loach, "The Function of Ceremonial," p. 53.
27. Hillam, *Crown, Orb, and Sceptre*, pps. 68–72.
28. There are no definitive sources for such rumors, and no firm dates which point to their origins. By the beginning of the seventeenth century they had become inflated, sensationalized after decades of polemic and theatrical performance.
29. He had begun collecting in earnest about 1588, at the same tine the Society of Antiquaries was founded. In 1642 the oath taken by Edward II was mentioned in a pamphlet against Charles I. it was found in "an old book in the Heralds Office, belonging to Clarencieux Hanley, who lived in Henry VIII's time." The pamphlet also mentions that the French oath is translated into both Latin and English. *A Remonstrance of the Lords and Commons Assembled in Parliament...* London: I. Wright, 1642. The Heralds Office was kept in Derby House, where the Society of Antiquarians met.
30. Sharpe, Kevin. *Sir Robert Cotton 1586–1631: History and Politics in Early Modern England*. Oxford: Oxford University Press, 1979, p. 64.
31. Sharpe, *Sir Robert Cotton*, pps. 57–58.
32. Despite his interest in the history of the subject, Cotton (along with the rest of the Antiquarian Society) agreed that dueling ought to be illegal. He bound the Society's papers, along with his own paper on the subject, in BL MS Cotton Titus C.i.
33. Tite, *Early Records*, p. 113.
34. Tite, *Early Records*, p. 113, and Sharpe, *Sir Robert Cotton*, pps. 70–71.
35. BL MS Cotton Tiberius E viii, vols. 100–110 ("The Coronation of K. Henry VIII. With the King's Oath Prefixed; Interlined by K. Henry VIII").
36. Sharpe, *Sir Robert Cotton*, p. 68.
37. Tite, *Early Records*, p. 113.
38. Sharpe, *Sir Robert Cotton*, p. 225.
39. Cotton possessed a large amount of material on antiquarian scholarship by Bale and Leland, among others. Bale's papers are found in BL MS Cotton Vitellius D iv.

40. BL MS Cotton Tiberius E viii, f. 313b.
41. Sharpe, *Sir Robert Cotton*, p. 80.
42. Sharpe, *Sir Robert Cotton*, p. 80.

Chapter 2

1. Walker asserts that "...nor is there anything in *The Governour* about the advantages of a peaceful foreign policy, no notes on effective diplomacy or advice on the best ways to stay on good terms with one's European neighbors, no models of conduct for neophyte ambassadors and envoys," in *Writing Under Tyranny*, p. 169.
2. Saul, Nigel. *The Three Richards*. London: Hambledon & London, 2005. In several introductory chapters, Saul outlines the ideals of medieval kingship, especially as they relate to the reigns of Richards I, II, and III.
3. Walker, *Writing Under Tyranny*, p. 142.
4. See Richard Helgerson's discussion of English nationhood during the sixteenth and seventeenth centuries in *Forms of Nationhood: The Elizabethan Writing of England*. Chicago: University of Chicago Press, 1002, pps. 1–18.
5. Wagner, Anne. "Idleness and the Ideal of the Gentleman." *History of Education Quarterly*, vol. 25, nos. 1–2 (Spring/Summer 1985), p. 42.
6. Berners, Dame Juliana. *The Book of St. Albans* (1496). New York: Abercrombie and Fitch, 1966; Capellanus, Andreas. *On Love* (thirteenth century), ed. and trans. P.G. Walsh. London: Duckworth, 1982; and Heltzel, Virgil B. *A Check List of Courtesy Books in the Newberry Library*. Chicago: Newberry Library, 1942. The book lists 1,539 entries held in the Newberry alone.
7. Wagner, "Idleness and the Ideal of the Gentleman," pps. 41–42.
8. For a fuller discussion of the conflict between the knight and the clerk, and its implications for the Tudor man of action, see Kelso, Ruth. *The Doctrine of the English Gentleman in the Sixteenth Century*, Urbana: University of Illinois Press, 1929, chapter VI.
9. Kelso, *Doctrine of the English Gentleman*, p. 119.
10. Siegel, Paul. "English Humanism and the New Tudor Aristocracy." *Journal of The History of Ideas*, vol. 13, no. 4 (October 1952), p. 458.
11. BL MS Cotton Cleopatra E iv. f. 260 (Letter from Thomas Elyot to Thomas Cromwell, 1536, after 2 July), reprinted in Wilson, K.J. "The Letters of Sir Thomas Elyot," *Studies in Philology*, vol. 73, no. 5, Texts and Studies, 1976, p. 32.
12. Walker, *Writing Under Tyranny*, p. 126.
13. Aristotle. *Nichomachean Ethics*, trans. H. Rachham, ed. E. Capps. Loeb Classical Library Series. New York: G.P. Putnam's Sons, 1926, II.iv.3.
14. Elyot, Thomas. *The Boke Named the Governour*. London: Thomas Bertheleti, 1531, III.vi.184b.
15. Elyot, *The Governour*, III.iv.179b.
16. Elyot, *The Governour*, III.iv. 182a.
17. Cicero, *De Officiis*, I.13; and Plato, *Republic*, trans. Paul Shorey. New York: G.P. Putnam's Sons, 1930–1935, II.4.
18. Elyot, *The Governour*, III.iv 181b–182a.
19. For a discussion of the concept of *fides*, see Kelso, *Doctrine of the English Gentleman*, pps. 78–80.
20. Norland, Howard. "More's and Elyot's Perspectives and Their Classical Antecedents." *Moreana*, vol. 40 (2003), nos. 153–54, p. 128.
21. Helgerson, *Forms of Nationhood*, pps. 131ff.
22. *Holy Bible, King James Version*. New York: NAL Penguin, Inc., 1974, Joshua 9:1–27. The episode makes up the entirety of the chapter.
23. Latin, from the Vulgate: *principes multitudinis* (Joshua 9:18). Tyndale's version, the subject of heresy accusations at the time, reads "Lords of the congregation."
24. The whole of Josh. 9:18 reads, "and the children of Israel smote them not, because the princes of the multitude had sworn unto them by the Lord God of Israel. And all the multitude murmured against the princes."
25. Norland, "More's and Elyot's Perspectives," p. 135.
26. Joshua 1:1.
27. Berners, *The Book of St. Albans*, e.vi. Later in the sixteenth century, Laurence Humphrey would posit that Biblical figures had noble qualities, which he linked to the "innate" nobility of Tudor Kings and Queens, in *Nobles, or of Nobylyte*. London: Thomas March, 1563. See also Kendrick, T.D. *British Antiquity*. London: Methuen and Co., 1950.
28. Norland, "More's and Elyot's Perspectives," p. 136.
29. The Geneva Bible, the most widely read version during the Elizabethan era, reads "princes of the congregation." This choice of words was used to encourage support for the Episcopate and eventually the Elizabethan settlement among English Protestants. Since

Elyot's book was reprinted well into the 1580s, it is likely that Elizabethan students of *The Governour* took Elyot's example of Joshua as advice to support Episcopal influence in governance.

30. Cicero, *De Officiis*, III.xxix.104.
31. Elyot, *The Governour*, III.vi.185a.
32. Cicero, *De Officiis*, III.xxix.107.
33. Aristotle, *Nichomachean Ethics*, V.x.4.
34. Lehmberg, Stanford. *Sir Thomas Elyot: Tudor Humanist*. Austin: University of Texas Press, 1960, pps. 30–31 and 101. Elyot only managed to hold onto his ambassadorship from late 1531 to June of 1532. The fact that this happened after the publication of *The Governour* suggests that its author failed to live up to his own theory. Elyot claimed to have left the Emperor's court because of the high cost of living, which was true. Yet, his failure to win the Emperor over to support of the King's Great Matter also suggests that Henry VIII found someone else for the job.
35. Cicero, *De Officiis*, III.xxviii.102.
36. See Lewis Einstein's important discussion of periods of change in the sixteenth century in *Tudor Ideals*. London: G. Bell and Sons, 1921, p. xv.
37. These models were well known to scholars of the time, and there had been earlier efforts to reconcile the two, mainly by the thirteenth-century followers of Aquinas and by many Italian humanists of the fourteenth and fifteenth centuries.
38. Despite Elyot's view of Greek democratic politics as an experimental form of governance, he nonetheless associates Greek institutionalism with a model view of the medieval political and theological institutions of previous generations. *The Governour*, I.xvii.
39. BL MS Cotton Vitellius B xxi, vols. 58–59 (Letter from Thomas Elyot to the Duke of Norfolk, 14 March 1532). Reprinted in Wilson, *Letters*, pps. 3–4.
40. Great Britain Public Record Office S.P. 1/75, f. 81 (Letter from Thomas Elyot to Sir John Hackett, 6 April 1533). Reprinted in Wilson, *Letters*, pps. 16–17.
41. This idea is essentially Florentine, but English humanists were heavily influenced by this hermeneutic. See Streuver, Nancy. *The Language of History in the Renaissance*. Princeton, NJ: Princeton University Press, 1970, p. 74.
42. Cicero, *De Officiis*, III.xxxi.112.

Chapter 3

1. See Greg Walker's discussion of the king's descent into tyranny during the 1530s and 40s, throughout *Writing Under Tyranny*.
2. This history is treated comprehensively in Jean DeLumeau's massive work, *Sin and Fear: The Emergence of a Western Guilt Culture, 13th–18th Centuries*, trans. Eric Nicholson. New York: St. Martin's Press, 1990.
3. Delumeau, *Sin and Fear*, p. 198.
4. Delumeau, *Sin and Fear*, p. 189.
5. Fourth Lateran Council of 1215. "Omnis Utriusque Sexus," complete text in Watkins, Oscar D. *A History of Penance*, vol. II. London, 1920, pps. 733–34 and 748–49.
6. Delumeau, *Sin and Fear*, p. 198.
7. Tentler, T.N. *Sin and Confession on the Eve of the Reformation*. Princeton, NJ: Princeton University Press, 1977, p. 297.
8. Greenblatt, Stephen. *Renaissance Self-Fashioning from More to Shakespeare*. Chicago: University of Chicago Press, 1980, p. 1.
9. Parentheses in MS.
10. Tentler, *Sin and Confession*, p. 59. Since Henry VIII differed with Lutheran theology, his effort here is distinctively English. Unlike Luther, Henry VIII accepted institutional satisfaction for penance, even if that institution was his own government rather than the Roman Church. He and his counselors (some of whom supported Protestantism more strongly than others) did, however, accept the idea promoted by Luther that confession was rooted in reason.
11. Tentler, *Sin and Confession*, p. 61.
12. Bernard, G.W. *The King's Reformation: Henry VIII and the Remaking of the English Church*. New Haven: Yale University Press, 2005, p. 504.
13. Delumeau, *Sin and Fear*, p. 198.
14. Tentler, *Sin and Confession*, p. 59.
15. Delumeau, *Sin and Fear*, p. 200.
16. British Library Manuscript Catalogue. Description of BL MS Stowe 15, ffs. 26–84.
17. BL MS Stowe 15, ffs. 3–5, 8a, 19b, and 88a.
18. BL MS Stowe 15, ffs. 9b–11b.
19. See Chapter I of this volume, "Defiance by Prerogative: The Coronation Oath of Henry VIII."
20. The most common sources from scripture used to justify the theological necessity of auricular confession are Mat. 16:19, Luke 17: 14, John 20: 22–23, and James 5:16. John

Notes — Chapter 4

11:44 was often used, but could at times be criticized as too implicit.
21. Tentler, *Sin and Confession*, pps. 109–10.
22. Tentler, *Sin and Confession*, p. 116.
23. Greenblatt, Stephen. *Renaissance Self-Fashioning*, p. 1.
24. 28 Henry VIII, c. 10 (The Act Extinguishing the Authority of the Bishop of Rome) made it illegal to refuse to answer questions touching the Supremacy. The act was meant to close any loopholes left by the refusal of Thomas More to swear to the Supremacy.
25. Delumeau, *Sin and Fear*, p. 297.
26. Years later, his daughter Elizabeth would continue this mindset. The Rainbow Portrait in the National Gallery in London shows Elizabeth I wearing a robe embroidered entirely with eyes and ears.
27. Greenblatt, *Renaissance Self-Fashioning*, p. 9.
28. Walker, *Writing Under Tyranny*, pps. 1–15.
29. Walker, *Writing Under Tyranny*, p. 15.
30. Walker, *Writing Under Tyranny*, p. 15.
31. Elton, G.R. *Reform and Reformation: England 1509–1558*. Cambridge, MA: Harvard University Press, 1977.
32. Elton, *Reform and Reformation*, p. 189.
33. Greenblatt, *Renaissance Self-Fashioning*, p. 9.
34. For a thorough discussion of the role of hatred within English communities in the sixteenth century see Jones, Norman. *The English Reformation: Religion and Cultural Adaptation*. Oxford: Blackwell Publishing, 2002, pps. 95–133.
35. Greenblatt, *Renaissance Self-Fashioning*, p. 5.
36. Walker, *Writing Under Tyranny*, p. 23.
37. Jones, Norman. *The English Reformation*, p. 134.
38. Parentheses in MS.
39. Parentheses in MS.
40. Ryrie, Alec. "Counting Sheep, Counting Shepherds: The Problem of Allegiance in the English Reformation." *The Beginnings of English Protestantism*, eds. Peter Marshall and Alec Ryrie. Cambridge: Cambridge University Press, 2002, p. 85.
41. Greenblatt, *Renaissance Self-Fashioning*, p. 2. This point is explicated throughout the book.
42. Greenblatt, *Renaissance Self-Fashioning*, p. 2.
43. Jones, Norman. *The English Reformation*, pps. 134–5.
44. British Library Manuscript Catalogue Description of MS Stowe 15.
45. See Agard, Arthur. *The Repertorie of Records, Remaining in the 4. Treasuries on the Receipt Side at Westminster, The Two Remembrances of the Exchequer: With a Briefe Introductive Index of the Records of the Chancery and Tower...* ed. Thomas Powell. London: Printed by B. Alsop and T. Fawcet, for B. Fisher, 1631, p. 123. This volume describes "[the] little book with the crucifix," which was preserved in the chest of Henry VIII's Remembrancer Christopher Moore, and is recorded as having been used for administering oaths. This description is in concordance with the British Library's provenance and thereby identifies the "little book" as MS Stowe 15.

Chapter 4

1. Woolf, D.R. "Speech, Text, and Time: The Sense of Hearing and the Sense of the Past in Renaissance England." *Albion*, no. 18, vol. 2 (Summer 1986), p. 193.
2. Woolf, "Speech, Text, and Time," p. 160.
3. 25 Henry VIII, cap. 22 (First Act of Succession).
4. Walker, *Writing Under Tyranny*, p. 24.
5. 25 Henry VIII, cap. 22; also Great Britain. *Statutes of the Realm*, vol. III. London: G. Eyre and A. Strahan, 1810–1828, p. 474.
6. For more discussion of the forms of Henrician fealty oaths, and on their various implications, see Chapter III of this volume, entitled, "Additions and Admissions: The Manipulation of Sworn Bond in the Henrician Fealty Oath."
7. Henry VIII. *A Glasse of the Truth*. London: Thomas Bertelet, 1532, p. 1a.
8. *A Glasse of the Truth*, A.iii.a.
9. *A Glasse of the Truth*, B.iii.a.
10. *A Glasse of the Truth*, C.vii.a.
11. *A Glasse of the Truth*, E.ii.b, and E.iii.a.
12. *A Glasse of the Truth*, E.viii.a.
13. *A Glasse of the Truth*, E.viii.a.
14. *A Glasse of the Truth*, E.viii.a, marginal note.
15. Warner, Christopher J. *Henry VIII's Divorce: Literature and the Politics of the Printing Press*. London: Boydell, 1998, p. 44.
16. Warner, *Henry VIII's Divorce*, p. 41.
17. Although the treatise was published anonymously, John Bale, a supporter of Protestant views and an expert bibliographer, attributes it to Swinnerton in his *Catalogus*, 2.

Notes — Chapter 4

76. The Huntington Library and British Library also identify the treatise as Swinnerton's.

18. Swinnerton, Thomas. *A Litel Treatise Ageynste the Mutterynge of Some Papists in Corners*. London: Thomas Bertelet, 1534, p. A.ii.b.

19. Swinnerton, *A Litel Treatise*, A.ii.b.

20. Swinnerton, *A Litel Treatise*, A.ii.b.

21. Swinnerton, *A Litel Treatise*, A.ii.b.

22. The call to those who have ears to hear is found especially in Mat. 13:9, Mark 4:9, 7:16, and 8:18, and Luke 8:8 and 14:35.

23. Swinnerton, *A Litel Treatise*, A.ix.a and b.

24. Swinnerton, *A Litel Treatise*, I.ix.b.

25. These were common folk beliefs in the sixteenth century, and the sayings can even be heard today. The Gally Halfpence was a Genoa coin whose use was banned by Henry IV in 1409. It became customary to associate the waning of Scotus' learning (or learning in general) with the changes in economy brought on by the banning of this foreign currency. The building of Tenterden Steeple had used up all the funds for the keeping up of the church at Sandwich Haven. The church stood near a shoal that was known for its inconveniently shifting sands. Both stories were used to illustrate the idea that one thing didn't necessarily follow another. They could also be used to presume that when one asks an absurd question, one gets an absurd answer. Thomas More and Hugh Latimer both used the example of Tenterden Steeple as an allegory in their polemical works. More, Thomas. "A Dialogue Concerning Heresies," *The Complete Works of Thomas More*. New Haven: Yale University Press, 1963, pps. 277a–278a; and Latimer, Hugh. "Last Sermon Preached Before Edward VI at Lent, Westminster," *Selected Sermons of Hugh Latimer*, ed. Allan G. Chester. Charlottesville: University of Virginia Press, 1968, p. 216.

26. Swinnerton, *A Litel Treatise*, B.ix.b.

27. Such as John Bale and Christopher St. German, both of whom enjoyed Cromwell's' patronage.

28. Sweet, A.H. "John de Feckenham and the Marian Reaction," *Persecution and Liberty: Essays in Honor of George Lincoln Burr*. London: Century Publishing Co., 1931, pps. 255–69; and Tudor, Philippa "John Feckenham and Tudor Religious Controversies," *The Cloister and The World: Essays in Medieval History in Honour of Barbara Harvey*, ed. John Blair and Brian Golding. Oxford: Oxford University Press, 1995, pps. 302–22.

29. Great Britain, Public Record Office. *Letters and Papers, Foreign and Domestic, of the Reign of Henry VIII*, vol. XXI–XXII. London: Longman, Green, Longman, & Roberts, 1862–1910, repr. 1965–1976, item 710.

30. Feckenham's treatise is now lost, but most of it is reprinted in Horne's answer to it; and some of it is also reprinted in Stapleton's attack on Horne's answer, and also in Bridges' subsequent defense of Horne.

31. Horne, Robert. *An Answeare Made by Rob. Bishoppe of Wynchester, to a Booke Entitled, the Declaration of Suche Scruples, and Staies of Conscience, Touching the Othe of the Supremacy...* London: Henry Wykes, 1566. Bishop Horne was not the only polemicist to produce a tract "answering" Feckenham's work: John Gough and Laurence Thomson both penned "answers" to Feckenham's objection to Gough's sermon of 15 January 1570. Gough, John. *The Aunswer of Iohn Gough Preacher, to Maister Fecknams Obiections Against His Sermon, Lately Preached in the Tower of London*. By Iohn Awdley, 1570; and Tomson, Laurence. *An Answere to Certein Assertions of M. Fecknam, Sometime Abbot of Westminster Which He Made of Late Against a Godly Sermon of M, Iohn Goughes, Preached in the Tower the xv of Ianuarie. Seen and Allowed*. London: Henry Bynneman, 1570. It is interesting to note that the validity of Tomson's book is determined in part by its having been *seen and allowed*, by those powers (possibly Cecil or Bacon, or their agents) which determine what is to be permitted in print.

32. Cross, Claire. *The Royal Supremacy in the Elizabethan Church*. London: Allen and Unwin, Ltd., 1969, p. 37.

33. Horne, *An Answeare...* Preface, p. 2.

34. Horne, *An Answeare...* A.iii.b.

35. Horne, *An Answeare...* A.iii.b.

36. A discussion of being "friend to the monarch" is found in Chapter II of this volume, entitled: "The Matter of Resources: Sworn Bond and Biblical Example In *The Boke Named the Governour*.

37. Horne, *An Answeare...* A.iv.a.

38. Horne, *An Answeare...* A.v.a.

39. Horne, *An Answeare...* A.v.a.

40. Great Britain, Public Record Office. *Calendar of State Papers and Manuscripts, Relating to English Affairs Existing in the Archives and Collection of Venice, and in Other Libraries of Northern Italy*, vol. VII. London: Longman,

Notes — Chapter 5

Green, Longman, Roberts, and Green, 1864, pps. 22–23; also Garret, Christina Hallowell. *The Marian Exiles: A Study in the Origins of Elizabethan Puritanism*. Cambridge: Cambridge University Press, 1938, pps. 134–36; and Starkey, David. *Elizabeth: The Struggle for the Throne*. New York: HarperCollins, 2001, p. 277.

41. David Starkey posits that since Feckenham knew the bill would pass in any case he preferred to abstain directly rather than prolong the debate, which he saw as self-defeating. Based on Feckenham's history, this is probably true, although Horne (and the Queen) certainly did not see it that way. Starkey, *Elizabeth: The Struggle for the Throne*, pps. 278–81; also *Proceedings in the Parliaments of Elizabeth I*, ed. T.E. Hartley. Leicester: Leicester University Press, 1981, vol. I, pps. 22–23.

42. Horne, *An Answeare*... B.v.a.

43. Horne, *An Answeare*... B.vi.b.

44. Horne, *An Answeare*... B.vi.b.

45. Gallagher, Lowell. *Medusa's Gaze: Casuistry and Conscience in the Renaissance*. Palo Alto: Stanford University Press, 1991, p. 6.

46. Gallagher, *Medusa's Gaze*, p. 10.

47. Gallagher, *Medusa's Gaze*, p. 2.

48. For a further discussion of auricular confession and its relation to the Henrician Supremacy see Chapter III of this volume, entitled, "Additions and Admissions: The Manipulation of Sworn Bond in the Henrician Fealty Oath."

49. Gallagher, *Medusa's Gaze*, p. 2.

50. *Proceedings in the Parliaments of Elizabeth I*, I, pps. 34 and 33–39; also Starkey, *Elizabeth: The Struggle for the Throne*, p. 277.

51. O'Connell, Marvin R. *Thomas Stapleton and the Counter Reformation*. New Haven: Yale University Press, 1964.

52. Stapleton, Thomas. *A Counterblast to M. Horne's Vayne Blaste Against M. Feckenham*. Louvain: Apud Ioannem Foulerum, 1567.

53. In opposition to Horne, Stapleton uses "king" rather than "emperor," in defiance of the Henrician effort to argue that England had always been an empire, and that the Tudors were not subject to papal authority.

54. Stapleton, *A Counterblast*... pps. 5b and 6a.

55. Stapleton, *A Counterblast*... p. 29a.

56. Stapleton, *A Counterblast*... p. 29a.

57. O'Connell, *Thomas Stapleton*, p. 193.

58. For a discussion of the monarch's obligations to the coronation oath, see Chapter I of this volume, entitled, "Defiance by Prerogative: The Coronations Oath of Henry VIII."

59. Emphasis Stapleton's.

60. Stapleton, *A Counterblast*... pps. 392a and b.

61. Stapleton, *A Counterblast*... p. 434a.

62. Bridges, John. *The Supremacie of Christian Princes*... London: Henry Bynneman for Humphrey Toye, 1573. The abbreviated title represents the first part of the book's title. The second part of the book is written against Thomas Sanders' *Visible Monarchie of the Romaine Church*.

63. Bridges, *The Supremacie of Christian Princes*... First Division, I.iii.

64. Bridges, *The Supremacie of Christian Princes*... First Division, K.

65. Bridges, *The Supremacie of Christian Princes*... First Division, K.iii. Emphasis is Bridges.

66. Hickman, David. "Religious Belief and Pious Practice Among London's Elizabethan Elite." *The Historical Journal*, vol. 42, no. 4 (December 1999), p. 946.

67. Starkey, *Elizabeth: The Struggle for the Throne*, p. 313.

68. Bridges, *The Supremacie of Christian Princes*... Second Division, Bii ff.

69. Bridges, *The Supremacie of Christian Princes*... Nineteenth Division, KKKK. iii. Much of what Bridges (and most everyone in Christian Europe, both Protestant and Catholic) believed about the Priscillianists was heavily influenced by popular legend and propaganda from Rome. To help dissolve the cult and defame its leader, the Church had accused Priscillian of sorcery and had depicted his followers as unapologetic liars.

70. Bridges, *The Supremacie of Christian Princes*... Twenty-Seventh Division, LL.iiii.

71. Starkey, *Elizabeth: The Struggle for the Throne*, p. 305.

72. *Proceedings in the Parliaments of Elizabeth I*, I. P. 36; also Starkey, *Elizabeth: The Struggle for the Throne*, p. 305.

73. *Proceedings in the Parliaments of Elizabeth I*, I. p. 36.

Chapter 5

1. The oath presented to More was an adapted form, different from that presented to others, and it had been presented to him in more than one draft before More's final refusal.

2. Harington especially was influenced by

Notes — Chapter 5

Erasmus's *Praise of Folly*, and also Rabelais, who, he points out, had been a groom of the stool "to some Prince of the blood." Harington, John. *A New Discourse on a Stale Subject, Called the Metamorphosis of Ajax* (1596), ed. Elizabeth Story Dunno. London: Routledge and Kegan Paul, 1962, p. 64.

3. For a comprehensive discussion of how More used the form of dialogue against various adversaries, see Pineas, Rainer. "Thomas More's Use of the Dialogue as a Weapon of Religious Controversy." *Studies in the Renaissance*, vol. 7, (1960), p. 197.

4. Pineas, Rainer. "Thomas More's Use of Humor as a Weapon of Religious Controversy." *Studies in Philology*, vol. 58, no. 2, Part I (April 1961), p. 113.

5. Martz, Louis. *Thomas More: The Search for the Inner Man*. New Haven: Yale University Press, 1990, p. 59

6. Wegemer, Gerard B. *Thomas More on Statesmanship*. Washington, D.C.: Catholic University Press, 1996, p. 25. Part of Wegemer's overall argument is that "like Plato and Augustine," More's political philosophy and its connection to humor cannot be found in any one place. His entire corpus much be considered in order to determine his views on the relationship between the individual and the state, and the role humor plays in that relationship. One of Wegemer's most important points is that we cannot fully understand More's politics unless we consider the times when he did not intend to be taken seriously.

7. Wegemer, *Thomas More on Statesmanship*, p. 25.

8. Wegemer, *Thomas More on Statesmanship*, p. 25.

9. Bale, John. *The First Two Partes of the Actes or Unchaste Examples of the Englyshe Votaryes, Gathered Out of Theyr Owne Legendes and Chronycles by Ihon Bale, and Dedicated to Oure Most Redoubted Soveraigne Kynge Edwarde the Syxte*. London: By John Tysdale, 1560, pps. 16b, and 18a.

10. *Kynge Johan* was revised several times before 1560.

11. Bale, John. *Kynge Johan*, ed. Barry Adams. San Marino: Huntington Library Press, 1969, 11. 1216 and 1222. For a discussion of sworn bond in Bale's *Kynge Johan* see Chapter VI of this volume, entitled, "Oath, Obligation, and Obedience: Sworn Fealty and Social Change in Three Plays About King John."

12. Bale, John. *The Apology of Iohan Bale Agaynste a Ranke Papyst: Aunswering Both Hym and Hys Doctours, That Neyther Their Vowes Nor Yet Their Priesthode Are of the Gospell, but of Antichrist*. S. Mierdman for John Day, 1550 (?), pps. 20 and 50.

13. Bale, John. *The Pageant of Popes: Contayninge the Lyves of All the Bishops of Rome, from the Beginninge of Them to the Year of Grace 1555... Written in Latin by Maister Bale, and Now Englished with Sondrye Additions by I.S*. Thomas Marshe, 1574.

14. For Bale's complete outline of this idea, see *The Image of Both Churches After the Most Wonderfull and Heavenly Revelacion of Sainct Iohn the Evangelist, Contayning a Very Frutefull Exposicion or Paraphrase Upon the Same...* London: Richard Jugge, 1548.

15. Fairfield, Leslie. *John Bale, Mythmaker for the English Reformation*. West Lafayette: Purdue University Press, 1976, pps. 106 and 109.

16. Harington, *A New Discourse...* p. 7.

17. Scott Warren, Jason. "The Privy Politics of Sir John Harington's *New Discourse on a Stale Subject, Called the Metamorphosis of Ajax*." *Studies in Philology*, vol. 93, no. 4 (Autumn 1996), p. 420.

18. Elizabeth I. "Text of the Bond of Association," *Collected Works*, ed. Leah Marcus, Janel Mueller and Mary Beth Rose. Chicago: University of Chicago Press, 2000.

19. Adiaphorism was an important matter of discussion among reformers, including Luther, Calvin, and Tyndale, among many others. Much of the discussion revolved around ceremonialism, and whether a particular ceremony was commanded or forbidden by Scripture. When it came to issues like sacramentalism and clerical marriage, many moderates (such as Thomas Cranmer and Stephen Gardiner) felt that if a sacrament or ritual was not forbidden by Scripture, it could be tolerated without being pronounced good or evil. A comprehensive discussion of this complex subject is found in Verkamp, Bernard. *The Indifferent Mean: Adiaphorism in the English Reformation to 1554*. Athens: Ohio University Press, 1997.

20. Despite each author's awareness of adiaphorism and its role in discussions of reform, and despite their attitudes toward others on the subject of moral neutrality, there is no consensus among traditionalists or among reformers concerning adiaphorism. As a post-philosophical, theological concept, adiaphorism was understood variously among individuals, and by groups large and small. Making deter-

Notes — Chapter 5

minations about faction or alliance based on this issue would be a mistake.

21. Verkamp devotes an entire chapter to this idea. *The Indifferent Mean*, pps. 61–92.

22. Guy, John. *A Daughter's Love: Thomas and Margaret More*. London: Fourth Estate, impr. HarperCollins, 2008, p. 235; and Rastell, William. *The Workes of Sir Thomas More Knight, Sometyme Lorde Chancellour of England, Wrytten by Him in the Englysh Tonge*. London: John Cawood, John Waly, and Richard Tottel, 1557, p. 1441, marginal note by William Rastell.

23. *The Correspondence of Sir Thomas More*, ed. Elizabeth Frances Rogers. Princeton: Princeton University Press, 1947, pps. 512–13.

24. *Correspondence*, pps. 512–13.

25. There has been much discussion about how much Margaret Roper contributed to the composition of the *Letter to Alice Alington*. William Rastell presumes that most of the work is More's, and John Guy, Louis Martz, and Peter Ackroyd agree. Although there is no doubt that Margaret Roper was extraordinarily clever, and that she contributed to the letter's general idea, the artfulness and skill of the writing points to More as its primary author.

26. Rastell, *The Workes of Sir Thomas More*, p. 1434.

27. Rastell, *The Workes of Sir Thomas More*, p. 1434.

28. Rastell, *The Workes of Sir Thomas More*, p. 1434.

29. Rastell, *The Workes of Sir Thomas More*, p. 1435.

30. Rastell, *The Workes of Sir Thomas More*, p. 1435.

31. Rastell, *The Workes of Sir Thomas More*, p. 1436.

32. Rastell, *The Workes of Sir Thomas More*, p. 1436.

33. Both More and Audley had served Cardinal Wolsey during the 1520s.

34. Rastell, *The Workes of Sir Thomas More*, p. 1436.

35. Rastell, *The Workes of Sir Thomas More*, p. 1436.

36. Rastell, *The Workes of Sir Thomas More*, p. 1437.

37. Rastell, *The Workes of Sir Thomas More*, p. 1437.

38. Rastell, *The Workes of Sir Thomas More*, p. 1438.

39. Rastell, *The Workes of Sir Thomas More*, p. 1438.

40. Rastell, *The Workes of Sir Thomas More*, pps. 1438–39.

41. Rastell, *The Workes of Sir Thomas More*, p. 1439.

42. Rastell, *The Workes of Sir Thomas More*, p. 1439.

43. Rastell, *The Workes of Sir Thomas More*, p. 1440.

44. Martz, *Thomas More: The Search for the Inner Man*, p. 60.

45. Simon Fish had provided statistics concerning parish revenues in *Supplication of the Beggars*.

46. Pineas, Rainer. "John Bale's Nondramatic Works of Religious Controversy." *Studies in the Renaissance*, vol. 9 (1962), p. 220.

47. Leslie Fairfield points out the amusing fact that amid Bale's condemnation of most chroniclers as liars, he was not above using the salacious gossip and lurid stories he found within the chronicles to pepper his own work. Fairfield, *John Bale, Mythmaker for the English Reformation*, p. 118.

48. Iohan Harryson [John Bale]. *Yet a Course at the Romyshe Foxe: A Disclosynge or Openyng of the Manne of Synne...* Zurich: Oliver Jacobson [A. Goinus], 1543, pps. 2a and 14b.

49. Bale, *Yet a Course at the Romyshe Foxe*, p. 26b.

50. See Appendix for Bale's version of the recantation it is reproduced in an abbreviated form in boldface throughout *Yet a Course at the Romyshe Foxe*, as Bale comments between the paragraphs. Alexander Seton's printing of the declaration had been issued a year earlier, and a copy is now held by the Lambeth Palace Library. *The Declaracion Made at Poules Crosse in the Cyte of London the Fourth Sonday of Advent*, by Alexander Seton and Mayster Willyam Tolwyn, Persone of S. Anthonynes in the sayd Cytye of London. London: Richard Lant, 1542.

51. Bale, *Yet a Course at the Romyshe Foxe*, pps. 2a and b.

52. Bale, *Yet a Course at the Romyshe Foxe*, pps. 25b and 26a.

53. Bale, *Yet a Course at the Romyshe Foxe*, p. 26b.

54. Bale, *Yet a Course at the Romyshe Foxe*, p. 27a, and marginal note.

55. Bale, *Yet a Course at the Romyshe Foxe*, p. 55b.

56. Bale, *Yet a Course at the Romyshe Foxe*, p. 47a.

57. Bale, *Yet a Course at the Romyshe Foxe*, p. 46b, parenthetical insert mine.

Notes — Chapter 5

58. For a discussion of the Tudor view of the Covenant, see Chapter II of this volume, entitled, "The Matter of Resources: Sworn Bond and Biblical Example in *The Boke Named the Governour.*"

59. Unfortunately, Bale is never far from Anti-Semitism in his discussions of the Old Testament forefathers. Soon after his praise for the Israelites' proper observance of sworn bond, he notes that because the Jews eventually placed too much trust in ceremonialism, God came to detest them. Bale, *Yet a Course at the Romyshe Foxe*, p. 78b.

60. Bale, *Yet a Course at the Romyshe Foxe*, p. 74b.

61. Throughout his work, Bale makes similar statements about the Mass, sacramentalism, pilgrimages, relics, and so on.

62. Bale, *Yet a Course at the Romyshe Foxe*, p. 80b.

63. Bale, *Yet a Course at the Romyshe Foxe*, p. 79b.

64. Bale, *Yet a Course at the Romyshe Foxe*, p. 79b.

65. One can contrast Bale's attitude toward Tolwyn with his nearly hagiographic attitudes toward John Oldcastle and Anne Askew, who refused to recant, and who willingly went to their deaths for their beliefs. See Bale, *A Brefe Chronycle Concernynge the Examinacyon and Death of the Blessed Martyr of Christ Sir John Oldcastle...* Antwerp: Hans Luft, 1544; and *The First Examinacyon of Anne Askewe, Latelye Martyred in Smythfielde, by the Romysh Popes Upholders...* Wesel: D. van der Straten, 1546.

66. Bale, *Yet a Course at the Romyshe Foxe*, p. 29b.

67. Bale, *Yet a Course at the Romyshe Foxe*, p. 92b.

68. Harington, *A New Discourse*, p. 5.

69. In the twenty-eighth canto, a king, a general, and a courtier devise a game by which they will test the chastity of women around the world to see if all women are as false as their own wives. The experiment proves that they are. Interestingly, Edmund Spenser includes an adapted version of this story in Book III, Canto VII of *The Faerie Queene*, published barely one year before Harington's translation of Ariosto. Spenser's version, however, avoids any discussion of the chastity of queens, and provides a general critique of the courtly love tradition instead.

70. The reference appears on p. 256 of Dunno's edition, but given the context it is difficult to determine whether Harington is making a serious reference to a real incident or a sarcastic response to a rumor that enhanced his reputation as a witty antagonist with an ability to influence others.

71. More had also referenced Harry Patenson, his family's jester, who, according to Margaret, had taken the oath. But again More's attitude is far different from Harington's: although More did not value the advice given or the examples provided by servants, he respected Patenson as a man who merely played the jester because it was his profession to do so. More did not believe that Patenson was actually a fool; he understood that self-preservation meant something different to a servant than it did to a former Lord Chancellor. *The Correspondence of Sir Thomas More*, ed. E.F. Rogers. Princeton: Princeton University Press, 1947, p. 529.

72. Bowers, Rick and Smith, Paul. "Wit, Humor, and Elizabethan Coping: Sir John Harington and the Metamorphosis of Ajax." *Humor*, vol. 17, issue 3 (2004), p. 183.

73. Scott-Warren, "The Privy Politics of Sir John Harington's *New Discourse...*," p. 414.

74. Harington, John. *A New Discourse...* Part III: "An Apologie..." (title page). London: Routledge and Kegan Paul, 1962; also Harington, John. *An Apologie...* London: Richard Field, 1596.

75. Harington, *An Apologie...* p. 206.

76. Harington, *An Apologie...* p. 208. Harington depicts his judges as pretentious men who know only rudimentary Latin and Greek, and who therefore sound out the "words" in English.

77. Harington, *An Apologie...* p. 209.

78. Harington, *An Apologie...* p. 211. Emphasis Harington's.

79. Harington, *An Apologie...* p. 213.

80. A common punishment for knavery or roguery.

81. This little remark is actually quite important, as English noblemen often bragged about ancestors who had been sent to the stake or gibbet. Elizabeth Dunno provides an anecdote told by a Venetian, of a foreigner who asked an English captain whether any of his family had ever been hanged or quartered. When the captain replied that he did not know of any, another Englishman whispered, "Don't be surprised, for he is not a gentleman." *Apologie*, pps. 215–16, n. 62; also Great Britain, Public Record Office. *Calendar of State Papers and Manuscripts, Relating to English Affairs Existing in the Archives and Col-*

lection of Venice, and in Other Libraries of Northern Italy, vol. VI. London: Longman, Green, Longman, Roberts, and Green, 1864, Part III, item 1672.

82. Harington, *An Apologie*, pps. 219–20.
83. Harington, *An Apologie*, pps. 221–22.
84. Harington, *An Apologie*, p. 222.
85. For a discussion of this issue and its connection to sworn bond, see Chapter IV of this volume, entitled, "Grudgings, Mutterings, and Horn Blasts: Aurality and Performativity in Reformation Polemic."
86. Harington, *An Apologie*, p. 227, n. 128.
87. Harington, *An Apologie*, p. 229, n. 135. Sir John Spenser was of no relation to the poet Edmund Spenser.
88. Harington, *An Apologie*, p. 213, n. 146.
89. Harington, *An Apologie*, p. 234, n. 157.
90. Harington, *An Apologie*, p. 237, n. 135. Dunno identifies this colloquialism as meaning, "someone who is good in a pinch."
91. Harington, *An Apologie*, p. 238, n, 187.
92. Harington, *An Apologie*, p. 240, n. 196.
93. Harington's joke concerning this man presumes that his lameness and Stoicism are related, but it is not known which came first.
94. Harington, *An Apologie*, pps. 241–54, for Harington's long rant against Markham.
95. Harington, *An Apologie*, p. 253.
96. Pronounced "shrewd."
97. Harington, *An Apologie*, p. 255.
98. Harington, *An Apologie*, p. 262.
99. Harington himself denied this very charge about five years later. *Apologie*, p. 262, n. 316.
100. Harington, *An Apologie*, p. 262.
101. Harington, *An Apologie*, p. 262, emphasis Harington's.
102. Scott Warren, "The Privy Politics of Sir John Harington's *New Discourse*...," p. 434.
103. Harington, *An Apologie*, p. 258.

Chapter 6

1. Henry VIII had been excommunicated twice: once in 1533 and again in 1538; ad Elizabeth I had been excommunicated in 1570.
2. *The Troublesome Raigne of John, King of England...* London: By T. Orwin for Sampson Clarke, 1591, title page.
3. Roger of Wendover. *Flowers of History, Comprising the History of England from the Descent of the Saxons to* A.D. *1235*, vol. ii. London: Henry G. Bohn, 1849, p. 250. The entire section on the reign of King John is full of statements of this type.
4. Capgrave, John. *The Chronicle of England*, ed. Francis Charles Hingeston. London: Longman, Brown, Green, Longman, and Roberts, 1858, p. 148; and Knighton, Henry. *Chronicon Henrici Knighton*, ed. J.R. Lumby, vol. i. London: Rolls Series, 1889–95, p. 187.
5. Given-Wilson, Chris. *Chronicles: The Writing of History in Medieval England.* London: Hambledon and London, 2004, p. 183.
6. Tyndale, William. *The Obedience of a Christian Man, and How Christian Rulers Ought to Governe...* Antwerp: J. Hoochstraten, 1528, fol. clvii, verso.
7. Holinshed, Raphael. *The First Volume of the Chronicles of England, Scotlande, and Irelande:...* London: Henry Bynneman for George Bishop, 1577, p. 565.
8. King John most likely died of dysentery, which had not been the result of poisoned peaches or ale, as rumors suggested.
9. Bale, John. *Actes of the Englishe Votaryes, Gathered Out of Theyr Owne Legendes and Chronicles...* London, 1548; *A Mysterye of Inyquyte Contayned Within the Hereticall Genealogye of Ponce Pantolabus.* Geneva [Antwerp]: By Mycheal Woode [A. Goinus], 1545; and *The Vocacyon of Johan Bale to the Bishiprick of Ossorie in Irelande...* Rome [Wesel] by J. Lambrecht for Hugh Singleton, 1553.
10. About the Chronicles, notably Wendover, Cromwell said that they were false, malicious, and heretical, and that King John had been falsely accused. See *L&P*, vol. vii, item 624.
11. Robinson, Marsha. "The Historiographic Methodology of *King John*," *King John: New Perspectives*, ed. Deborah T. Curren-Aquino. Newark: University of Delaware Press, 1989, p. 30.
12. Vaughan, Virginia. "King John: A Study in Subversion and Containment," *King John: New Perspectives*, p. 63.
13. The king's sworn obligation to his people is outlined in the coronation oath. See Chapter I of this volume, entitled, "Defiance by Prerogative: The Coronation Oath of Henry VIII."
14. For a further discussion of this issue, see Chapter II of this volume, entitled, "The Matter of Resources: Sworn Bond and Biblical Example in *The Boke Named the Governour*."

Notes — Chapter 6

15. A comprehensive discussion of the ideals of medieval kingship and the relationship between the three estates is found in *The Three Richards*, by Nigel Saul. London: Hambledon and London, 2005. In several introductory chapters Saul discusses these ideals in terms of how they were either upheld or neglected by Richards I, II, and III. Interestingly, Saul's discussion uses the legacy of John Lackland as "Bad King John" to provide a contrast with the heroic myth of John's older brother Richard Cordelion.
16. Translated in Norgate, Kate. *John Lackland*. London: Macmillan, 1902, pps. 391–92.
17. Wendover, *Flowers of History*, ii, p. 181.
18. Bale, John. *Kynge Johan*, ed. Barry Adams. San Marino: Huntington Library Press, 1969, I. 22–24.
19. Bale, *Kynge Johan*, I. 510–14.
20. For a further discussion of Bale's polemic and cynicism, see Chapter V of this volume, entitled, "Credibility Among Cynics: Coerced Sworn Bond in More, Bale, and Harington."
21. XXV Hen. VIII c. 19 (Submission of the Clergy).
22. Bale, *Kynge Johan*, I. 519–21.
23. Bale, *Kynge Johan*, I. 522–23.
24. For a further discussion of this issue, see Chapter III of this volume, entitled, "Additions and Admissions: The Manipulation of Sworn Bond in the Henrician Fealty Oath."
25. Anonymous. *The Troublesome Raigne of John, Kinge of England*, ed. J.W. Sider. New York: Garland Publishing, 1979, I.i.159–162.
26. *Troublesome Raigne*, I.i. 211–12.
27. *Troublesome Raigne*, I.i. 238–9.
28. Shakespeare, William. *King John*, ed. Claire McEachern. New York: Penguin Books, 2000, I.i. 245.
29. Groves, Beatrice. "Memory, Composition, and the Relationship of *King John* to *The Troublesome Raigne of King John*," *Comparative Drama*, vol. 38, issues 2/3, 2004, pps. 277–291.
30. Greenblatt, *Renaissance Self-Fashioning*, Introduction.
31. *Troublesome Raigne*, I.i. 372–74.
32. *King John*, I.i.184. The Bastard has a separate, no less intriguing, but fully developed, relationship with sworn bond. It revolves around his newly established relationship with the dead Richard Cordelion, and with the continuing development of his persona. It is a subject deserving of a separate study.
33. *King John*, II.i. 236–40.
34. It is also likely that the succession issue is omitted from *Kynge Johan* because of the controversies surrounding the Tudor succession in 1539, when the play was first performed. After the divorce of Katherine of Aragon, the execution of Anne Boleyn, and the death of Jane Seymour, the subject may have been too delicate to raise. Both Mary and Elizabeth had been declared illegitimate, and Edward was the sole (and sickly) heir. The same may have been true as Bale revised *Kynge Johan* for a possible performance before Elizabeth I at Ipswich just after her succession. Moreover, Henry VIII had not been the eldest child of Henry VII and Elizabeth of York; the first Prince of Wales had been his brother Arthur.
35. *Troublesome Raigne*, I.i.100–104.
36. *Troublesome Raigne*, I.i. 105–107.
37. *King John*, III.i. 9–10.
38. *Troublesome Raigne*, I.ii. 462–67.
39. *King John*, III.i. 60–61.
40. *King John*, III.i. 107.
41. Hamel, Guy. "*King John* and *The Troublesome Raigne*: A Reexamination," *King John, New Perspectives*, p. 48.
42. Hamel, "*King John* and *The Troublesome Raigne*: A Reexamination," p. 50.
43. Bale, *Kynge Johan*, I. 619–23.
44. Bale, *Kynge Johan*, II. 1184–85.
45. Bale, *Kynge Johan*, II. 1216 and 1222.
46. Bale, *Kynge Johan*, II. 1658–65.
47. Bale, *Kynge Johan*, II. 173ff.
48. Bale, *Kynge Johan*, II. 1957–58.
49. *Troublesome Raigne*, I.iii. 67.
50. *Troublesome Raigne*, I.iii. 79–82.
51. *King John*, III.i. 147–8.
52. It is also likely that such depictions were considered antiquated by the 1590s, although the plays of Shakespeare and many others of the period do contain scenes of fabliau-related comedy, reminiscent of the cycle plays.
53. Bale, *Kynge Johan*, II. 1473–76.
54. Bale, *Kynge Johan*, II. 1479–87.
55. *Troublesome Raigne*, II.xi. 199 and 213–15.
56. *Troublesome Raigne*, II.xi. 222–24.
57. *Troublesome Raigne*, II.xi. 227.
58. Holinshed records that the nobles at St. Edmundsbury had sworn to make war upon John until he agreed to address their grievances. *Troublesome Raigne* adapts that situation, and makes it about allegiance to Lewes instead.

Notes — Chapter 6

59. *Troublesome Raigne*, II.xvi. 22–23.
60. *King John*, V.ii. 1–2.
61. *King John*, V.ii. 6.
62. *King John*, V.ii. 9–15.
63. Klause, John. "New Sources for Shakespeare's *King John*: The Writings of Robert Southwell," *Studies in Philology*, vol. 98, no. 4, Autumn 2001, p. 423.
64. Because this chapter's focus is on King John and his three estates in England, I will not be discussing the relationship between King Philip, the Dauphin, the French nobles, and Pandulph. Although French traditions concerning these principles are similar, they are not identical.
65. *Troublesome Raigne*, II.i. 269–72.
66. *Troublesome Raigne*, II.i. 273–75.
67. *Troublesome Raigne*, II.i. 538–39.
68. *King John*, IV.ii. 141–52.
69. See Chapter I of this volume, entitled, "Defiance by Prerogative: The Coronation Path of Henry VIII," for a discussion of this legend.
70. *King John*, IV.ii. 9.
71. As Barbara Traister points out, the coronation oath, as an emblem of the ceremonial body of kingship, establishes that the monarch is invested from the moment of the previous sovereign's death. Rather than doubly establishing his right to rule, King John's second coronation threatens to argue the converse: that he had not been invested from the moment of Richard's death, and that perhaps Arthur had. Traister, Barbara. "The King's One Body: Unceremonial Kingship in *King John*," *King John, New Perspectives*, p. 93.
72. *Troublesome Raigne*, II.x. 21–23.
73. Hamel, "*King John* and *The Troublesome Raigne*," p. 52.
74. *King John*, IV.i. 58–59.
75. *Troublesome Raigne*, I.vii.81–126, for the entire exchange between Arthur and Hubert.
76. Hubert's decision is based on the outstanding principle that even if a king were a tyrant, his subjects were obligated to obey him. Providence would punish such a king and his kingdom at a later date, and his subjects would then be free to place the blame on the king for the misfortune of the realm. See Gautier, Léon. *Chivalry* (1898), trans. D.C. Dunning. New York: Barnes and Noble, 1968; Rosenwein, Barbara. *Anger's Past: The Social Uses of an Emotion in the Middle Ages*. Ithaca: Cornell University Press, 1998; and Walker, Greg, *Writing Under Tyranny*.

77. Bale, *Kynge Johan*, I. 103–4.
78. *King John*, IV.ii. 208–209, and 231–36.
79. Bale, *A Disclosynge or Openynge of the Manne of Synne*, p. 46.
80. *King John*, V.vii. 32–33.
81. *Troublesome Raigne*, II.x. 186–87.
82. *Troublesome Raigne*, II.xv. 76–79.
83. *Troublesome Raigne*, II.xv. 144–47.
84. Kantorowicz, Ernst Hartwig. *The King's Two Bodies: A Study in Medieval Political Theology*. Princeton, NJ: Princeton University Press, 1957.
85. Jones, Robert C. *These Valiant Dead: Renewing the Past in Shakespeare's Histories*. Iowa City: University of Iowa Press, 1991, p. 50.
86. *Troublesome Raigne*, II.xv. 138.
87. Melun, one of the French lords, reveals his conscience and informs the English barons that the Dauphin seeks to have them killed as soon as the battle is over. He laments his false oath, made doubly treacherous because his grandfather had been an Englishman.
88. *Troublesome Raigne*, II.xvi. 20–23.
89. Only recusants extended this regard to Mary I, and they did so at their peril.
90. *King John*, V.iv. 49–57.
91. *King John*, V.ii. 128–29.
92. For a comprehensive discussion of Imperyall Majestie, his function and symbolism both inside and outside the play, see Cervone, Thea. "The King's Phantom: Staging Majesty in Bale's *Kynge Johan*," *Studies in Medievalism* XVII. Cambridge: D.S. Brewer, 2009, pps. 185–202.
93. Bale, *Kynge Johan*, II. 2287–90.
94. Bale, *Kynge Johan*, II. 2303–04.
95. Bale, *Kynge Johan*, II. 2309–14.
96. Bale, *Kynge Johan*, II. 2435.
97. Bale, *Kynge Johan*, II. 2497.
98. Although Sedycyon's speech contains elements familiar to the rite of auricular confession, Bale was against the practice, which, in any case, had yet to be banned by Henry VIII. Here, Sedycyon's "confession" to Imperyall Majestie appears as an admission of his crimes to a figure who represents both God and King rather than the Church. Clergye remains silent during Sedycyon's admission.
99. Hogdon, Barbara. *The End Crowns All: Closure and Contradiction in Shakespeare's Histories*. Princeton, NJ: Princeton University Press, p. 32.
100. Cranmer, Thomas. *Works*, vol. ii, ed.

the Rev. John Edmund Cox for the Parker Society. Cambridge: Cambridge University Press, 1844–46, pps. 126–27; and Sibly, John. "The Anomalous Case of *King John*," *English Literary History* vol. 33, no. 4 (December 1966), pps. 415–421.

Chapter 7

1. McClaren, Anne. "The Quest for a King: Gender, Marriage, and Succession in Elizabethan England." *Journal of British Studies*, vol. 41, no. 3 (July 2002), p. 263.
2. Millican, Charles B. "Spenser and the Arthurian Tradition," *The Review of English Studies*, vol. 6, no. 22 (1930), p. 167.
3. For a discussion of the continuous reinterpretation of the misogyny of the Arthurian legend see Noble, James. "Tintagel: The Best of English Twinkie," *King Arthur in Popular Culture*, ed. Elizabeth Sklar and Donald Hoffman. Jefferson, NC: McFarland, 2002, pps. 36ff.
4. 25 Henry VIII, c. 19 (Act in Restraint of Appeals, Preamble).
5. Millican, Charles. *Spenser and the Table Round: A Study in the Contemporaneous Background for Spenser's Use of the Arthurian Legend*. Cambridge, MA: Harvard University Press, 1932, p. 94.
6. Here, Amoret is an exception, since she is already married to Scudamore.
7. 1596 version.
8. Alpers, Paul. *The Poetry of the Faerie Queene*. Princeton, NJ: Princeton University Press, 1967, p. 113.
9. Leslie, Michael. *Spenser's "Fierce Warres and Faithfull Loves": Martial and Chivalric Symbolism in the Faerie Queene*. Cambridge: D.S. Brewer/Barnes and Noble, 1983, p. 135; Schofield, William. *Chivalry in English Literature*. Cambridge, MA: Harvard University Press, 1912, p. 5; and Gautier, Léon. *Chivalry*, p. 144ff.
10. Britomart actually swears three times in Book III: she swears two platonic leagues with other knights and one oath in anger outside Malbecco's castle. None of these oaths, however, are love vows, and none of them describe espousal or betrothal.
11. Spenser, Edmund. *The Faerie Queene*, ed. Thomas P. Roche and C. Patrick O'Donnell. New York: Penguin Classic Edition, 1979, III.ii.33.5–7.
12. *FQ*, III.ii.46.8–9.
13. *FQ*, III.iii.57.6.

14. Britomart embodies many of Castiglione's "virtues of the minde," including wisdom, temperance, and sobriety of mood. Castiglione also provides a source for Britomart's ability to overcome physical illness with nightly prowess. He states that reason has so much force in a worthy person, "she maketh the sense always to obey ... so that althoughe ye spirites and the sinews, and the bones have no reason in them, yet when there springeth in us ye motion of minde ... all ye members are in a readinesse, the feet to renne, ye handees to take or to doe that which the kinde thinketh upon." Castiglione, Baldassare. *The Courtyer ... Done into Englyshe by Thomas Hoby*. London: William Seres, 1561, O.o.ii and Yy.iiii.
15. T.G.A. Nelson, "Doing Things with Words: Another Look at Marriage Rites and Spousals in Renaissance Drama and Fiction." *Studies in Philology*, vol. 95, no. 4 (Autumn 1998), p. 359.
16. *FQ*, III.iii.26.1–2.
17. The pneumatic gaze is a binding mystical and erotic element between two partners. It is based on Platonic, Aristotelian, and Galenic theory and is adapted in the works of Marcilio Ficino, Pico della Mirandola, and Giordano Bruno. Spenser was familiar with the works of these Italian authors. See Couliano, Ioan. *Eros and Magic in the Renaissance*. Chicago: University of Chicago Press, 1986.
18. This image corresponds to the dysfunctional image of the narcissistic lover present in Couliano's discussion of Ficino (vis-à-vis Carl Jung), although Spenser avoids this type of metaphor. Couliano, *Eros and Magic in the Renaissance*, p. 32.
19. Lethbridge, J.B. *Shakespeare and Spenser: Attractive Opposites*. Manchester: Manchester University Press, 2008, pps. 239–40.
20. Dawson, Lesel. *Lovesickness and Gender in Early Modern Literature*. Oxford: Oxford University Press, 2008, p. 128.
21. Britomart meets Sir Guyon before she tells Redcrosse her story as a flashback.
22. *FQ*, III.ii.12.
23. Berners, *The Book of St. Albans*, p. F.iii.
24. Redcrosse marries Una in *FQ*, I.xii.
25. For an example of abuse within the courtly love system, see Andreas Capellanus' dialogue between a lover and a noblewoman. Capellanus, *On Love*, I. Cap. C.
26. *FQ*, III.ii.27.6. "Perdy" is a mild oath that does not affect Britomart's character.
27. See Berners and Castiglione for the

issue of restraint for knights. *The Courtyer*, p. Y.y.iii, and *The Book of St. Albans*, pps. F.ii–iii.

28. *FQ*, III.i.28.2–6.

29. Redcrosse's situation actually poses a conundrum where bonds of espousal are concerned. In I.xii Redcrosse marries Una, and the espousals are witnessed and validated by Una's father, the King of Eden. After a short time, Redcrosse is required to leave Una in the charge of her parents while he serves Gloriana, the Faerie Queene, for six years. Here the chivalric bond between a knight and his monarch trumps the bond of espousal between husband and wife. Indeed, Spenser acknowledges this fact in I.i.3.4–5, when he states that Redcrosse's mission to slay the dragon is meant "To winne him worship, and her grace to have/Which of all earthly things he most did crave." Because his monarch is female, the metaphor is even more suggestive: Redcrosse is "married" to his queen moreso than to his wife.

30. *FQ*, III.iii.62.8.
31. *FQ*, III.iv.4.4.
32. *FQ*, III.vi.3.6–9.

33. Amoret is indeed rescued in III.xii, but the wedding and Amoret's abduction are not described until IV.i.3.5, in a flashback sequence.

34. Nelson, "Doing Things with Words," p. 365.

35. *FQ*, IV.i.2.

36. Wells, Marion. *The Secret Wound: Love-Melancholy and Early Modern Romance*. Palo Alto, CA: Stanford University Press, 2007, p. 244.

37. Wells, The Secret Wound, p. 244.
38. Wells, The Secret Wound, p. 248.

39. Wells describes Busyrane as "...a sinister alter ego for Scudamore, spiriting away the beloved whom he desires only as an inaccessible object of his own mind." *The Secret Wound*, p. 251.

40. *FQ*, III.xi.20.4.
41. *FQ*, III.xi.20.4.

42. Nelson, "Doing Things with Words," p. 365; and Stone, Lawrence. *Road to Divorce: England 1530–1987*. Oxford: Oxford University Press, 1990.

43. *FQ*, III.xii.36–38.

44. The so-called "courtly love vow" can be difficult to define. Many *lais* and romances depict ambiguous or equivocal vows which are meant to provoke or escalate dramatic tension, as in Beroul's *Tristan and Isolde*, or Chretien's *Knight of the Cart*. The marriage of the lovers usually represents resolution and permanence, as in Chretien's *Erec and Enide* or Marie De France's *Guigemar* (although Marie is not above revoking a marriage vow when it interferes with true love, as in *Le Fresne*).

45. *FQ*, III.xii.46 (1590 text).
46. *FQ*, III.xii.45 (1596 text).
47. *FQ*, III.v.10.3.
48. *FQ*, III.v.10.5–9.

49. See Chrétien de Troyes, *Lancelot, Knight of the Cart*, and Sir Thomas Malory, *The Noble Tale of the Sankgreal*, for two key examples. In the first example, Lancelot debases himself and searches to the point of exhaustion until he rescues Guinevere from Meleagant's capture. In the second, Guinevere waits seven years until Lancelot returns from his quest. Chrétien de Troyes, "Lancelot, Knight of the Cart," *Arthurian Romances*, ed. and trans. William W. Kibler. New York: Penguin Books, 2004; and Malory, Sir Thomas. "The Noble Tale of the Sankgreal," *Le Mort Darthur*, ed. Stephen Shepard. New York: W.W. Norton & Co., 2004.

50. The dates for such a practice are divided along religious lines, however; in Catholic Europe the practice ended in 1563, but in Protestant England it continued until 1753. See Nelson, "Doing Things with Words," p. 353.

51. Nelson, "Doing Things with Words," pps. 353 and 365.

52. Nelson, "Doing Things with Words," p. 372.

53. Nelson, "Doing Things with Words," p. 372.

54. *FQ*, III.v.8.2–6.
55. *FQ*, IV.xii.29.4–6.
56. *FQ*, IV. xii.32. 2.
57. *FQ*, IV.vi.12ff.
58. *FQ*, IV.vi.41.6–9.
59. *FQ*, IV.vi.41.5.
60. *FQ*, IV.vi.46.8–9.

61. McLaren, Anne. "The Quest for a King," pps. 266–68.

62. McLaren, Anne. "The Quest for a King," pps. 270 and 279.

Bibliography

Primary Sources

Agard, Arthur. *The Repertorie of Records, Remaining in the 4. Treasuries on the Receipt Side at Westminster, the Two Remembrancers of the Exchequer: With a Briefe Introductive Index of the Records of the Chancery and Tower...* ed. Thomas Powell. Printed by B. Alsop and T. Fawcet, for B. Fisher, 1631.

Anonymous. *The Troublesome Raigne of John, King of England...* London: By T. Orwin for Sampson Clarke, London, 1591.

Aristotle. *Nichomachean Ethics*, ed. E. Capps, trans. H. Rachham. Loeb Classical Library Series. New York: G.P. Putnam's, 1926.

Augustine, Saint, Bishop of Hippo. *De Doctrina Christiana*. Oxford: Clarendon Press, 1995.

Bale, John. *The Apology of Iohan Bale Agaynste a Ranke Papyst: Anuswering Both Hym and Hys Doctours, That Neyther Their Vowes Nor Yet Their Priesthode Are of the Gospell, but of Antichrist.* S. Mierdman for John Day, 1550.

_____. *A Brefe Chronycle Concernynge the Examinacyon and Death of the Blessed Martyr of Christ Syr Iohan Oldecastell the Lorde Cobham, Collected Togyther by Iohan Bale.* Antwerp: Hans Luft [?] 1544.

_____. *The First Examinacyon of Anne Askewe, Latelye Martyred in Smythfelde, by the Romysh Popes Vpholders, with the Elucydacyon of Iohan Bale.* Wesel: Printed by D. van der Straten, 1546.

_____. *The First Two Partes of the Actes or Vnchaste Examples of the Englyshe Votaryes, Gathered Out of Theyr Owne Legendes and Chronycles by Ihon Bale, and Dedicated to Oure Most Redoubted Soueraigne Kyng Edwarde the Syxte.* London: By John Tysdale, 1560.

_____. *The Image of Both Churches After the Moste Wonderfull and Heauenly Reuelacion of Sainct Iohn the Euangelist, Contayning a Very Frutefull Exposicion or Paraphrase Vpon the Same. Wherein It Is Conferred with the Other Scriptures, and Most Auctorised Historyes.* London: Richard Jugge, 1548.

_____. *Kynge Johan*, ed. Barry Adams. San Marino: Huntington Library Press, 1969.

_____. *A Mysterye of Inyquyte Contayned Within the Heretycall Genealogye of Ponce Pantolabus*, An, M.D.xlii. Geneua [i.e. Antwerp]: By Mycheal Woode [i.e. A. Goinus], 1545.

_____. *The Pageant of Popes: Contayninge the Lyues of All the Bishops of Rome, from the Beginning of Them to the Yeare of Grace 1555...* Written in Latin by Maister Bale, and Now Englished with Sondrye Additions by I.S Thomas Marshe, 1574.

_____. *The Vocacyon of Ioha[n] Bale to the Bishiprick of Ossorie in Irelande His Persecu-

Bibliography

cions in Ye Same, & Finall Delyueraunce... [Imprinted in Rome [i.e. Wesel?]: [i.e. by J. Lambrecht? for Hugh Singleton], 1553.

_____. *Yet a Course at the Romyshe Foxe: A Dyclosynge or Openinge of the Manne of Synne, Contayned in the Late Declaration of the Popes Olde Faythe Made by Edmond Bonner Bysshopp of London...* Zurich: Oliver Jacobson [A. Goinus], 1543.

Berners, Dame Juliana. *The Book of St. Albans* (1496). New York: Abercrombie and Fitch, 1966.

Bridges, John. *The Supremacie of Christian Princes; Over All Persons Throughout Their Dominions, in All Causes So Wel Ecclesiastical as Temporall, Both Against the Counterblast of Thomas Stapleton, Replying on the Reverend Father in Christe, Robert Bishop of Winchester...* London: Henry Byneman for Humphrey Toye, 1573.

British Library MS Add. 19398, f. 44.

British Library MS Autogr. 32, 654 f. 58 (Addition to Lord Metford's proclamation on invading Scotland).

British Library MS Cotton Cleopatra E. iv., fol. 260 (Letter from Sir Thomas Elyot to Thomas Cromwell.)

British Library MS Cotton Cleopatra E vi f. 185 (Draft of The Act in Restraint of Appeals).

British Library MS Cotton Tiberius E viii f. 100a (Coronation Oath, Anomalous Form, with Autograph Emendations by Henry VIII).

British Library MS Cotton Tiberius E viii, fol. 313b. (Descriptions of the destruction of the shrine of Thomas Becket).

British Library MS Cotton Titus C. I (Papers of the Antiquarian Society).

British Library MS Cotton Vespasian C. vii f. 71 (Additions to instructions for Imperial Ambassadors Sir Philip Hoby and Sir Thomas Wyatt).

British Library MS Cotton Vitellius D iv (John Bale's papers).

MS Cotton Vitellius B. xxi, fols. 58–59 (Letter from Sir Thomas Elyot to the Duke of Norfolk).

British Library MS Harley 283 fol. 75r (Birth announcement of Elizabeth I).

British Library MS Harley 6986 f. 8 (Letter to the Earl of Shrewsbury).

British Library MS Kings 9 f. 231b (Notes to Anne Boleyn in a psalter).

British Library MS Kings 2 A xvi (Autograph notes in a psalter).

British Library MS Stowe 15. Manuscript Catalogue Description, *www.bl.uk/catalogues/manuscripts*.

British Library MS Stowe 15, ffs. 3–5, 8, 9b–11b, 19b, and 88.

Capellanus, Andreas. *On Love* (Thirteenth Century), ed. and trans. P.G. Walsh. London: Duckworth, 1982.

Capgrave, John. *The Chronicle of England*, ed. Francis Charles Hingeston. London: Longman, Brown, Green, Longmans, and Roberts, 1858.

Castiglione, Baldassare. *The Courtyer ... done into Englyshe by Thomas Hoby*. London: William Seres, 1561.

Chrétien de Troyes. "Lancelot, Knight of the Cart," *Arthurian Romances*, ed. and trans. William W. Kibler. New York: Penguin Books, 2004.

Cicero, M. Tullius. *De Legibus*, trans. Clinton Walker Keyes. Loeb Classical Library Series. New York: Putnam, 1928, II.viii.19, and II.ix.22. [0]

_____. *De Officiis*, Trans. Walter Miller, Ed. T.E. Page. Loeb Classical Library Series. New York: Macmillan, 1913.

Corpus Inscriptionum Latinarum, editione altera. Berolini: Apud. G. Reimerum and W. de Gruyter, 1893.

Bibliography

The Correspondence of Sir Thomas More, ed. Elizabeth Frances Rogers. Princeton, NJ: Princeton University Press, 1947.

Cranmer, Thomas. *Works*, vol. II, ed. the Rev. John Edmund Cox for the Parker Society. Cambridge University Press, 1844-46.

Elizabeth I. "Text of the Bond of Association," *Collected Works*, eds. Leah Marcus, Janel Mueller and Mary Beth Rose. Chicago: University of Chicago Press.

Elyot, Sir Thomas. *The Boke Named the Governour*. London: Thomas Bertheleti, 1531.

Fourth Lateran Council of 1215. "Omnis Utriusque Sexus," complete text in Great Britain, Public Record Office. *Letters and Papers, Foreign and Domestic, of the Reign of Henry VIII*, vols. XXI-XXII. London: Longman, Green, Longman & Roberts, 1862-1910, repr. 1965-1976.

Gough, John. *The Aunswer of Iohn Gough Preacher, to Maister Fecknams Obiections Against His Sermon, Lately Preached in the Tower of London*. By Iohn Awdley, 1570.

Great Britain. *Statutes of the Realm*, vol. III. London: G. Eyre and A. Strahan, 1810-1828.

Great Britain, Public Record Office. *Calendar of State Papers and Manuscripts, Relating to English Affairs Existing in the Archives and Collection of Venice, and in Other Libraries of Northern Italy*, vol. VI. London: Longman, Green, Longman, Roberts, and Green, 1864.

Great Britain Public Record Office. S.P. 1/75, fol. 81 (Letter from Sir Thomas Elyot to Sir John Hackett).

Harington, John. *An Apologie...* London: Richard Field, 1596.

———. *A New Discourse on a Stale Subject, Called the Metamorphosis of Ajax* (1596), ed. Elizabeth Story Dunno. London: Routledge and Kegan Paul, 1962.

Heltzel, Virgil B. *A Check List of Courtesy Books in the Newberry Library*. Chicago: Newberry Library, 1942.

Holinshed, Raphael. *The Firste Volume of the Chronicles of England, Scotlande, and Irelande: Conteyning, the Description and Chronicles of England, from the First Inhabiting Vnto the Conquest...* London: Henry Bynneman for George Bishop, 1577.

Holy Bible, King James Version. New York: NAL Penguin, 1974.

Horne, Robert. *An Answeare...* London: Henry Wykes, 1566.

Humphrey, Laurence. *The Nobles or of Nobilitye: The Original Nature, Dutyes, Right and Christian Institucion Thereof, Three Books*. London: Thomas Marshe, 1563.

Inscriptiones Latinae Selectae, ed. Hermann Dessau. Berolini: Apud. Weidmannos, 1892-1916.

Knighton, Henry. *Chronicon Henrici Knighton*, ed. J.R. Lumby, vol. i. London: Rolls Series, 1889-95.

Latimer, Hugh. "Last Sermon Preached before Edward VI, at Lent, Westminster." *Selected Sermons of Hugh Latimer*, ed. Allan G. Chester. Charlottesville: University of Virginia Press, 1968.

Malory, Thomas. "The Noble Tale of the Sankgreal," *Le Morte Darthur*, ed. Stephen Shepard. New York: W.W. Norton, 2004.

Marie De France. *The Lais of Marie de France*. Ed. and trans. Glyn S. Burgess and Keith Busby. New York: Penguin, 2003.

More, Sir Thomas. "A Dialogue Concerning Heresies." *The Complete Works of Thomas More*, New Haven: Yale University Press, 1963.

Plato. *Republic*, trans. Paul Shorey. New York: G.P. Putnam's, 1930-1935.

Proceedings in the Parliaments of Elizabeth I, ed. T.E. Hartley. Leicester: Leicester University Press, 1981.

Bibliography

Prynne, William. *The Signal Loyalty and Devotion of God's True Saints and Pious Christians Towards Their Kings*. 2 vols. London: T. Childs, Printer, 1660.

Rastell, William. *The Workes of Sir Thomas More Knyght, Sometyme Lorde Chancellour of England, Wrytten by Him in the Englysh Tonge*. London: John Cawood, John Waly, and Richard Tottel, 1557.

A Remonstrance of the Lords and Commons Assembled in Parliament... London: By I. Wright, 1642.

Roger of Wendover. *Flowers of History, Comprising the History of England from the Descent of the Saxons to* A.D. *1235*, vol. ii. London: Henry G. Bohn, 1849.

Seton, Alexander. *The Declaracion Made at Poules Crosse in the Cytye of London the Fourth Sonday of Aduent,* by Alexander Seyton and Mayster Willyam Tolwyn, Persone of S. Anthonynes in the Sayd Cytye of London, London: Rychard Lant, [1542?].

Shakespeare, William. *King John*, ed. Claire McEachern. New York: Penguin Books, 2000.

Stapleton, Thomas. *A Counterblast to M. Horne's Vayne Blaste Against M. Feckenham*. Louvain: Apud Ioannem Foulerum, 1567.

Swinnerton, Thomas. *A Litel Treatise Ageynste the Mutterynge of Some Papists in Corners*. London: Thomas Bertelet, 1534.

Tomson, Laurence. *An Ansvvere to Certein Assertions of M. Fecknam, Sometime Abbot of Westminster Which He Made of Late Against a Godly Sermon of M. Iohn Goughes, Preached in the Tower the xv. of Ianuarie*. Seen and allowed. London: Henry Bynneman, 1570.

Tyndale, William. *The Obedience of a Christen Man, and How Christen Rulers Ought to Gouerne...* Antwerp: J. Hoochstraten, 1528.

25 Henry VIII, c. 19 (Act in Restraint of Appeals, Premable).

25 Henry VIII, c. 22 (First Act of Succession)

28 Henry VIII. c. 10 (The Act Extinguishing the Authority of the Bishop of Rome).

Secondary Sources

Alpers, Paul. *The Poetry of the Faerie Queene*. Princeton, NJ: Princeton University Press, 1967.

Austin, J.L. *How to Do Things with Words*, eds. J.O. Urmson and Marina Sbisa. New Haven, CT: Harvard University Press, 1975.

Bartlett, Robert. *Trial by Fire and Water: The Medieval Judicial Ordeal*. Oxford: Clarendon Press, 1986.

Bernard, G.W. *The King's Reformation: Henry VIII and the Remaking of the English Church*. New Haven: Yale University Press, 2005.

Bowers, Rick, and Paul Smith. "Wit, Humor, and Elizabethan Coping: Sir John Harington and the Metamorphosis of Ajax." *Humor*, vol. 17, issue 3 (2004).

Canfield, J. Douglas. *Word as Bond in English Literature from the Middle Ages to the Restoration*. Philadelphia: University of Pennsylvania Press, 1989.

Condren, Conal. *Argument and Authority in Early Modern England: The Presupposition of Oaths and Offices*. Cambridge: Cambridge University Press, 2006.

Couliano, Ioan. *Eros and Magic in the Renaissance*. Chicago: University of Chicago, 1986.

Cross, Claire. *The Royal Supremacy in the Elizabethan Church*. London: Allen and Unwin, 1969.

Bibliography

Dawson, Lesel. *Lovesickness and Gender in Early Modern Literature*. Oxford: Oxford University Press, 2008.

DeLumeau, Jean. *Sin and Fear: The Emergence of a Western Guilt Culture 13th–18th Centuries*, trans. Eric Nicholson. New York: St. Martin's Press, 1990.

Duffy Eamon. *The Stripping of the Altars*. New Haven: Yale University Press, 1992.

Einstein, Lewis. *Tudor Ideals*. London: G. Bell, 1921.

Ellis, Henry. *English Coronation Records*, ed. Leopold G. Wickham-Legge. Westminster: A. Constable, 1901.

———. *Original Letters, Illustrative of English History*. London: Harding, Triphook & Lepard, 1824;

Elton, G.R. *Reform and Reformation: England 1509–1558*. Cambridge, MA: Harvard University Press, 1979.

English Historical Documents, ed. Dorothy Whitelock. New York: Oxford University Press, 1979.

Fairfield, Leslie. *John Bale Mythmaker for the English Reformation*. Purdue University Press, 1976.

Gallagher, Lowell. *Medusa's Gaze: Casuistry and Conscience in the Renaissance*. Stanford: Stanford University Press, 1991, p. 6.

Garret, Christina H. *The Marian Exiles: A Study in the Origins of Elizabethan Puritanism*. Cambridge: Cambridge University Press, 1938.

Gautier, Léon. *Chivalry*. (1898), trans. D.C. Dunning. New York: Barnes and Noble, 1968.

Given-Wilson, Chris. *Chronicles: The Writing of History in Medieval England*. London: Hambledon and London, 2004.

Greenblatt, Stephen. *Renaissance Self-Fashioning from More to Shakespeare*. Chicago: University of Chicago Press, 1980.

Groves, Beatrice. "Memory, Composition, and the Relationship of *King John* to *The Troublesome Raigne of King John*," *Comparative Drama*, vol. 38, issues 2/3, 2004.

Guy, John. *A Daughter's Love: Thomas and Margaret More*. London: Fourth Estate, impr. HarperCollins, 2008.

———. *Tudor England*. Oxford: Oxford University Press, 1988.

Hamel, Guy. "*King John* and *The Troublesome Raigne*: A Reexamination," *King John, New Perspectives*, ed. Deborah T. Curren-Aquino. Newark: University of Delaware Press, 1989.

Helgerson, Richard. *Forms of Nationhood: The Elizabethan Writing of England*. Chicago: University of Chicago Press, 1992.

Henry VIII and His Afterlives. Eds. Mark Rankin, Christopher Haighley, and John N. King. Cambridge: Cambridge University Press, 2009.

Hickman, David. "Religious Belief and Pious Practice Among London's Elizabethan Elite." *The Historical Journal*, vol. 42, no. 4 (Dec. 1999).

Hillam, David. *Crown, Orb, and Sceptre: True Stories of English Coronations*. Gloucestershire: Sutton, 2001.

Hogdon, Barbara. *The End Crowns All: Closure and Contradiction in Shakespeare's Histories*. Princeton, NJ: Princeton University Press, 1991.

Jones, Norman. *The English Reformation: Religion and Cultural Adaptation*. Oxford: Blackwell, 2002.

Jones, Robert C. *These Valiant Dead: Renewing the Past in Shakespeare's Histories*. Iowa City: University of Iowa Press, 1991.

Bibliography

Jones, William. *Crowns and Coronations*. London: Chatto & Windus, 1902.
Kantorowicz, Ernst Hartwig. *The King's Two Bodies; A Study in Mediaeval Political Theology*. Princeton, NJ: Princeton University Press, 1957.
Kelso, Ruth. *The Doctrine of the English Gentleman in the Sixteenth Century*. Urbana: University of Illinois Press, 1929.
Kendrick, T.D. *British Antiquity*. London: Methuen, 1950.
Kerrigan, William. *Shakespeare's Promises*. Baltimore: Johns Hopkins University Press, 1999.
Klause, John. "New Sources for Shakespeare's *King John*: The Writings of Robert Southwell," *Studies in Philology*, vol. 98, no. 4, Autumn 2001.
Lehmberg, Stanford. *The Reformation Parliament, 1529–1536*. Cambridge: Cambridge University Press, 1970.
_____. *Sir Thomas Elyot—Tudor Humanist*. Austin: University of Texas Press, 1960.
Leslie, Michael. *Spenser's "Fierce Warres and Faithfull Loves": Martial and Chivalric Symbolism in the Faerie Queene*. Cambridge: D.S. Brewer/Barnes and Noble, 1983.
Lethbridge, J.B. *Shakespeare and Spenser: Attractive Opposites*. Manchester: Manchester University Press, 2008.
Lipscomb, Susannah. *1536: The Year That Changed Henry VIII*. London: Lion, 2009.
Loach, Jennifer. "The Function of Ceremonial in the Reign of Henry VIII," *Past and Present* no. 142 (Feb. 1994).
Martz, Louis. *Thomas More: The Search for the Inner Man*. New Haven: Yale University Press, 1990.
McClaren, Anne. "The Quest for a King: Gender, Marriage, and Succession in Elizabethan England. *Journal of British Studies*, vol. 41, no. 3 (July 2002).
Millican, Charles B. "Spenser and the Arthurian Tradition," *The Review of English Studies*, vol. 6, no. 22 (1930).
_____. *Spenser and the Table Round: A Study in the Contemporary Background for Spenser's Use of the Arthurian Legend*. Cambridge: Harvard University Press, 1932.
Nelson T.G.A. "Doing Things with Words: Another Look at Marriage Rites and Spousals in Renaissance Drama and Fiction." *Studies in Philology*, vol. 95, no. 4 (Autumn 1998).
Noble, James. "Tintagel: The Best of English Twinkie," *King Arthur in Popular Culture*, eds. Elizabeth Sklar and Donald Hoffman. Jefferson, NC: McFarland, 2002.
Norgate, Kate. *John Lackland*. London: Macmillan, 1902.
Norland, Howard. "More's and Elyot's Perspectives and Their Classical Antecedents." *Moreana* 40 (2003), nos. 153–4.
O'Connell, Marvin R. *Thomas Stapleton and the Counter Reformation*. New Haven: Yale University Press, 1964.
Oscar, D. *History of Penance*, vol. II, London: Longmans, Green, 1920.
Pineas, Rainer. "John Bale's Nondramatic Works of Religious Controversy." *Studies in the Renaissance*, vol. 9 (1962).
_____. "Thomas More's Use of the Dialogue as a Weapon of Religious Controversy." *Studies in the Renaissance*, vol. 7, 1960.
_____. "Thomas More's Use of Humor as a Weapon of Religious Controversy." *Studies in Philology*, vol. 58, no. 2, Part 1 (April 1961).
Ratcliffe, Edward C. *The English Coronation Service*. London: Skeffington, 1936.
Robinson, Marsha. "The Historiographic Methodology of *King John*," *King John: New*

Bibliography

Perspectives. Ed. Deborah T. Curren-Aquino. Newark: University of Delaware Press, 1989.

Rosenwein, Barbara. *Anger's Past: The Social Uses of an Emotion in the Middle Ages*. Ithaca: Cornell University Press, 1998.

Ryrie, Alec. "Counting Sheep, Counting Shepherds: The Problem of Allegiance in the English Reformation." *The Beginnings of English Protestantism*, eds. Peter Marshall and Alec Ryrie. Cambridge: Cambridge University Press, 2002.

Saul, Nigel. *The Three Richards*. New York: Hambledon & London, 2005.

Sawyer, P.H. *Anglo-Saxon Charters: An Annotated List and Bibliography*. London: Royal Historical Society, 1968, p. 236.

Scanlon, Larry. *Narrative, Authority and Power: The Medieval Exemplum and the Chaucerian Tradition*. Cambridge: Cambridge University Press, 1994.

Schofield, William Henry. *Chivalry in English Literature*. Cambridge, MA: Harvard University Press, 1912.

Schramm, Percy. *A History of the English Coronation*, Trans. Leopold G. Wickham-Legge. Oxford: Clarendon Press, 1937.

Scott-Warren, Jason. "The Privy Politics of Sir John Harington's *New Discourse on a Stale Subject, Called the Metamorphosis of Ajax*." *Studies in Philology*, vol. 93, no. 4 (Autumn 1996).

Sharpe, Kevin. *Sir Robert Cotton 1586–1631: History and Politics in Early Modern England*. Oxford: Oxford University Press, 1979.

Shelton, Jo Anne. *As the Romans Did: A Sourcebook in Roman Social History*, 2nd ed., Oxford: Oxford University Press, 1998.

Shirley, Frances. *Swearing and Perjury in Shakespeare's Plays*. Allen & Unwin, 1979.

Shuger, Deborah. *Habits of Thought in the English Renaissance*. Berkeley: University of California Press, 1990, p. 9.

Siegel, Paul. "English Humanism and the New Tudor Aristocracy." *Journal of the History of Ideas*, vol. 13, no. 4 (October 1952).

Starkey, David. *Elizabeth: The Struggle for the Throne*. New York: HarperCollins, 2001.

Stone, Lawrence. *Road to Divorce: England 1530–1987*. Oxford: Oxford University Press, 1990.

Streuver, Nancy. *The Language of History in the Renaissance*. Princeton, NJ: Princeton University Press, 1970.

Strong, Roy. *Coronation: A History of Kingship and the British Monarchy*. London: HarperCollins, 2005.

Sweet, A. H. "John de Feckenham and the Marian Reaction," *Persecution and Liberty: Essays in Honor of George Lincoln Burr*. London: Century, 1931.

Tentler, T.N. *Sin and Confession on the Eve of the Reformation*. Princeton, NJ: Princeton University Press, 1977.

Tite, Colin G. *The Early Records of Sir Robert Cotton's Library*. London: The British Library 2003.

Traister, Barbara. "The King's One Body: Unceremonial Kingship in King John," *King John: New Perspectives*. Ed. Deborah T. Curren-Aquino. Newark: University of Delaware Press, 1988.

Tudor, Philippa "John Feckenham and Tudor Religious Controversies," *The Cloister and the World: Essays in Medieval History in Honour of Barbara Harvey*, eds. John Blair and Brian Golding. Oxford: Oxford University Press, 1995.

Bibliography

Vallance, Edward. *Revolutionary England and the National Covenant.* Woodbridge, Suffolk, UK: Boydell Press, 2005.

Vaughan, Virginia. "King John: A Study in Subversion and Containment," *King John: New Perspectives*, ed. Deborah T. Curren-Aquino. Newark: University of Delaware Press, 1989.

Verkamp, Bernard. *The Indifferent Mean: Adiaphorism in the English Reformation to 1554.* Athens: Ohio University Press, 1997.

Wagner, Anne. "Idleness and the Ideal of the Gentleman." *History of Education Quarterly*, vol. 25, nos. 1–2 (Spring-Summer, 1985).

Walker, Greg. *Writing Under Tyranny.* Oxford: Oxford University Press, 2005.

Warner, Christopher J. *Henry VIII's Divorce: Literature and the Politics of the Printing Press.* London: Boydell, 1998.

Watkins, Oscar D. *History of Penance*, vol. II, London, 1920.

Wegemer, Gerard B. *Thomas More on Statesmanship.* Washington, DC: Catholic University of America Press, 1996.

Wells, Marion. *The Secret Wound: Love-Melancholy and Early Modern Romance.* Palo Alto, CA: Stanford University Press, 2007.

Wilson, K.J. "The Letters of Sir Thomas Elyot," *Studies in Philology*, vol. 73, no. 5, Texts and Studies, 1976.

Woolf, D.R. "Speech, Text, and Time: The Sense of Hearing and the Sense of the Past in Renaissance England." *Albion*, no. 18, vol. 2, Summer 1986.

Index

acedia 178
Act Extinguishing the Authority of the Bishop of Rome 196, 210
Act in Restraint of Appeals 24, 26–28, 35
Acts of Supremacy and Succession 7, 13, 14, 32, 47, 73, 76, 78, 80, 85, 110, 142, 164, 210
adiaphorism 109, 110, 199
Aesop 111, 114
Agard, Arthur 196, 207
Alington, Alice 15, 111–113, 116, 118, 200; *see also* More, Sir Thomas
Alington, Giles 111
Alpers, Paul 171, 205, 210
Ariosto, Lodovico 125, 201
Aristotle 42, 45, 49–52, 54, 79, 105, 205
Arthurian legend 28, 31, 107, 169, 170, 172, 177, 181, 183, 186, 205
Arundel, Matthew 130
Askew, Anne 73; *see also* Bale, John
Audley, Thomas 15, 27, 37, 53, 102, 105, 111–117, 131, 200
Augustine, Saint 192, 199, 207
auricular confession 14, 57, 60, 61, 63, 68, 91, 195, 198, 204
Austin, J.L. 191, 210

Bale, John 102–133, 134–167, 207; *Actes of the Englyshe Votaryes* 106, 107, 199, 137, 202, 207; *Apology* 198, 199, 202; *Brefe Chronicle* 199, 201, 207; *First Examincacyon of Anne Askew* 199, 203, 207; *Kynge Johan* 106, 134–167; 199, 207; *Pageant of Popes* 137, 199, 207; *Vocacyon of Iohan Bale* 137, 208; *Yet a Course at the Romyshe Foxe* 102–133, 208
Bartlett, Robert 1, 191, 192

Barton, Elizabeth 73, 166
Baynton, Sir Edward 130
Becket, Thomas 35, 193
Berin, John 130
Bernard, G.W. 195, 210
Berners, Dame Juliana 41, 48, 175, 194, 205, 208
Boleyn, Anne 26, 28, 118, 166, 193
bond of association 109
Bonner, Edmund 15, 97, 102, 106, 107, 110, 118–124, 131
Bowers, Rick 190, 201, 208
Boyer, Robert 33, 47
Bridges, John 15, 77–101, 197, 198, 208
Bruno, Giordano 205

caesaropapism 7, 136
Canfield, J. Douglas 1, 191, 210
Capellanus, Andreas 41, 194, 205, 208
Capgrave, John 120, 136, 202, 208
Carthusians 113
Castiglione, Baldassare 126, 205, 208
casuistry 90, 91
Cathedral of Notre Dame 31
Charles I, King of England 36, 193
Charles V, Holy Roman Emperor 40, 43, 51, 114, 195
chivalry 17, 46, 52, 159, 160, 168, 169, 172, 173, 175, 176, 179, 180, 185, 206
Chrétien de Troyes 206, 208
Cicero 12, 42, 45, 50–52, 54, 208; *De Legibus* 8, 9, 208; *De Officiis* 8, 49, 54, 191, 192, 208
Clement VII 137
Condren, Conal 1, 191, 210
Corpus Inscriptionum Latinarum 191
Cotton, Sir Robert 3, 13, 20, 26, 33–36, 193

Index

Couliano, Ioan 205, 210
Council of Trent 183
courtly love tradition 17, 41, 168, 169, 176, 177, 180, 181, 183, 184, 201, 205, 206
Cranmer 15, 51, 53, 61, 67, 84, 86, 102, 105, 112, 167, 199, 204, 209
Cromwell, Thomas 15, 27, 73, 43, 44, 53, 60, 71, 72, 76, 85, 102, 105, 111–113, 135, 137, 164, 162, 197, 202
Cross, Claire 197, 210
crucifix 74, 75

Dauce, William 111
Dawson, Lesel 205, 211
Dee, John 170
DeLumeau, Jean 195, 211
divine right of kings 136, 144, 145, 150, 156, 159, 161, 164
Duffy, Eamon 1, 191, 211
Dunstan, Saint 30

Edgar, King of England 30
Edith 30
Edmund, Saint 29
Edward I, King of England 19, 25, 62
Edward II, King of England 25, 36, 187, 193
Edward III, King of England 34, 169
Edward IV, King of England 62
Edward VI, King of England 32
Edwy, King of England 43
Einstein, Lewis 195, 211
Elizabeth I, Queen of England 14, 28, 34, 77, 78, 86, 87, 89, 91, 92, 97–100, 134, 153, 160, 162, 167, 169, 170, 172, 185, 196, 202
Elizabethan betrothal laws 177–179, 182, 183
Ellis, Henry 192, 211
Elton, G.R. 7, 191, 196, 211
Elyot, Sir Thomas 13, 194, 195, 209; *The Boke Named the Governour* 38–55
energia 79
entrelacement 171
Erasmus, Desiderius 44, 53, 103, 126; *Praise of Folly* 199

Fairfield, Leslie 199, 200, 211
Feckenham, John 14, 15, 78, 87–92, 94–97, 197, 198
Ficino, Marcilio 205
Fisher, John 66, 73
Fourth Lateran Council of 1215 195, 209

Foxe, John 137, 139; *Acts and Monuments* 137
Franks 10, 26, 192
Frith, John 73

Gallagher, Lowell 90, 198
gally halfpenny 85, 197
Gardiner, Stephen 199
Garret, Christina 198, 211
Gautier, Léon 204, 205, 211
gentilesse 168, 169, 180, 181, 183
Geoffrey of Monmouth 28, 199
Given-Wilson, Chris 136, 202, 211
Gough, John 197, 209
Greenblatt, Stephen 58, 66, 68, 72, 196, 211
Grey, Lady Jane 86, 186
Groves, Beatrice 143, 203, 211
Guy, John 193, 200, 211

Haighley, Christopher 7–8, 211
Hamel, Guy 147, 158, 203, 204, 211
Happe, Peter 8
Harington, Sir John 15, 198–202; *A New Discourse on a Stale Subject...Part III. An Apologie...* 102–133, 209
Helgerson, Richard 194, 211
Henry V, King of England 33
Henry VI, King of England 31, 33, 35, 36, 62
Henry VII, King of England 62, 203; Lytlington Ordo 24, 25
Henry VIII, King of England 6, 7, 13, 14, 17, 19–37, 38, 41, 48, 56–76, 77, 81, 82, 86, 89, 90, 93, 111, 114, 118–120, 134, 137, 142, 159, 164, 167, 169; *A Glasse of the Truthe* 78, 80–83; Great Matter 7, 14, 43, 47, 67, 80–82, 195
Heron, Giles 111
Hickman, David 97, 198, 211
Hillam, David 193, 211
Hoak, Dale 7–8, 211
Hogdon, Barbara 166, 204, 211
Holinshed, Raphael 136, 203, 209
Holy Maid of Kent *see* Barton, Elizabeth
Horne, Robert 15, 78, 86–95, 197, 198, 209
Horsey, Ralph 130
humanism 42–44, 81, 107, 195
Humphrey, Lawrence 194, 209

Innocent III 30, 134, 137
Inscriptiones Latinae Selectae 191, 209

Index

Isabel 31
Israelites 42, 47, 51, 126, 201

Jones, Norman 70, 73, 196, 211
Jones, Robert 204, 211
Jones, William 192, 212

Kantorowicz, Ernst Hartwig 204, 212
Katherine of Aragon 32, 59, 81, 82, 166, 203
Kelso, Ruth 42, 194, 212
Kendrick, T.D. 194, 212
Kerrigan, William 1, 191, 212
King, John N. 7–8, 211
Klause, John 154, 161, 204, 212
Knighton, Henry 136, 209

Langton, Stephen 136, 140, 150, 161
Latimer, Hugh 61, 86, 197, 209
Lehmberg, Stanford 195, 212
Leland, John 28, 31, 34, 35, 106, 119, 169, 193
Leslie, Michael 205, 212
Lethbridge, J.B. 205, 212
Lipscomb, Susannah 8, 191, 212
Loach, Jennifer 30, 193, 212
London Round Table 169
Lytlington Ordo *see* Henry VII

Machiavelli, Niccolò 40
Magna Carta 23, 24, 31, 134, 136, 140
Malory, Sir Thomas 206, 209
Marie de France 206, 209
Markham, Thomas 130–131
Martz, Louis 105, 199, 200, 212
Mary I, Queen of England 14, 6, 72, 78, 88, 89, 91, 95, 203
McClaren, Anne 205, 206, 212
Merlin 107, 172–175
Millican, Charles B. 205, 212
Mirandola, Pico della 205
Moore, Christopher 73
More, Sir Thomas 2, 6, 15, 23, 43, 53, 66, 73, 102–133, 194, 196, 198–201, 209; correspondence 201, 209; *Dialogue Concerning Heresies* 105, 106, 209; *Dialogue of Comfort Against Tribulation* 106, 111, 117, 209; *Letter to Alice Alington* 2, 102, 104–106, 110, 113–117, 128, 200, 209
Mulcaster, Richard 169, 170

Nelson, T.G.A. 205, 206

Noble, James 205, 212
Norland, Howard 46, 194, 212

oaths, types: Abrahamic covenant 6, 11, 122; Anglo-Saxon 10–12, 22, 170; Oath of Supremacy 15, 43, 77, 83, 92, 96, 112; Oath of Uniformity 86; ordeals 10–12, 109, 192; Romano-British 8–11; Teutonic 9–11
O'Connell, Marvin 198, 212
Oldcastle, John 199
Ong, Walter J. 79

Parr, Katherine 174, 175, 178
Peeter, Sir John of Stonden 129
Petrarch 174, 175, 178
Pineas, Rainer 105, 199, 200, 212
Plato 44, 46, 105, 106, 126, 205
Portman, Sir Hugh 130
priscilianism 98–99
Prynne, William 192, 210

Rankin, Mark 7–8, 211
Rastell, William 200, 210
Ratcliffe, Edward 25, 212
regicide 161
Rich, Richard 102
Richard I, Cordelion, King of England 29, 33, 145, 146, 163
Richard II, King of England 33, 36
Richard III, King of England 31, 62
Robinson, Marsha 183, 202, 212
Roger of Wendover 136, 140, 202
Roper, Margaret 2, 15, 102, 103, 106, 111–113, 116, 117
Rosenwein, Barbara 204, 213
Ryrie, Alec 7–8, 72, 197, 211, 213

St. Paul's Cathedral 31
Sampoole, George 130
Saul, Nigel 193, 194, 203, 213
Sawyer, P.H. 192, 213
Scanlon, Larry 192, 213
Schofield, William 205, 213
Schramm, Percy 24, 25, 192, 193, 213
Scott-Warren, Jason 126, 132, 201, 202, 213
Seton, Alexander 200, 206
Seymour, Jane 6, 32, 59, 60, 70, 118, 203
Shakespeare, William 1, 2, 16, 35, 174, 191, 202–205, 210; *King John* 134–167
Sharpe, Kevin 33, 35, 215
Sheldon, Ralph 130

Index

Shelton, Jo Anne 191, 213
Shirley, Frances 1, 191, 213
Shuger, Deborah 191, 213
Siegel, Paul 43, 194, 213
Smith, Paul 190, 201, 208
Society of Antiquaries 33
Spenser, Edmund 16, 17, 35, 108; *The Faerie Queene* 16, 17, 168–186, 201, 205, 206, 210
Spenser, Sir John 129
Stanhope, Thomas 129
Stapleton, Thomas 15, 78, 197; *A Counterblast to M. Horne's Vayne Blast Against Feckenham* 91–97
Starkey, David 198, 213
Starkey, Ralph 33, 47
Stone, Lawrence 206, 213
Streuver, Nancy 195, 213
Strong, Roy 192, 213
Sweet, A.H. 197, 213
Swinnerton, Thomas 78, 83–85, 87, 196

Tate, Francis 33, 47
Tenterden steeple 85, 197
Tentler, T.N. 195, 196, 213
Tite, Colin 33, 34, 192, 193, 213
Tolwyn, William 15, 102, 107, 118–124, 130, 131, 188, 189, 201
Tomson, Laurence 197, 210

Traister, Barbara 204, 213
Treason Act 59, 67, 80, 196
The Troublesome Raigne of King John 2, 134–167, 207
Tudor, Phillipa 197, 213
Tyndale, William 43, 104, 117, 118, 136, 137, 194, 199
tyranny 7–8, 20, 40, 66–68, 80, 82, 105, 123, 140, 161, 195, 204

Vallance, Edward 1, 191, 214
Vaughan, Virginia 202, 214
Verkamp, Bernard 200, 214

Wagner, Anne 41, 42, 194, 214
Walker, Greg 8, 44, 67, 69, 80, 191, 194–196
Walter, Hubert 140
Warner, Christopher 82, 196, 214
Watkins, Oscar D. 195, 212, 214
Wegemer, Gerard 199, 214
Wells, Marion 178, 206, 214
Westminster Abbey 9, 31, 86, 87, 89, 90
Westminster Palace 73, 76
Willoughby, Francis 130
Wilson, K.J. 194, 195, 214
Wolsey, Thomas 26, 114, 115, 200
Woolf, D.R. 78, 196, 214

www.ingramcontent.com/pod-product-compliance
Ingram Content Group UK Ltd.
Pitfield, Milton Keynes, MK11 3LW, UK
UKHW041955140426
5217IPUK00015B/808